AF894376

BECOME A MILLIONAIRE IN ONE YEAR

The Practical Guide to Turning a Thousand into

Holiday Car Boat Deposit House or

Millions

(in crypto or any financial market)

By Lisa N Edwards

Obviously, this is not a fiction novel, but Lisa also writes these.

Fiction Novels

Can't Fight Fate
Chasing Butterflies
Seed of the Sunflower

BECOME A MILLIONAIRE IN ONE YEAR

The Practical Guide to Turning a Thousand into

Holiday Car Boat Deposit House or

Millions

(in crypto or any financial market)

Lisa N Edwards

BECOME A MILLIONAIRE IN ONE YEAR
The Practical Guide to Turning a Thousand into Holiday Car Boat Deposit House Millions
(in crypto or any financial market)
by Lisa N Edwards

ISBN: 978-0-6486443-0-9 PRINT Standard Colour

Published by Visual Media Group
Docklands Melbourne Australia 3008
vmg@visualmediagroup.com.au
www.visualmediagroup.com.au

Cataloguing-in-Publication data is available from the National Library of Australia

Money is only a tool.

It will take you wherever you wish, but it will not replace you as the driver.

Ayn Rand

DISCLAIMER

The following disclaimer applies to the book titled "Become a Millionaire in One Year! The Practical Guide to Turning a Thousand into Millions" (hereinafter referred to as "the Book"). By reading and utilising the information provided in this Book, you acknowledge and agree to the terms set forth in this disclaimer.

1. No Financial Advice: The Book is intended to provide general information and guidance on wealth accumulation strategies and financial principles. However, it is not intended to be a substitute for professional financial advice. The author although a professional trader is not a certified financial advisor, and the information contained in the Book should not be interpreted as personalised financial advice or recommendations. Before making any financial decisions, it is recommended that you consult with a qualified financial advisor.
2. Individual Results: The strategies and techniques outlined in the Book are based on the author's experiences and research. While efforts have been made to provide accurate and up-to-date information, the author makes no guarantee regarding the effectiveness of the strategies outlined in the Book. Individual results may vary, and the author does not guarantee that readers will achieve the same level of financial success or become millionaires within a specific time frame.
3. Risks and Liabilities: The strategies presented in the Book involve various risks, including but not limited to financial risks and market fluctuations. Readers are solely responsible for their financial decisions and should exercise caution and conduct thorough research before engaging in any investment or business activities. The author and publisher disclaim any liability for any financial loss, damages, or negative consequences arising directly or indirectly from the use or application of the information presented in the Book.
4. External Links and Recommendations: The Book may contain references to external websites, products, or services for informational purposes. The author and publisher do not endorse or guarantee the accuracy, reliability, or suitability of any external resources mentioned in the Book. Readers should exercise their own discretion and undertake independent research before relying on any external links, products, or services mentioned in the Book.
5. Legal and Tax Advice: The Book does not provide legal or tax advice. The author and publisher are not liable for any legal or tax consequences that may arise from the implementation of the strategies outlined in the Book. Readers should consult with qualified legal and tax professionals regarding their specific circumstances and any legal or tax implications related to their financial decisions.
6. Personal Responsibility: The information presented in the Book is intended to be educational and motivational. However, readers are solely responsible for their actions and decisions based on the information provided. The author and publisher are not responsible for any outcomes or consequences resulting from the implementation of the strategies presented in the Book.
7. Intellectual Property: All intellectual property rights related to the Book, including but not limited to copyrights and trademarks, belong to the author and publisher. No part of the Book may be reproduced, distributed, or transmitted in any form or by any means without the prior written permission of the author and publisher.

By reading and utilising the information provided in the Book, you acknowledge that you have read, understood, and agreed to the terms and conditions set forth in this disclaimer.

Published Date: 17 December 2023 Author: Lisa N Edwards
Publisher: Visual Media Group - Books P/L

The Only Way to Make Money

Is Make Your Own!

Lisa N Edwards

ABOUT THE AUTHOR

Lisa N. Edwards

Trader and Cryptocurrency Influencer

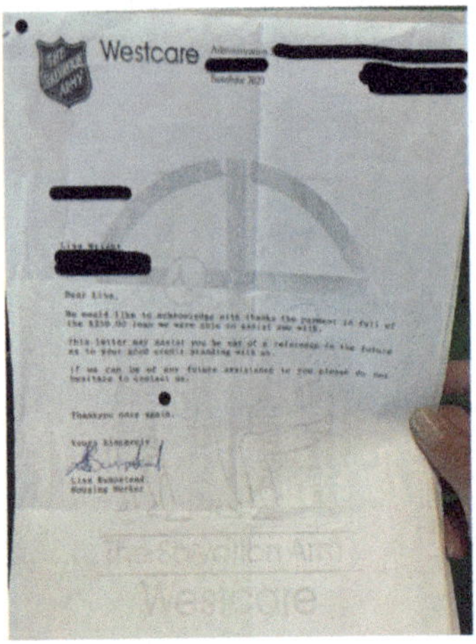

Westcare [redacted]

[redacted]

[redacted]

Lisa N Edwards is a trusted name in the cryptocurrency world, known for her boundless energy, and positive attitude.

She was just 16 when she learned to trade. It all started during her part-time job at KFC when a regular customer, who happened to be a junior analyst took her under his wing. Lisa was excited to tell him she had placed highly amongst the top competitors in the Australian Westpac Bank Math Competition at her school.

This young analyst saw potential in Lisa and decided to be her mentor. He armed her with the skills to not only boost her minimum wages but also seemingly conjure money out of thin air. This has helped her on many occasions to turn small amounts of income into much larger sums to buy almost anything she wants.

Those skills have proven to be a lifeline for her on numerous occasions, allowing her to turn small amounts of income into substantial sums.

Take, for example, the time she moved from Brisbane to Melbourne, Australia, with her baby daughter, they found themselves couch-surfing at friends' places while she searched for work. But then, a stroke of luck. Someone mentioned a loan program at The Salvation Army, affectionately known as the SALVOS in Australia. (Pictured) And guess what? While navigating the challenges of couch-surfing, she utilised her trading prowess to secure her own rental property. She covered rent, bond, and even put food on the table!

And then, more importantly, repaid the Salvos!

As a mother of five, and at times a single mother, this skillset has proved invaluable over the years. It's a true testament to her resilience and resourcefulness. She's been able to provide for her family and make ends meet through thick and thin.

Flash forward to now, Lisa is the Managing Partner of Visual Media Group, which boasts a portfolio of leading brands in the crypto space, all created from ideas she has had, to make the crypto world less toxic and more female friendly, and a space for everyone whatever age or gender to learn and grow.

She's a seasoned trader with 30 years of experience in stocks, commodities, and 10 years in cryptocurrency trading. A skilled Elliott Wave specialist, Lisa's expertise goes beyond just EW - she also uses various other methods like support and resistance, volume profile, Fibonacci, or Lisanachi as she affectionately calls it and chart indicators. She's a force to be reckoned with and has ranked among the top traders on Trading View with previous experience heading discords and trading groups as well as significant crypto funds for both private and public clients.

Lisa's impact extends beyond the trading floor. She's a multi-talented storyteller and actress with extensive experience in the media and film industries, including previous ownership of a modelling, acting, and casting agency and is an award-winning screenwriter and novelist.

Her passion for human psychology, both in her creative works and as a trader, makes her an insightful expert in understanding what moves the market. With 10 years hearing stories of success and failure, she knows how to get you to the next level. Her drive to succeed and a refusal to give up, makes Lisa proof that the sky's the limit for those who dare to dream big!

Visual Media Group Brands:
https://visualmediagroup.com.au/
GSIC - https://gettingstartedincrypto.com/
Thousand to Millions - compound trading strategy site.
https://thousandtomillions.com/
Personal Links
All my links - https://linktr.ee/LisaNEdwards

Money is only a tool.

It will take you wherever you wish, but it will not replace you as the driver.

Ayn Rand

DISCLAIMER

The following disclaimer applies to the book titled "Become a Millionaire in One Year! The Practical Guide to Turning a Thousand into Millions" (hereinafter referred to as "the Book"). By reading and utilising the information provided in this Book, you acknowledge and agree to the terms set forth in this disclaimer.

1. No Financial Advice: The Book is intended to provide general information and guidance on wealth accumulation strategies and financial principles. However, it is not intended to be a substitute for professional financial advice. The author although a professional trader is not a certified financial advisor, and the information contained in the Book should not be interpreted as personalised financial advice or recommendations. Before making any financial decisions, it is recommended that you consult with a qualified financial advisor.
2. Individual Results: The strategies and techniques outlined in the Book are based on the author's experiences and research. While efforts have been made to provide accurate and up-to-date information, the author makes no guarantee regarding the effectiveness of the strategies outlined in the Book. Individual results may vary, and the author does not guarantee that readers will achieve the same level of financial success or become millionaires within a specific time frame.
3. Risks and Liabilities: The strategies presented in the Book involve various risks, including but not limited to financial risks and market fluctuations. Readers are solely responsible for their financial decisions and should exercise caution and conduct thorough research before engaging in any investment or business activities. The author and publisher disclaim any liability for any financial loss, damages, or negative consequences arising directly or indirectly from the use or application of the information presented in the Book.
4. External Links and Recommendations: The Book may contain references to external websites, products, or services for informational purposes. The author and publisher do not endorse or guarantee the accuracy, reliability, or suitability of any external resources mentioned in the Book. Readers should exercise their own discretion and undertake independent research before relying on any external links, products, or services mentioned in the Book.
5. Legal and Tax Advice: The Book does not provide legal or tax advice. The author and publisher are not liable for any legal or tax consequences that may arise from the implementation of the strategies outlined in the Book. Readers should consult with qualified legal and tax professionals regarding their specific circumstances and any legal or tax implications related to their financial decisions.
6. Personal Responsibility: The information presented in the Book is intended to be educational and motivational. However, readers are solely responsible for their actions and decisions based on the information provided. The author and publisher are not responsible for any outcomes or consequences resulting from the implementation of the strategies presented in the Book.
7. Intellectual Property: All intellectual property rights related to the Book, including but not limited to copyrights and trademarks, belong to the author and publisher. No part of the Book may be reproduced, distributed, or transmitted in any form or by any means without the prior written permission of the author and publisher.

By reading and utilising the information provided in the Book, you acknowledge that you have read, understood, and agreed to the terms and conditions set forth in this disclaimer.

Published Date: 17 December 2023 Author: Lisa N Edwards
Publisher: Visual Media Group - Books P/L

Acknowledgements

Thank you, Josh Taylor; he's the person no one sees in the background doing all the stuff I hate to do; it doesn't go unseen by me. I love him and appreciate him.

Thank you to ***GSIC, CRYPTO TWITTER****, and the whole crypto, Blockchain Web3, and Web2.5 because some people can't do 3. There are so many amazing people that I connect with daily. You are always there, SALTY & SWEET; you all helped me believe I could, and those that didn't, I blocked, haha.*

Why can't there be a BLOCK button in real life 😊

There are always so many people to thank for the inspiration to my words. While I can't name them all here, I hope they know who they are...

THANK YOU!

"Every life is a story. Thank you for being part of mine."

Lisa

CONTENTS

SECTION 2 - THE MARKETS
ALL MARKETS, NOT JUST CRYPTO

CHAPTER BREAKDOWN

1. The Power of Compound Trading
2. Cultivating a Wealth Mindset
3. SMART - Goal Setting and Visualisation
4. Embracing Growth Mindset
5. Mastering the Art of Delayed Gratification
6. Importance of Your Surroundings
7. Setting Financial Goals: Charting Your Path to 1 MILLION
8. Mastering Risk by Understanding Position Sizing
9. Understanding Liquidity
10. Developing a Solid Trading Plan
11. Developing Trading Rules and Strategies
12. Fundamental Analysis and Market Research
13. Fundamental Analysis in Cryptocurrency
14. Fundamentals of Stock Market Trading
15. Trading the High Volatility Cryptocurrency Market
16. The Art of Portfolio Management
17. Sustaining Momentum to One Million
18. The Next Level – Scaling up YOUR Wealth

SECTION 3 – TECHNICAL ANALYSIS
TRADE LIKE LISA – BE LIKE LISA

CHAPTER BREAKDOWN

1. Technical Analysis: Be Like Lisa - Trade Like Lisa
2. Elliott Wave Theory and Historical Price Action
3. Oscillators and Momentum Indicators
4. Timing the Market
5. Navigating Market Volatility
6. The Psychology of Successful Trading
7. LISANACCI – FIBONACCI "Lisa Style"

SECTION 4 - PRACTICAL CRYPTO LEARNING

10-week beginner trading course for crypto

- Week 1: Introduction to Crypto Trading
- Week 2: Technical Analysis
- Week 3: Fundamental Analysis
- Week 4: Risk Management
- Week 5: Trading Strategies
- Week 6: Market Psychology
- Week 7: Trading Psychology
- Week 8: Cryptocurrency Investment
- Week 9: Technical Tools
- Week 10: Final Review and Assessment

"Money is multiplied in practical value depending on the number of W's you control in your life:

What you do. When you do it, and with Whom you do it."

Tim Ferris

"I trained 4 years to run only 9 seconds.

There are people who do not see results in 2 months, give up and leave. Sometimes failure is sought by oneself."

Usain Bolt

This quote is the only quote entered twice, and as you read you will understand why.

INTRODUCTION TO MINDSET

In a world driven by money and financial aspirations, few dreams are as universally captivating as transforming a modest sum into a staggering fortune. The journey from $1,000 to $1,000,000 may seem insurmountable, but it is an achievable feat with the right knowledge, mindset, and strategy.

Welcome to "The Practical Guide to Turning a Thousand into Holiday, Car, Boat, Deposit, House, Millions!" - a transformative handbook designed to unlock the secrets of compound trading, and the mindset needed to achieve and practical ideas to get you there.

This book is not just another pie-in-the-sky promise; it is a strategic roadmap crafted by a financial visionary who has made her fortune in the real world. Inside these pages, you will find the distilled wisdom in the realm of wealth creation and the ability to find the necessary balance between want and need. The ability to know and trust in yourself and your ability to learn and succeed.

Robert T. Kiyosaki, renowned author of the best-selling book "Rich Dad Poor Dad," once said, "Compound interest is the eighth wonder of the world. He who understands it earns it; he who doesn't pays it." With his profound understanding of the power of compounding, Kiyosaki recognises the potential for exponential growth that lies within our grasp, waiting to be harnessed.

Warren Buffett, one of the most successful investors of all time, echoes this sentiment with his timeless advice: "The stock market is a device for transferring money from the impatient to the patient." Through years of disciplined investing and shrewd decision-making, Buffett has amassed a fortune and built an investment empire that stands as a testament to the potential of compound trading.

Drawing on the teachings and experiences of these two financial luminaries, this book takes a hands-on approach, providing practical advice, actionable strategies, and invaluable insights into the art of turning a modest sum into a life-changing fortune. Whether you are an experienced trader seeking to enhance your skills or a beginner eager to embark on your wealth-building journey, this guide is designed to equip you with the tools and knowledge you need to succeed.

By exploring fundamental concepts, risk management techniques, crypto and stock selection strategies, and the art of timing the market, " The Practical Guide to Turning a Thousand into Holiday, Car, Boat, Deposit, House, Millions!" demystifies the world of compound trading and empowers you to navigate the financial landscape with confidence.

So, prepare to embark on an extraordinary adventure. Whether you aspire to build a secure future for yourself, achieve financial independence, or leave a lasting legacy, the principles and wisdom shared within these pages will serve as your guiding light. Let us journey together towards the realisation of your wildest financial dreams.

Remember, as Robert T. Kiyosaki aptly puts it, "The more you learn, the more you earn." It is time to unlock the hidden potential of your capital and harness the power of compound trading to transform your $1,000 into an awe-inspiring $1,000,000.

Always remember...

"You Never Fail Until You Stop Trying."

WHAT IS YOUR WHY?

This is the most important question you can answer, and if it is to just get rich, put this book down, or close it on your browser or iPad if an eBook. Close it now and do some self-reflection.

If you are thinking about becoming a "Crypto Bros," and looking for what is known as WIFE CHANGING MONEY in the crypto space, have the conversation with your wife or girlfriend before you even start learning. This book isn't a guide to inflating your ego or acquiring superficial connections with individuals who lack depth, all because you believe you can buy them with your newfound wealth. I want you to contemplate the profound implications of this.

He's so handsome, that wallet looks good on you, how many Bitcoins do you have? She's so young and pretty let me be your crypto sugar daddy. This isn't the purpose for writing this guide.

Just because you can afford someone or something... Doesn't mean you value it!

Have that heart-to-heart conversation about what this journey might mean for your relationship with your significant other. All this is a bit unconventional, isn't it? But it makes sense. You both need to want this, have combined dreams, or this is a ticket to heartbreak.

And if you're single, what's your motivation?

The question of motivation takes on a unique dimension. Without the immediate responsibility of a partner or family, your motivation becomes a canvas upon which you can paint the future of your dreams.

It's an opportunity to define not only what you want to achieve financially but also who you want to become as an individual. Your financial goals can encompass personal growth, self-discovery, and the pursuit of passions that ignite your soul. It's a chance to create a life that is not just prosperous in terms of material wealth, but also rich in experiences, personal fulfilment, and the freedom to chart your own course.

Being single offers you the freedom to explore uncharted territories, take calculated risks, and seize opportunities that align with your deepest desires. So, if you're single, ask yourself, "What's my motivation?" and let it be the driving force behind a future that's uniquely yours. But if you are in a happy relation don't make yourself single, that is not the intention here.

I want you to reflect deeply on what this means to you…

It's quite interesting to begin with such a strong statement. Essentially, what I'm saying in this question, is, "What is your motivation for entering the world of cryptocurrencies?"

Consider why a person might feel compelled to walk away from a relationship just because they've hit it big financially. It's almost a cautionary tale – a warning against letting material wealth distort your priorities and your sense of self-worth.

I do know mindset is absolutely crucial. And we will expand on this as we progress through the pages It's like a litmus test for your intentions. And I'm not mincing words either – if your sole purpose is to get rich quick, then please stop right here, put the book down and back away!

I am urging you to take a step back and really think about your reasons and motivation for money.

This opening chapter serves as a stark reminder that wealth, or the ability to afford something or someone, doesn't equate to valuing them. Money can buy many things, but it can't buy love, respect, or genuine human connections.

In a way, this book is not just about cryptocurrencies; it's about values, relationships, and the human side of financial success. It's about keeping your feet on the ground even as you explore the potential riches in the world of crypto. Quite a thought-provoking start, wouldn't you say?

As the author, I want to emphasise the gravity of this question. It's not just a passing thought; it's the crux of everything I'm about to share with you. If your sole motivation for delving into the world of cryptocurrencies is to amass wealth rapidly, I'll say it again, I implore you to stop right here.

Always remember: Just because you possess the means to acquire something, or someone doesn't automatically translate into genuine value. Money is a powerful tool, but it can't purchase authentic love, respect, or meaningful human bonds.

This book isn't solely about cryptocurrencies; it's a journey through values, relationships, and the human aspect of financial prosperity. It's a reminder to stay grounded as you explore the potential riches within the crypto world. It's a thought-provoking start to what I hope will be a transformative journey for you.

Additionally, it's crucial to underscore the significance of having your own financial independence. While we explore the intricacies of wealth and its role in our lives, it's equally essential to recognise the value of self-sufficiency. Having your own money isn't just about financial security; it's about personal empowerment and the ability to make choices that align with your goals and aspirations. It fosters a sense of autonomy and self-confidence that can be invaluable in any relationship or life circumstance.

So, as we navigate the world of cryptocurrencies and financial success, remember that your financial independence is a cornerstone upon which you can build a more fulfilling and self-determined future.

Always remember…

"Don't Let Your DREAMS, be dreams."

THE LAW OF SUCCESS PHILOSOPHY

As we delve into the world of success, it's crucial to understand that success is not a random stroke of luck or a distant dream that only a fortunate few can attain. Instead, it's a journey that begins within the corridors of your mind. The Law of Success Philosophy teaches us that we have the power to control our thoughts, making us the masters of our fate. Fate is a concept I have pondered, both here in a mostly technical book, and in my fiction novels.

Fate is a concept that refers to the idea that events in a person's life are predetermined and beyond their control. My fiction novels explore the concept of giving a psychic the power to choose your destiny, by implanting thoughts and ideas, which shape the ideas in your mind. It suggests that there is a fixed, preordained course of events or a predetermined outcome that will occur regardless of one's actions or choices. Fate is often associated with the belief that there is a higher power or force, such as destiny or providence, which guides the course of a person's life.

The concept of fate has been a recurring theme in various cultures and religions throughout history. Some people believe in a predetermined fate that governs their lives, while others subscribe to the idea of free will, which suggests that individuals have the power to make choices and shape their own destinies.

The belief in fate can vary greatly among individuals and cultures, and it often intersects with philosophical, religious, and existential questions about the nature of life, choice, and the role of external forces in shaping one's journey. Ultimately, whether one believes in fate or not is a matter of personal belief and perspective.

I now believe in the power of choice and believe that my choices and actions will bring the lessons and necessary growth to move forward with my dreams and goals, even as these change, I have an inner knowing that I will achieve everything I set my mind to. I also believe that anything meant for me will be and if not, I will be ok in myself to move forward and continue my learning and growth.

Imagine for a moment that your mind is a canvas, and every thought you have is a brushstroke. What you paint on this canvas becomes your reality. As you read through this book, I want you to picture what your life looks like 5, 10, or even 30 years from now. Envision it vividly, with the firm belief that if you can think it, you can see it. If you believe it, you can achieve it.

But this journey towards success is not a mere wishful thinking exercise. It's about igniting a burning desire to succeed within you. Wishing for money, a new car, a new house, or whatever you desire will not magically bring these things to life. The universe or praying to your God doesn't respond to vague wishes; it responds to purposeful actions.

To turn your dreams into reality, you must instigate a plan and put it into practice. Success doesn't happen by chance; it's a product of deliberate and persistent effort. There's a saying I love that encapsulates this idea: "Don't let your dreams be dreams." It's a call to action, an invitation to turn your dreams into concrete goals and then into achievements.

The path to success is not always smooth; it's often riddled with obstacles, setbacks, and challenges. But it's your persistence and a clear, positive mindset that will see you through. Success is not reserved for those who have never encountered difficulties but for those who keep going when everything seems against them. This is where the "You never fail until you stop trying" mindset enters your realm, can you keep going when the world seems against you, at the extreme, debt collectors knocking at your door, or potential life changing results from a failed business looming. Can you reach your goals without the support of the people around you; can you continue to grow when people are trying to tear you down and your world apart?

This is where you will need to dig deep and find the deep belief and trust within yourself to know and understand you are enough and the only person you need to succeed.

Success is not the exclusive domain of those who have never faced adversity but belongs to those who keep marching forward even when the world seems set against them. In this book you will define what success means to you. Is it a Car, Boat, Deposit, House, Millions or is it just the peace of mind of knowing whatever happens you will be, ok?

Maintaining a positive outlook and a clear focus on your goals or desires is the key. It's about believing in yourself, your abilities, and your vision even when others doubt you or when circumstances appear bleak. It's about knowing that setbacks are not permanent but temporary detours on your road to success.

In the Law of Success Philosophy, you are the architect of your destiny. You hold the power to shape your life according to your dreams and aspirations. So, as you continue your journey through this book, remember that success is not an abstract concept; it's a tangible reality waiting for you to claim it. It begins with your thoughts, fuelled by your burning desire, and brought to life through your persistent actions.

Don't let your dreams be dreams; make them your reality.

"If you have no critics, you'll likely have no success."

Malcolm X

"Setting goals is the first step in turning the invisible into the visible."

Tony Robbins

MONEY, WHAT'S THE BIG DEAL?

Alright, let's talk about money. We use it every day, but have you ever stopped to think about what it really is? Money isn't just the coins jangling in your pocket or the notes you hand over at the shops. It's a whole system that makes our modern world tick.

First off, money comes in various shapes and sizes. You've got your old-school paper notes and shiny coins, but these days, a lot of our money is digital. Think about the numbers in your bank account – that's money too. Even those plastic cards in your wallet, whether debit or credit, are a way of carrying around your money without the need for cash.

And then there's the buzzword of the decade: cryptocurrencies like Bitcoin. They're like digital money but a bit more mysterious and decentralised. Some people (like me) reckon they're the future of money. And we can deeper dive into this as the book proceeds.

What Does Money Do? And what's the point of all this money stuff?

Well, money serves many important roles in everyday life:

- Buy Stuff: The most obvious one – you use money to buy things. No more trading your chickens for a new phone; just hand over some cash or swipe your card.

- Keep Score: Money acts as a way to measure the value of stuff. Ever notice how prices are always in pounds or dollars? That's because money gives us a common language to talk about the worth of things. Notice I say worth, as we have touched on, worth does not equal value. You and your emotions place the value on something, not a monetary figure.

- Savings: You can save money for a rainy day. Instead of stashing potatoes under your mattress, you can put money in a bank and earn a bit more over time. Well, a tiny bit, as banks don't actually want you to save or make money. They want you to take loans as this is where they make their money.
- Pay Later: Money lets you make promises about future payments. Got a mortgage, credit card or a loan? Those are agreements that say you'll pay back a certain amount of money over time.

"It doesn't matter how slowly you go as long as you don't stop."

Confucius

THE ENERGY OF MONEY!

Money, oh money! It's a subject that gets everyone talking, and for good reason. We either have lots of it, or not enough, it causes relationship stressors and often insecurities.

ABBA wrote songs about it, Money, Money Money, sure is funny in a rich man's world, and we learned in the movie, Scarface, that Tony Montana believed, "you gotta make the money first. Then when you get the money, you get the power. Then when you get the power, then you get the women." Money energy is often ego driven.

The energy of money is a captivating and perplexing concept that permeates our lives in myriad ways. It's not merely the tangible notes and coins but a force that influences our decisions, emotions, and aspirations. It's the engine that drives economies, shapes destinies, and fuels dreams. In this chapter, we're delving deep into the enigmatic essence of money, exploring what it truly means to understand the energy it carries.

What is money? It's not just bits of paper and coins or cryptocurrency; it's got this mysterious energy that's hard to pin down. So, let's take a deep dive into what exactly we mean when we talk about the energy of money.

"There is nothing either good or bad, but thinking makes it so."

Quote from William Shakespeare's Hamlet ACT II, Scene 2

"ENERGY IS CURRENCY."

When you 'PAY' attention to something, you're buying an experience – it's an investment so 'spend' your time carefully and only on things that will bring you a good return. Be selective. Treat your time with as much care as your finances. It's equally as VALUABLE!

Infinity Healing Official

UNDERSTANDING THE ENERGY OF MONEY

The energy of money isn't something you can hold in your hand or put in your wallet. It's more like the vibes it gives off, the way it makes us feel, and the thoughts we attach to it.

Money demands respect, and I don't mean that if you have lots of money, you are instantly a respectable person; I am talking about the thoughts and emotions behind money.

To get a handle on this concept, let's break it down a bit:

1. Swapping Valuc

At its most basic, money is like a universal coupon for trading stuff. You give it, and you get something in return. It's like the middleman in the grand exchange of goods, services, and ideas. Money doesn't play favourites; it's just a tool for making things happen.

2. Emotions and Beliefs

Now, here's where it gets interesting. Money has this knack for stirring up feelings. Some people see it as a ticket to freedom and success, while others associate it with fear or greed. These feelings aren't random; they're tied to our life experiences, family upbringing, and what society has drummed into our heads about money.

3. Intentions and Goals

What you do with your money tells a lot about you. Are you hoarding it like a dragon guarding its treasure, or are you using it to make a difference in the world? The energy of money is all about the intentions you have behind earning, spending, and saving it.

"Money is life energy that we exchange and use as a result of the service we provided to the universe."

Deepak Chopra

GOING WITH THE FLOW

Think of money like a river, always moving. You're standing by the riverbank, and you have a say in where it goes. Just like a river, money can be a force for good or bad, creating abundance or scarcity. To ride the money wave effectively, consider these principles:

1. Thinking Abundance

Start by thinking there's plenty to go around. An abundance mindset is all about seeing opportunities instead of roadblocks. When you shift your focus from lack to abundance, your financial situation can change dramatically. Think of that money flow as what goes out is always replaced; you can start to believe that the money that goes out is always replenished by 3 times, 10 times, or even 100 times more. That bit is up to you, but as we're thinking of money as a river always moving, imagine the river receiving rains, the banks filling up, and sometimes this flow overflowing, while at other times it gets dammed up, or even runs dry. It's all about the ebb and flow of the financial river.

2. Spending with a Purpose

Mindful spending is about knowing where your money goes. It's about spending in ways that match your values and priorities. When you spend consciously, your money becomes a tool for achieving what truly matters to you. And if you are not sure what this is, go back and reread, "What is Your Why?"

Abraham Hicks, a renowned teacher of the Law of Attraction, has provided invaluable insights into the power of our thoughts and emotions in shaping our reality. One fascinating exercise that Abraham Hicks often recommends is mentally spending $100 as a means of demonstrating the principles of the Law of Attraction.

The Law of Attraction, in a nutshell, asserts that like attracts like. In other words, the energy you emit through your thoughts and feelings will draw similar energy or experiences into your life. Therefore, if you consistently focus on lack and scarcity, you are likely to attract more of the same. Conversely, if you focus on abundance and prosperity, you are more likely to manifest these into your life.

Now, let's delve into the exercise of mentally spending $100, as advised by Abraham Hicks. This exercise is designed to shift your thoughts and emotions from a state of scarcity to one of abundance, thereby aligning your energy with your desired financial reality.

1. Imagine the Possibilities: Take a moment to close your eyes and imagine you have $100 in your pocket, and if you have the financial means, go, and withdraw $100 from an ATM. Visualise or feel the crisp bills and feel the texture of the money. Allow yourself to fully experience the sensation of having this money at your disposal.

2. Mentally Allocate the Funds: Next, mentally allocate this $100 to various expenses or desires. You might allocate some for bills, some for savings, and some for leisure activities or treats. The key is to distribute this imaginary money in a way that feels abundant and joyful.

3. Feel the Abundance: As you go through this exercise, pay close attention to how it makes you feel. Embrace the emotions of abundance, gratitude, and excitement. The Law of Attraction is highly responsive to our emotions, so it's crucial to genuinely feel the positivity associated with this exercise.

4. Maintain the Vibration: After completing the exercise, try to maintain this elevated emotional state throughout your day. Continue to carry the feeling of abundance with you as you go about your tasks and interactions. Go for a walk to your local shopping centre or mall, and as you window shop, think, I could buy and, and that, oh and look, wow, I could buy that, smile to yourself.

The idea behind this exercise is that by mentally spending $100 with a sense of abundance and positivity, you are sending out a powerful signal to the universe. You are telling the universe that you are open to receiving and that you believe in the abundance of resources available to you.

Abraham Hicks often emphasises the importance of aligning your thoughts, emotions, and beliefs with your desires. By consistently practising exercises like mentally spending $100 with an attitude of abundance, you are reprogramming your subconscious mind and raising your vibrational frequency to attract more financial prosperity into your life.

Ok so for some of you reading this, you may be thinking this is just woo woo and doesn't work for me, that's your thing Lisa. I'm not saying that the Law of Attraction is a magical solution, but if you think of it as a powerful tool that, when used consistently and with genuine belief, can help you shift your financial reality and, more importantly, your mindset and opinion of money.

As Abraham Hicks teaches, your thoughts are the starting point for creating the life you desire, and by adopting a mindset of abundance, you can manifest positive financial changes in your life.

3. Giving Back

Generosity is akin to casting a pebble into the flowing river of money. When you extend a helping hand to others, whether through charitable donations, acts of kindness, or gestures of goodwill, you initiate a ripple effect of positive energy that can, quite unexpectedly, circle back to enrich your own life.

Consider the act of giving to charity, for instance. When you contribute to a cause you're passionate about, you're not only making a tangible difference in the lives of those in need but also setting in motion a chain of positive events. Your donation may fund a crucial medical breakthrough, support education for underprivileged children, or provide relief to disaster-stricken communities. These acts of generosity, even on a small scale, contribute to a collective effort that can create lasting, positive change in the world.

Moreover, the energy you put out into the universe through your generosity doesn't dissipate into nothingness. Instead, it reverberates through the interconnected web of human experiences. Your goodwill can inspire others to pay it forward, creating a domino effect of kindness and compassion. It's as though your initial pebble sets off a series of ripples, touching more lives than you might ever know.

But the beauty of generosity doesn't stop there. The positive energy you release into the world tends to find its way back to you, often when you least expect it. This isn't about expecting a direct return on your investment; it's about the universe recognising your kindness and responding in kind. It might manifest as unexpected opportunities, acts of kindness from others when you need them most, or a general sense of contentment and fulfilment that permeates your life.

In essence, generosity is a powerful way to tap into the energetic flow of the universe. It aligns you with a cycle of abundance, where giving freely opens the door to receiving abundantly. It's a reminder that we are all interconnected, and the positive energy we put into the world has a way of coming back to us, often in the most delightful and unexpected ways.

So, as you navigate the river of money and life, consider the impact of your generosity. Be the pebble skipping across the water that sets off ripples of positivity, knowing that in doing so, you not only make the world a better place but also invite the flow of abundance and goodwill back into your own life.

4. Smart Investing

Investing wisely is akin to planting seeds that have the potential to grow into magnificent money trees. It's a strategic approach to financial growth, one that harnesses the power of compounding, and it's a bit like having nature work its magic in your financial garden. Let's explore this concept in more detail.

Imagine your initial investment as the seeds you sow in the fertile soil of the financial market. These seeds come in various forms, such as stocks, bonds, real estate, or mutual funds and cryptocurrency. Each

seed represents a portion of your capital, and your goal is to choose them wisely, considering factors like risk tolerance, financial goals, and market conditions.
Much like the patient gardener who waters and nurtures their seeds, you, as an investor or trader, must tend to your investments with care and precision. Understanding when and what to invest in is akin to selecting the right plants for your garden. Timing plays a pivotal role in the world of trading, much like a gardener who plans and prepares for spring during the dormant months of winter. Just as sowing seeds in the middle of summer would be ill-advised and would likely lead to no spring flowers, making impulsive investment decisions can lead to less-than-optimal outcomes. Strategic planning and a keen awareness of market cycles are your tools for cultivating a thriving financial garden.

This involves vigilant monitoring of your trades and portfolio, staying abreast of market trends, and making occasional adjustments to ensure that your investments remain in harmony with your long-term objectives.

You are investing your money, and you want to see that grow, just as a garden requires precise timing for planting, with seeds sown at the wrong time failing to flourish, this too shows a strong resemblance with trading and investing. Investments demand a strategic approach. Rushed or untimely decisions can lead to missed opportunities or unnecessary risks, akin to planting delicate flower seeds in the dead of winter amidst the frost. In both gardening and investing, patience, foresight, and the right timing are the keys to reaping a bountiful harvest.

Now, here's where the magic happens: compound trading is the concept of reinvesting your earnings or returns into your portfolio. It's like the tree you planted yielding fruit, and instead of consuming all the fruit, you take some of the seeds and replant those, allowing the production of even more in the future.

Compounding is the secret sauce that transforms your modest initial investment into a flourishing money tree. It works by earning returns not only on your original investment but also on the returns generated over time. This compounding effect can significantly accelerate your wealth growth.

Consider this scenario: You invest $1,000, and it generates a 10% return on the first trade. You now have $1,100 and instead of cashing out those earnings, you reinvest them, and in the second trade, you earn another 10% return. However, this time, your return isn't just on your initial investment but on the total amount, including all trades. You now have a profit of $110 on this second trade, showing 10% growth on the invested amount. And $1,210 in total to roll into the third trade. Now as the trades progress, this compounding effect can lead to exponential growth.

Investing wisely and harnessing the power of compound trading isn't a get-rich-quick scheme. It's a long-term strategy that requires patience and discipline. Money trees don't grow overnight, but with time and consistent care, they can provide you with an abundant harvest.

Compound trading is like tending to your own money garden. You plant the seeds of your investments, nurture them with patience and knowledge, and watch them grow into flourishing money trees. The power of compounding is your ally in this journey, multiplying your wealth over time. So, as you embark on your investment journey, remember that with the right approach and a long-term perspective, your financial garden can yield bountiful results.

It's essential to have a clear financial goal. With this strategy and by visualising, you will be able to put clear action behind your monetary goals and dreams.

"Doubt kills more dreams than failure ever will."

Suzy Kassem

PUTTING THE ENERGY OF MONEY INTO ACTION

Let me tell you about Sarah. She used to live week to week, but she turned her financial life around by:

- Changing Her Mindset: Sarah stopped seeing money as a scarce resource and started believing in her ability to create abundance through her skills and hard work.
- Mindful Spending: She took a hard look at her spending habits, trimmed the fat, and directed her money towards savings and investments that matched her goals.
- Giving Back: Sarah started donating part of her income to causes she cared about, which gave her a sense of purpose and fulfilment.
- Investing Wisely: She educated herself about investing and built a diverse portfolio that steadily grew over time.

Through these steps, Sarah not only improved her financial situation but also changed her whole vibe about money. It went from being a source of stress to a tool for empowerment and positive change.

The energy of money is a bit like catching smoke – it's elusive but not impossible to understand. By exploring its various aspects and learning how to make it work for you, you can turn your relationship with money from one of stress and scarcity into one of abundance and purpose. In the chapters ahead, we'll dive into practical strategies for building a healthier and more prosperous connection with the energy of money.

Visualisation works most powerfully when you realise that it is already a reality on the unseen level. It's already there."

Eckhart Tolle

VISUALISING YOUR PATH TO SUCCESS

In the pursuit of your dreams and goals, it's crucial to do more than simply wish for them. You must visualise them with crystal clarity, making every detail tangible and vivid in your mind's eye. Think of it as plotting a course on a map; the more specific your destination, the easier it is to reach. Let's explore this concept further.

Consider, for instance, the goal of acquiring a new car. It's not enough to vaguely wish for it; you must visualise the exact amount of money needed. I want you to take a proactive step by visiting a car dealership, sitting down, and comprehending all the intricacies of your desired vehicle. Understand the various options, add-ons, and features that will constitute the total cost of your purchase. Get a detailed quote in writing. Factor in a 10% buffer for potential inflation. With this precise figure in mind, start visualising that new car

Your goal might not be an entire car or house but simply a substantial deposit. We all know that securing a loan becomes easier with a larger down payment. Pursuing this method sets you on the path towards your desired achievement, be it a car, boat, or house.

The key here is to make the image of your goal crystal clear. This clarity simplifies the journey toward your destination because you know exactly where you're headed. Imagine it as entering a destination into a mapping app. You receive step-by-step directions and an estimated time of arrival. The beauty of modern map apps is that they allow for occasional detours while still guiding you to your endpoint. These detours, as you'll discover on your journey, often yield valuable learning experiences, provided you don't lose sight of your destination.

Moreover, be definite about what you want and why you're striving to achieve it. There's psychology behind this clarity of purpose—it fuels your determination and helps you overcome obstacles. After all, you can't reach your destination if you don't have one.

Lastly, remember that a dream is just a dream if you don't put in the effort to turn it into reality. And an important factor to remember is that YOUR dreams are just that, and while you may get help along the way, like the messages in this book, ultimately reaching the destination is within your power. So, determine what actions you'll take to achieve your dreams and goals. As the saying goes, "A dream without a plan is just a wish." Your goals are within reach, but it's your commitment and purposeful actions that will transform them from dreams into tangible achievements.

"Every skill you acquire doubles your odds for success."

Scott Adams

THE POWER OF IMAGINATION

Visualisation is a potent mental tool that allows you to paint a vivid mental picture of your desired outcomes. It's not just about daydreaming or fantasising; it's a deliberate and structured process of mentally rehearsing success. When you visualise, you engage your senses—seeing, hearing, feeling, and even smelling and tasting—as if your goals were already a reality.

For instance, when you visualise owning that new car, it's not just about seeing it in your driveway. It's about feeling the smooth leather seats, hearing the purr of the engine, smelling the new car scent, and experiencing the joy and pride that comes with owning it. This sensory-rich experience imprints your subconscious mind with a clear image of what you're working towards, making it feel more achievable and real.

Let's open the gateway to achievement.

Visualisation is a remarkable mental technique that bridges the gap between imagination and accomplishment. It's a dynamic process that engages your mind's eye to craft a detailed mental representation of your desired goals. This practice goes far beyond mere daydreaming or wishful thinking; it's a structured and deliberate exercise that simulates success in your mind's theatre. Think of something as simple as a butterfly, and you will likely see many, then maybe ask to see a yellow car; I'm sure many will drive past. This is the power of Visualisation in everyday life. It's amazing really!

When you embark on a visualisation journey, you are essentially activating all your senses to create a profound and multisensory experience. It's like taking a mental test drive of your dreams. For example, let's revisit the idea of owning a new car. Visualisation involves not only seeing that car parked in your driveway, but it goes much deeper.

"People begin to become successful the minute they decide to be."

Harvey MacKay

THE SENSE OF SUCCESS

- Sight: You vividly see the gleaming exterior, the elegant curves, and the radiant paintwork. You observe how it sparkles in the sunlight, and you take in every intricate detail, from the sleek headlights to the polished alloy wheels.

- Sound: You hear the satisfying click as you unlock the car, the gentle hum of the engine as it purrs to life, and the smooth swish of the tires on the road as you take it for a spin. You listen to your favourite music playing on the top-notch sound system.

- Touch: You feel the supple leather seats beneath your fingertips, the reassuring grip of the steering wheel in your hands, and the cool touch of the dashboard as you explore the vehicle's features.

- Smell: You inhale the intoxicating scent of a brand-new car— the fresh upholstery, the hint of new plastic, and that distinctive new car aroma that signifies the beginning of a thrilling journey.

- Taste: While taste might not be directly associated with a car, it can be an element in other visualisations. For instance, if your goal is to embark on a culinary adventure, you might imagine savouring exotic flavours and tasting success in every bite.

The Subconscious Connection needs to be wired into your active thoughts. This sensory-rich experience during visualisation is not just a mental exercise; it's a process that deeply imprints your subconscious mind. Your subconscious doesn't distinguish between reality and what you vividly imagine. As far as your subconscious is concerned, what you've envisioned during visualisation is as real as any tangible experience.

This creates a powerful alignment between your conscious desires and your subconscious beliefs. And by consistently practicing visualisation, you instil a profound sense of belief in your ability to achieve your goals. You begin to view your aspirations as not just possibilities but inevitabilities. This newfound confidence becomes a driving force, motivating you to take the necessary actions to turn your dreams into concrete achievements.

When you can clearly see and feel your desired outcomes in your mind, you're better equipped to navigate the challenges and setbacks that may arise along the way.

Visualisation is not a passive act; it's an active step towards your aspirations. It's the ignition key that starts the engine of your ambition, propelling you forward with a sense of purpose and determination. So, close your eyes, imagine your dreams in vivid detail, and watch as your goals transition from mere ideas to tangible realities.

Incorporating visualisation into your daily routine is like unlocking a secret treasure chest on your journey to success. It's a potent tool that transcends wishful thinking and propels you towards your goals with unwavering purpose and determination. In this chapter, we'll explore the profound impact of visualisation on your aspirations and how it can guide you through the twists and turns of your path to achievement.

One of the first remarkable aspects of visualisation is its ability to crystallise your goals. Think of it as a mental blueprint for your future. When you take the time to visualise your desires, you're essentially bringing them into sharp focus. It's like adjusting the lens on a camera to capture a clear, high-definition image.

By clearly defining what you want and how you intend to get there, you're not only setting yourself up for success but also enhancing your motivation. This newfound clarity acts as a beacon, guiding your actions and decisions towards your desired destination.

Give yourself the clarity of purpose. We all know that person on a deep search for purpose, whether that is to serve others, be it as a Doctor or Nurse, or perhaps the desire to follow dreams and become a famous actor, or whether that search for a sense of purpose becomes an all-consuming and overwhelming search for inner peace.

What if I told you, purpose could change, and while you may not be one of those people that is sure, you can walk through life with the knowledge you have many different purposes to many different places, people, and things, not one fixed purpose, and maybe that is true freedom.

Choice is always freedom, and that should give you a sense of excitement rather than the stress of the unknown and change the way you look at this.

Along the way there is always going to be challenges and mountains to climb. Life's journey is rarely a straight road devoid of obstacles. Along the path to success, you're bound to encounter challenges and setbacks. This is where the power of visualisation truly shines.

When you've vividly imagined your goals, you've essentially rehearsed success in your mind. You've seen yourself triumphing over obstacles, overcoming hurdles, and emerging victorious. This mental rehearsal equips you with the resilience and determination needed to face adversity head-on.

Rather than seeing setbacks as insurmountable roadblocks, you view them as temporary detours. Just as a seasoned traveller might adjust their route to reach their destination, they may take a drive to the beach on their journey to a snowcapped mountain, you too can adapt your approach when faced with unexpected challenges. Visualisation becomes your compass, helping you stay on course and maintain your enthusiasm, even in the face of adversity.

We learn by doing, and by practising, dreams require action to be achieved and guess what, life is not a Disney movie, and no one is going to save you or achieve YOUR dreams, except you, and this is where these techniques will become invaluable now and as your life evolves.

Visualisation is not a passive exercise; it's an active step towards your aspirations. It's the ignition key that starts the engine of your ambition. Just as a car doesn't move forward until the key is turned, your goals remain stagnant until you activate them with visualisation.

When you close your eyes and immerse yourself in the vivid details of your dreams, you're sending a powerful message to your subconscious mind. You're saying, "This is what I want, and I believe it's possible." "There's my new car, I love that red colour!"
This unwavering belief becomes the driving force behind your actions.

Visualisation propels you forward with a sense of purpose and determination. It's not just a fleeting daydream; it's a deliberate and structured process that primes your mind for success. As you consistently practice visualisation, you'll find yourself naturally gravitating towards actions that align with your goals. It's as if you've set your internal compass to a specific direction, and your actions follow suit. It's like taking the blueprints of your dreams and constructing them in the physical world.

By repeatedly visualising your desired outcomes, you're training your mind to work tirelessly towards those goals, even when you're not consciously aware of it. It becomes a part of your subconscious programming, influencing your decisions, actions, and the way you perceive opportunities.

So, as you embark on your journey towards success, remember that visualisation is not just a mental exercise; it's a dynamic force that can shape your destiny. Embrace it as a powerful ally in your pursuit of greatness. Close your eyes, imagine your dreams in vivid detail, and watch as your goals transition from mere ideas to tangible realities.

With the transformative power of visualisation, your journey becomes not just a path to success but a thrilling adventure towards self-realisation and purpose. So, start programming those coordinates into that GPS navigation system and the more precise your destination coordinates, the more efficiently you can chart your course. When you set clear and specific goals, you create a roadmap for your journey.

For example, if you're aiming to buy a new house, specifying details like the number of bedrooms, the neighbourhood, and the architectural style not only makes the goal more tangible but also guides your actions. You know what kind of properties to explore, which neighbourhoods to focus on, and what budget to work towards.

Overcoming Obstacles: The Detours on Your Journey

No journey is without its detours and challenges. In the pursuit of your goals, you'll encounter setbacks, unexpected expenses, and moments of doubt. These are the moments where your clarity of purpose and determination become your guiding stars.

Consider these obstacles as temporary roadblocks, not dead ends. Just like a GPS recalculates your route when you take a wrong turn, you, too, can adjust your approach. Perhaps you need to revise your strategy and seek additional training or explore new opportunities. These detours often provide the most valuable lessons and can even lead to a better route to your destination.

The Psychology of Commitment: Turning Dreams into Achievements

Your unwavering commitment to your goals is the driving force behind their realisation. When you're definite about what you want and most importantly why you want it, you tap into a deep well of motivation.

This psychological commitment keeps you focused and resilient in the face of adversity. Think of your commitment as the fuel that propels you forward on your journey. It helps you push through challenges, maintain your enthusiasm, and stay the course when distractions and doubts arise.

Achievement of your dreams and goals is not a matter of chance or luck but rather a deliberate and structured process that begins with a clear mental image of what you want, progresses with precise goal setting, and gains momentum through proactive steps and unwavering commitment. Along the way, you'll face detours and challenges, but your determination and clarity of purpose will guide you to your destination.

Remember, your dreams are within reach, and with the right mindset and actions, you can transform them from mere fantasies into tangible achievements.

"Success is not the key to happiness.

Happiness is the key to success.

If you love what you are doing, you will be successful."

Albert Schweitzer

THE WOLF YOU FEED

The Two Wolves story, often falsely attributed to Cherokee or other Native American origins, is believed to be a Christian parable written by non-Indigenous authors possibly from Bible times. It tells of an elder using a metaphor of two wolves in conflict to teach inner struggles to a younger person. When asked which wolf prevails, the elder responds, "whichever one you feed." While various versions exist, often using imagery of white vs. black and good vs. evil, like the devil and angel on your shoulder, the story's typically fabricated origin makes it widely regarded as fakelore.

"One wolf is evil - it represents anger, jealousy, greed, resentment, lies, inferiority, and ego. The other wolf is good - it represents joy, peace, love, hope, humility, kindness, empathy, and truth.

The wolf that wins is the one you feed."

UNKNOWN

This is something we are all guilty of at times; we all have moments of despair when the world feels like it is closing in, and that negative bias takes over. Let's delve into the meaning of "The Wolf You Feed" and how overcoming this negative bias will not only aid you on your journey but also transform your life. By cultivating a positive mindset, not only will you find your own path illuminated, but you will also become a magnet for others. People will be naturally drawn to your optimism, creating a ripple effect of positivity in your life and the lives of those around you.

In the heart of a tranquil village, nestled amidst rolling hills and lush forests, there lived an old storyteller named Alistair. Alistair was known far and wide for his wisdom, and his stories were like gems of guidance for the villagers. His favourite tale, one he told under the shade of an ancient oak tree, was the fable of "The Wolf You Feed."

The Fable of the Two Wolves

One crisp autumn evening, as the sun dipped below the horizon, casting a golden hue across the village, Alistair gathered the villagers around the flickering fire. He began his story with a solemn tone, "Once upon a time, in a village much like our own, there lived a young boy named Liam."

"Liam was a curious lad, and like all of us, he had two wolves within him. These wolves were not of flesh and blood but of a different nature. One was the Wolf of Negativity, sly and cunning, feeding on doubt, fear, and anger. The other was the Wolf of Positivity, gentle and kind, nourished by hope, love, and joy."

"As the days passed, Liam discovered that he could choose which wolf to feed. Whenever he harboured bitterness, envy, or negativity in his heart, the Wolf of Negativity grew stronger. But when he embraced gratitude, kindness, and optimism, it was the Wolf of Positivity that thrived."

The Power of Choice

Alistair paused, letting the firelight dance in the villagers' eyes. "You see, dear friends," he continued, "Liam's story is not just his alone; it's a reflection of all our lives. Each day, we face choices that influence which wolf we feed within ourselves."

The villagers nodded in agreement, for they knew the truth in Alistair's words. Life was indeed a series of choices, and the wolves within represented the choices they made.

Lessons from the Fable

Alistair went on to share the wisdom embedded in the fable:

Self-Awareness: The first step to feeding the right wolf is self-awareness. Recognise your emotions, thoughts, and actions. Are they nurturing the Wolf of Positivity or strengthening the Wolf of Negativity?

Choose Wisely: Life presents us with countless opportunities to choose our responses. When faced with adversity, choose to hope over despair, love over hatred, and forgiveness over grudges.

Practice Gratitude: Cultivate a heart of gratitude. Focus on the blessings in your life, no matter how small they may seem. Gratitude is food for the Wolf of Positivity.

Surround Yourself with Positivity: Seek the company of those who uplift you, who inspire you to be a better person. Positive relationships and environments nurture the Wolf of Positivity.

Daily Nourishment: Just as a garden requires daily care, feeding the Wolf of Positivity is an ongoing process. Small acts of kindness, self-compassion, and positivity compound over time.

As the night sky filled with stars, and the fire's glow illuminated the faces of the villagers, Alistair concluded his tale. "Remember, dear friends, the fable of the Wolf You Feed is a reminder that the choices we make shape our character and our destiny. Choose wisely, for it is the wolf you feed that will ultimately define your journey."
The villagers left the gathering with hearts and minds aglow, their spirits inspired to nurture the Wolf of Positivity within, for they knew that in doing so, they could transform not only their own lives but also their beloved village. And under the guidance of Alistair's wisdom, they set forth on a path of conscious choices and abundant positivity.

The fable of the Two Wolves serves as a timeless metaphor for the inner conflicts we all face. The central message, "whichever one you

feed," reminds us of the power of our choices in shaping our character and destiny.
We are urged to engage in introspection and deliberately select thoughts, emotions, and actions that resonate with our loftiest aspirations. This advice is especially pertinent when venturing into the realms of trading and investing, where maintaining a positive mindset can be just as pivotal as the decisions we make. By nurturing the positive facets within ourselves, we pave the way for personal growth, resilience, and inner harmony.

The enduring allure of this parable stems from its capacity to kindle mindfulness regarding our choices, recognising their profound influence in shaping the trajectories of our lives. This awareness holds particular significance in the intricate realms of trading and investment, where the interplay of choices and mindset can chart the course towards financial success and fulfilment.

"We suffer more from imagination than in reality."

Seneca

THE ORIGINS OF SUFFERING

In the intricate tapestry of human existence, suffering has been a perennial companion. From the trials of everyday life to the challenges faced in the trading, understanding the roots of suffering is paramount, because if you know where your trigger points are, you can change the outcome. In this chapter, we deep dive into the age-old concept that attachment and craving lie at the heart of suffering, affecting not only our personal lives but also our trading endeavours.

The Human Condition

Suffering is an inherent aspect of the human condition. Whether it's the pain of loss, the anguish of unfulfilled desires, or the stress of uncertainty, suffering can manifest in countless forms. In relationships you'll see these manifest as arguments and broken promises. In the realm of trading, these emotional struggles are amplified as financial stakes loom large. As your balance grows, so will the attachment and craving to have the things you want and to be where you want to be, patience and understanding will be thrown out the window. And this is where the mistakes and frustrations creep in, after all there is a lot more on the line here, the risks are greater? Or are they?

The Roots of Suffering

Buddhist philosophy, among others, teaches that the root of suffering is attachment and craving. Attachment is our deep-seated desire to cling to things, people, or outcomes, believing they are the sources of our happiness. Craving, on the other hand, is the insatiable longing for more, driven by the belief that acquiring more material possessions or wealth will bring contentment.

In trading, these tendencies can be particularly potent. Traders often become attached to their positions, desperately hoping they will turn profitable. The craving for quick gains can lead to impulsive decisions, heightening the emotional rollercoaster that comes with financial markets. This is often where sloppy trading takes over and mistakes follow in quick succession.

The Illusion of Control

Both in life and trading, attachment and craving are rooted in the illusion of control. We often convince ourselves that by holding onto people, possessions, or specific outcomes, we can shape our destinies. However, life's unpredictability and the inherent volatility of financial markets challenge this illusion.

In trading, the illusion of control can lead to overtrading, revenge trading, or stubbornly holding onto losing positions, all of which can result in significant losses and emotional turmoil.

Letting Go

The path to alleviating suffering lies in the practice of letting go. In life, it means releasing our attachment to specific outcomes and embracing the impermanence of all things.

In trading, it involves detaching emotionally from individual trades and recognising that losses are an integral part of the journey. As we progress, it is the ability to trust in yourself and know the trade has been set up to the best of your ability, and the rest is outside of your control.

Mindful Trading

Mindfulness, a practice borrowed from ancient traditions, can be a powerful tool in both life and trading. By cultivating mindfulness, we learn to observe our thoughts and emotions without judgment, allowing us to respond rationally rather than react emotionally. Keep a journal, it is a valuable tool to know and understand to change the patterns that will develop as your balance grows.

Traders sometimes struggle with closing losing trades due to several psychological and emotional factors. Here are some reasons why traders may not close trades when they should and believe the market will reverse in their favour:

- Hope and Optimism: Traders often hold onto losing positions because they hope the market will turn around and the trade will become profitable. This optimism can lead to a reluctance to accept losses.

- Fear of Regret: Traders may fear the regret of closing a trade prematurely only to see it reverse in their favour shortly after. This fear can lead them to delay closing losing positions.

- Overconfidence: This can make traders believe they are right, and the market is wrong. This cognitive bias can lead to holding onto losing positions longer than necessary.

- Sunk Cost Fallacy: Traders sometimes fall into the trap of considering the money already invested in a losing trade as a "sunk cost." They may feel compelled to continue with the trade, hoping to recover their losses.

- Loss Aversion: Human psychology tends to weigh losses more heavily than gains. Traders may hold onto losing positions to avoid realising a loss, even if it means risking further losses.

- Greed: This can drive traders to hold onto losing positions in the hope of making larger profits. This can be particularly risky as it may lead to larger losses.

- Lack of Discipline: Some traders lack discipline in adhering to their trading plan, which includes setting stop-loss orders or OCO's to limit losses. Without such discipline, they may hold onto losing positions.

- Confirmation Bias: Traders may seek out information that confirms their belief that the trade will turn around, ignoring contrary signals or information that suggests otherwise.

- Emotional Attachment: Traders can become emotionally attached to a trade, especially if they have invested a significant amount of time and effort in analysing it. This emotional attachment can cloud their judgment.

- Lack of Experience: Inexperienced traders may not have developed the skills and knowledge to recognise when a trade is unlikely to turn profitable. They may hold onto losing positions due to inexperience.

Be brave. Take risks. Nothing can substitute experience.

Paulo Coelho

To overcome these challenges once your balance starts growing, successful traders often employ risk management strategies, such as setting stop-loss orders, diversifying their portfolios, and adhering to a well-defined trading plan. They also cultivate emotional discipline and realistic expectations, understanding that losses are an inevitable part of trading. Ultimately, the ability to close losing trades promptly and objectively is a crucial skill for long-term success in the financial markets.

In exploring the origins of suffering in life and trading, we uncover profound insights into the human psyche. Attachment and craving, rooted in the illusion of control, are at the heart of our emotional turmoil. By embracing the practice of letting go and adopting mindfulness, we can navigate the turbulent waters of trading and life with greater equanimity.

As we continue our journey, let us remember that understanding the roots of suffering is the first step towards transcending it. The Trading world is where fortunes rise and fall, this wisdom can be the difference between turmoil and tranquillity, between financial ruin and sustainable success.

You've got to know where to hold ém, know where to fold ém, know when to walk away. And know when to run.

You never count your money when you're sitting at the table. There'll be time enough for counting when the dealing's done.

Kenny Rogers

The sage advice of Kenny Rogers' timeless song, "The Gambler," holds profound significance on your path to maintaining a balanced mindset in the world of trading. It's about discerning when a trade is favourable, recognising when it's time to take a step back from the market, and, most importantly, grasping that the pursuit of wealth should never be your primary objective. It's NEVER about the money!

As your trading portfolio expands, it becomes increasingly crucial not to become overly fixated on the numerical values. Recall that your journey likely commenced with a mere one thousand dollars. Success in trading should not be solely gauged by the size of your account but rather by your capacity to make sound, well-informed decisions and maintain a composed demeanour, regardless of the financial stakes involved.

If, along the way, you find yourself becoming preoccupied with money as the ultimate goal, it's time to revisit your initial motivations – your "why." Why did you embark on this trading journey in the first place? What drove you to take this path? Reconnecting with your original purpose can serve as a compass, guiding you back to a mindset where your focus transcends mere financial gains. In the end, it's the ability to stay true to your purpose and make prudent choices that truly defines your success in the world of trading. Choices are what make your life what it is, it is ALWAYS within your power!

"Be inspired when you see someone else succeed, envy will only make you doubt yourself."

Bhawna Gautam

THE GREEN EYED MONSTER

Let's navigate the perils of comparison and envy, by exploring how these habits affect trading, life, social media, and psychology.

The Allure and Pitfalls

In this chapter, we embark on a journey to unravel the intricate web of comparison and envy, examining how these tendencies impact various facets of our lives. From trading to the intricacies of human psychology, these habits have a far-reaching influence on our well-being.

Let's delve into the allure and perils of these emotions and how they shape our experiences and may influence your trading as you progress and stop you from being the best you can be.

The Temptation of Measuring Success

Trading, especially in the ever-evolving world of cryptocurrency, is a minefield where success can be elusive. It's natural for traders to assess their progress by comparing their portfolios and outcomes to others.

However, this habit of benchmarking can lead to unnecessary stress and anxiety. Remember, every trading journey is unique, and what works for one trader may not work for another. Instead of fixating on comparing your returns to peers, concentrate on honing your trading strategy, mastering risk management, and embracing continuous learning.

In trading, it's not about who has the most but who makes the wisest decisions. Comparing can be futile, as you never truly know another person's goals or needs.

Life: Navigating the Sea of Expectations

The habits of comparison and envy often manifest in our personal and professional spheres. It's easy to fall into the trap of measuring our achievements against societal norms or the accomplishments of others. Recently, I've heard various comparisons from different individuals: "My younger brother just bought a house," or "All my friends are having babies, and I'm not starting."

Remember that everyone's journey is unique, and it's important to define success on your terms. Celebrate your own milestones and cherish the experiences that shape your life. Embrace your individual path, for it is distinct and valuable.

Social Media: The Highlight Reel vs. Reality

In today's era dominated by social media, the habits of comparison and envy have found fertile ground. As we scroll through carefully curated feeds, we are often bombarded by images of seemingly perfect lives led by friends, celebrities, and influencers. It's easy to feel inadequate in comparison. However, it's essential to remember that social media often presents a distorted reality. People showcase their best moments while concealing their struggles.

This phenomenon is particularly prevalent among traders, with some flaunting their massive gains. While it may be tempting to shift your strategy based on their apparent success, I urge you to exercise caution. To combat the corrosive effects of envy, curate your online experience. Follow accounts that inspire and uplift you, and don't hesitate to take breaks from social media to reconnect with the tangible world, where authenticity thrives.

"In order to be irreplaceable, one must always be different."

Coco Chanel

Psychology: The Battle Within

Envy is a fundamental human emotion, but when it becomes a recurring pattern, it can erode our mental well-being. Within the realm of psychology, experts stress the importance of self-awareness. Recognise when you're comparing yourself to others and acknowledge those feelings without judgment. Consider journaling your thoughts, as this practice can help dispel negative biases. Shift your focus toward gratitude for what you have and set achievable goals aligned with your values. Often, the journey begins with smaller, more attainable goals, and that's perfectly valid.

When envy becomes an entrenched habit, and you find yourself trapped in your own thoughts, seeking professional help is a wise choice. It's a sign of strength, not weakness, to seek guidance when comparison and envy become overwhelming.

Tall Poppy Syndrome

Australians are known for their "tall poppy syndrome," where success is often met with envy or criticism. It's essential to understand that celebrating your achievements doesn't equate to boasting. However, constant comparison to others can lead to self-doubt and envy.

Embrace your wins, but also acknowledge that everyone faces their unique challenges. Value humility and remember to stay grounded while supporting others on their journeys. Embrace your uniqueness, whether you're navigating trading, enjoying the ups and downs of life, scrolling through social media, or managing your mental well-being.

Comparison and envy can be subtle thieves of joy, so set your own path, embrace your journey, and shine as the distinctive star you are. Here's to a life free from the shackles of envy and comparison!

Embrace Your Unique Journey

In a world that celebrates individuality, remember that your path is uniquely yours. Whether you're navigating the complexities of trading, savouring the nuances of life, engaging with social media, or tending to your psychological well-being, the habits of comparison and envy can dim the brilliance of your journey.

Embrace your uniqueness, set your own benchmarks, and find contentment in the authenticity of your path. There's no need to measure yourself against others; you're already a distinctive star in your own constellation. Here's to a life liberated from the chains of envy and comparison!

"I am my problem, but also my solution."

Unknown

AM I THE PROBLEM?

Sometimes you start to wonder if you are the problem or obstacle in the way to finding your own success and happiness.

It's easy to get caught up in the whirlwind of excitement and anxiety. As traders, we often find ourselves asking the same recurring question: "Where is this trade going?" It's a question that echoes in our minds, a relentless whisper that can keep us up at night. But what if, instead of constantly seeking external answers, we turned inward to ask a different question: "Am I the problem?"

This chapter challenges you to embark on a journey of self-reflection, to let go of ego and embrace trust, not just in the market but in yourself. It urges you to stop obsessing over the direction of a trade and to consider a radical alternative: exiting immediately and pulling the stop loss. This may sound counterintuitive, but it's a step towards acknowledging that sometimes, the problem isn't the market; it's us.

Trading, like any relationship, demands trust and respect. If you can't trust the trade, if doubt and anxiety cloud your judgment, why are you placing it in the first place? The Law of Success, as we've explored in previous chapters, teaches us that our thoughts and feelings have a profound impact on our outcomes. When you approach trading with uncertainty and fear, you attract more of the same. Like always attracts like.

Imagine the trade as if it were a relationship. In a healthy partnership, you trust your significant other to make decisions without your constant supervision. You trust that they will remain trustworthy and respectful of you. This trust forms the foundation of the relationship, allowing it to thrive and grow. Similarly, in trading, you must trust the process and your ability to make informed decisions.

Building this inner knowing is crucial on your path to becoming a successful trader and achieving your dreams and goals. It involves a deep understanding of the market, a solid grasp of your trading strategy, and most importantly, self-confidence.

Let's delve deeper into these key aspects:

1. Understanding the Market: Knowledge is power in the trading world. It's essential to continually educate yourself about the financial instruments you trade, market dynamics, and economic indicators. The more you understand, the more confident you become. Remember, ignorance breeds anxiety.

2. Mastering Your Trading Strategy: Your trading strategy is your roadmap. It should be based on sound principles and thoroughly tested. When you trust your strategy, you can execute trades with conviction, even in the face of uncertainty and in any market, Bull, or Bear.

3. Developing Self-Confidence: Trusting yourself is perhaps the most challenging aspect of trading. It requires you to overcome self-doubt and build a mindset that fosters resilience and adaptability. Confidence comes from experience, so keep trading and learning from your successes and failures.

As you cultivate these elements, you'll notice a profound shift in your trading mindset. You'll stop obsessing over the market's every move and start trusting your instincts. You'll develop a sense of inner calm that allows you to make rational decisions, even in volatile situations. But remember, this journey isn't without its challenges. It's not about eliminating all doubt and fear; it's about managing them. Healthy scepticism can be a valuable tool in risk management. The key is finding the right balance between trust and caution.

The question, "Am I the problem?" is not an indictment of your abilities but an invitation to self-improvement. By letting go of ego, embracing trust, and building an inner knowing, you can transform yourself into a successful trader who attracts positive thoughts and experiences. Trading, like any relationship, is a journey of growth and self-discovery. If there's no growth eventually a tree dies, so keep learning, the more you invest in yourself, the greater your chances of achieving your trading dreams and goals. So, take a deep breath, trust the process, and embark on this transformative journey with confidence.

TRUSTING THE TRADE

Uncertainty reigns supreme and markets can change direction in the blink of an eye, there is one concept that stands out as both a challenge and a necessity: trust. Trusting the trade is not just about having faith in the market; it's about believing in yourself, knowing that you are in control, and accepting that whatever happens is okay.

The Illusion of Certainty

Let's start by addressing a common misconception in the trading world: the illusion of certainty. Many traders mistakenly believe that they can predict the future with 100% accuracy, that they can always pinpoint the exact direction a trade will take. This belief is akin to thinking that in a relationship, you can be certain your partner will never stray, never make a mistake, never change, or never want something different to you.

In both trading and relationships, this level of certainty is an illusion. Life is filled with variables, and there are no guarantees. Just as you can't control every aspect of your partner's life, you can't control every market fluctuation. But that doesn't mean you're powerless. It means you must shift your focus from trying to predict the unpredictable to mastering your own actions and reactions.

Trusting Yourself

Trusting the trade begins with trusting yourself. Just as you trust your judgment when choosing a partner, why are you with them otherwise? You must trust your skills and instincts as a trader. This self-reliance is the cornerstone of successful trading. When you believe in your ability to analyse markets, formulate strategies, and make informed decisions, you're better equipped to handle the inevitable ups and downs.

Building this self-trust is an ongoing process. It requires education, practice, and a healthy dose of self-awareness. Start by thoroughly understanding your trading strategy. Know its strengths and weaknesses and be prepared to adapt when necessary. Trust that you've put in the work to develop a strategy that aligns with your goals.

The Parallel with Relationships

To illustrate the concept of trusting the trade, let's draw a parallel with relationships. When your partner goes out for the evening, you trust your choice in that person. You believe they will return home, even though they may not come straight back. They might stop by the kebab shop or engage in a meaningless conversation with a stranger. Despite these uncertainties, you trust they will come home and have respect for your relationship.

In trading, think of the market as your partner. It may take unexpected turns, fluctuating up and down before reaching your desired sell price. Just as in a relationship, waves may rock the boat, but you know how to adjust your sails. If the market goes in the opposite direction, it's not the end of the world. Adjust your strategy.

In both trading and relationships, trust is cultivated during the moments when we're not actively monitoring. Whether it's your partner enjoying a night out with friends, firmly declining unwanted advances, or your own decision to step away from the trading screens, trust develops in these unseen moments.

You understand that in any scenario, there's the option to make a choice: to either continue nurturing the relationship or, if necessary, to end it. Similarly, in trading, it's the recognition that your carefully planned trade will either progress towards its targets or be limited by the stop loss you've set. Trust is not solely built on what you witness in real-time but also on the confidence that you've made choices and preparations to safeguard your interests in the larger context.

Managing Uncertainty

Uncertainty is an inherent part of both trading and life. Instead of fearing it, embrace it. Understand that not every trade will go your way, just as not every aspect of a relationship will be perfect. But it's how you respond to these uncertainties that defines your success.

In trading, you have tools at your disposal to manage uncertainty, such as setting stop losses and adjusting your positions. These tools are like the trust you have in your partner to come home; they provide a safety net.

Trusting the trade is a journey of self-discovery and empowerment. It's about letting go of the need for absolute certainty and focusing on what you can control—yourself and your actions. Just as in a relationship, trust in trading can weather storms and uncertainties. When you trust yourself and your trading strategy, you'll find the confidence to navigate the ever-changing landscape of the markets.

Remember, a trade going against you is not the end of the world; just like your partner taking that detour for a kebab, it's an opportunity to learn and adapt. Trust the process, trust yourself, and embrace the journey of trading with a mindset of self-reliance and resilience.

"If you spend too much time thinking about a thing, you'll never get it done."

Bruce Lee

"Trust is a core currency of any relationship. Sometimes our need to control and micromanage everything erodes our confidence in ourselves and others.

The TRUTH: people are much more capable than we think. A hearty does of trust is often what's needed to unlock magic. Go ahead, have faith."

Kris Carr

THE CURRENCY OF TRUST

In the complex landscape of human dynamics and financial markets, trust plays an unexpectedly central role. In this chapter, we embark on a thought-provoking journey that draws parallels between the trust we invest in relationships and the trust we extend in trading. By examining these two seemingly disparate areas of life, we uncover profound insights into the essence of trust itself and its transformative power.

What is the Currency of Trust?

Trust is the currency of both relationships and trading, a valuable asset that fuels our interactions and decisions. In relationships, trust forms the very fabric of connections, while in trading, it shapes our investment choices and strategies. Without trust, both domains would be barren landscapes, devoid of the human touch that makes them thrive.

Trust is the cornerstone of both personal relationships and trading. It's a precious currency that must be given freely because without trust, our interactions and investments are like ships adrift without a compass.

Consider this: you can't shatter trust if it never existed; instead, you inadvertently nurture your own insecurities. In the realm of relationships, self-esteem is bolstered not only by the connections we embrace but also by the knowledge that we have the autonomy to choose. It's akin to the freedom of a bird released into the open sky, yet it willingly returns home.

Similarly, in trading, trust in oneself is paramount. It's about understanding how you'll react with each trade, and this self-trust is the compass that guides you on the journey from one thousand to a million.

Both in trading and relationships, without the trust that you can make informed decisions, the path forward remains uncertain and fraught with doubt.

Building and Breaking Trust

In relationships, trust is built over time through shared experiences, open communication, and a consistent display of reliability. Similarly, in trading, trust is cultivated by conducting diligent research, making informed decisions, and adhering to a well-defined strategy. It's a precious commodity that requires nurturing and can be shattered in an instant.

"Trust takes years to build and seconds to break."

Unknown

Feeding Insecurities

This goes back to the chapter of 'The Wolf You Feed," refusing to extend trust in either realm has strikingly similar consequences.

In relationships, withholding trust can lead to insecurities, creating a climate of doubt and suspicion. Similarly, in trading, constant scepticism can hinder progress, leaving investors paralysed by their own fears and uncertainties. It's a self-perpetuating cycle that often prevents us from reaching our full potential.

Self-Esteem and Choices

One of the most profound aspects of trust in both relationships and trading is its impact on self-esteem. In relationships, self-esteem is bolstered not only by the love and trust of those we embrace but also by the knowledge that we have choices. The ability to turn away, knowing we are wanted, provides a sense of empowerment and self-worth. In trading, self-esteem is elevated when we have the confidence to make choices, manage risks, and chart our own path to financial success.

The Freedom of Trust

Imagine trust as a bird in the palm of your hand. Just as in relationships, where trust allows us to give and receive love freely, in trading, it grants us the freedom to make calculated decisions without the burden of constant doubt. Hold onto the bird too tightly in your hand you could kill it or at least bruise its wings keeping it down unable to fly. But letting the bird taking flight, trusting it will return but also knowing if it doesn't you are still ok.

In trading sitting and watching the trades every move only makes you second guess the overall process. Yes, markets fluctuate, sideways, and yes it goes up and down, trust in your well-formed decisions and use of a stop loss ensure your overall success.

Trust in both realms offers us the opportunity to explore new horizons while knowing we have a secure home to return to.

"A bird sitting in a tree isn't afraid of the branch breaking, because the trust is not in the branch, but in its own ability to fly."

Unknown

This exploration of trust in relationships and trading shows how trust is the lifeblood of both realms, how it can be built and broken, and how withholding it can lead to insecurities. We've also discovered that trust, whether in relationships or trading, has the power to enhance self-esteem and empower us to make choices.

Ultimately, this chapter highlights the universality of trust as a fundamental human experience, one that transcends the boundaries between matters of the heart and the intricacies of financial markets.

Trust, like the bird taking flight, enables us to navigate the world with confidence, knowing that we can always return to the secure embrace of our relationships or the soundness of our investment strategies.

The timeless adage "Knowledge is Power" extends its wisdom beyond the realm of mere information. It harbours a profound truth about trust and decision-making. When we delve deeper into the quote, we uncover a fundamental principle: true empowerment comes from a deep understanding of the motives that underlie every action. It is this understanding that allows us to trust ourselves to make the most suitable choices for our own well-being.

In essence, knowledge provides us with the clarity and discernment needed to navigate the complexities of life, enabling us to align our decisions with our values and aspirations. When we grasp the motives behind our own actions and those of others, trust becomes not just a word but a cornerstone of our ability to thrive and make informed choices that resonate with our authentic selves.

"Knowledge is Power."

Unknown

THE PARADOX OF BEING REPLACEABLE

This chapter delves into a fascinating paradox: the duality of being irreplaceable while acknowledging our own replaceability. It explores how this profound notion influences our decisions and perspectives in both trading and relationships.

The pursuit of being irreplaceable is an unwavering driving force for traders alike. Tirelessly seeking to decipher unique strategies, and identify niche opportunities, and gain a competitive edge in the market.

They are the ones who can spot trends before the masses, analyse data with precision, and adapt swiftly to changing conditions. This relentless pursuit often involves tireless research, discipline, and an unquenchable thirst for knowledge - perhaps why you are still reading.

Yet, amidst this quest for irreplaceability, traders must remain acutely aware of their replaceability. Markets are vast, and no single trader is indispensable. The market operates independently, shifting and evolving with or without any one trader's hopes, fears, or aspirations. Accepting this reality is humbling but vital for sound decision-making.

The delicate dance between irreplaceability and replaceability is akin to the value we place on individuals and their unique qualities. What I value may not hold the same value for you. Even though I may be irreplaceable in certain aspects, there may always be a younger, smarter, or more versatile version of me, for variety is the spice of life, isn't it?

At the core of this paradox lies the concept of value. In trading, relationships, and business, value is the currency that sets us apart. When traders offer unique insights, relationships are built on trust and genuine connection, and businesses provide products or services that genuinely enhance lives, they become irreplaceable in their respective domains. Their value proposition distinguishes them, making them sought after and cherished.

However, value is not static. It is a dynamic force that can wax and wane over time. Traders must consistently adapt their strategies to stay relevant in shifting markets. Charles Darwin's principle that "It is not the strongest of the species that survives, nor the most intelligent; it is the one most responsive to change" encapsulates the essence of adaptability's importance in survival and success.

The Darwinian principle of adaptability reigns supreme, be it in trading or relationships. Survival and success do not hinge solely on strength or intelligence but on the ability to navigate change effectively.

Adaptability is paramount in trading. Markets shift, and strategies must evolve. Successful traders embrace change, adjusting their approaches to emerging trends and opportunities. Similarly, in relationships, the strongest bonds form when partners support each other's growth and adapt communication to nurture their connection.

The saying "Adapt or Fade" underscores the importance of flexibility and resilience in both trading and relationships. Those who heed this principle are better positioned for lasting success and fulfillment.
In relationships, maintaining the value of a connection requires ongoing effort, communication, and shared growth. In business, the ability to innovate and deliver evolving value propositions ensures relevance. And in trading, continued learning and skill development are essential as market seasons change.

Acknowledging that value can fluctuate helps individuals and entities strike a balance between their irreplaceable qualities and their replaceability. It fuels the drive to continually enhance the value they bring, fostering resilience and adaptability in the face of change. In essence, the perception of irreplaceability and replaceability is inextricably linked to the value one offers, making it a cornerstone of success in these diverse domains.

The notion of being irreplaceable is woven into the very fabric of human connections. We strive to be the ones who understand our partners like no one else, offering unwavering support and bringing joy and love into their lives. We cherish the belief that our bond is unique, incomparable, and irreplaceable.

However, this belief is balanced by the understanding that we are, in fact, replaceable. Relationships can end, partners can change, and circumstances can evolve. Recognising our replaceability isn't about devaluing ourselves but about acknowledging the fluidity of life and love. It's about realising that, in the grand tapestry of existence, each of us plays a role, but the world continues to turn with or without us.

Embracing the paradox of being irreplaceable yet replaceable is an exercise in humility, especially when success brings newfound wealth. Temptation is everywhere, but staying grounded reminds us to continually refine our skills and foster adaptability, preventing complacency or overconfidence.

We are encouraged to cherish each moment and nurture our connections, communicating openly and treating loved ones with kindness and respect. This fosters empathy, understanding that our presence enriches others' lives while recognising that life's journeys can lead in unexpected directions, embracing impermanence as the only constant.

In the intricate dance of trading and relationships, the paradox of being irreplaceable yet replaceable is a delicate balance. It's a reminder that, while we strive for excellence and depth, we are part of a larger tapestry. Embracing this paradox empowers us to make wise choices, nurture connections, and appreciate the precious moments shared with others.

Taking this concept further into the realm of business, the paradox of being irreplaceable yet replaceable gains a unique dimension. Entrepreneurs and professionals aspire to build companies and brands synonymous with excellence and innovation, striving to become leaders in their industries. This pursuit fuels the drive to create groundbreaking products, offer exceptional services, and forge lasting customer relationships.

However, the market dynamics are ever-changing, requiring businesses to remain adaptable and open to evolution. Recognising their replaceability serves as a catalyst for constant improvement and innovation, urging businesses to stay attuned to customer needs, embrace new technologies, and remain agile in an ever-shifting landscape.

In essence, the perception of irreplaceability and replaceability is inextricably linked to the value one offers, making it a cornerstone of success in these diverse domains. This profound concept influences our decisions and perspectives in trading, relationships, and business, reminding us of the impermanence of life and the need for adaptability and resilience in the face of change.

Embracing this paradox empowers us to make wise choices, nurture our connections, and continually enhance the value we offer in all areas of our existence.

"It is not the strongest of the species that survives, nor the most intelligent that survives.

It is the one that is the most adaptable to change, that lives within the means available and works co-operatively against common threats."

Charles Darwin

ANALYSIS PARALYSIS

Trusting your choices is a pivotal aspect of both trading and life in general. When you decide in trading, whether it's entering a trade or setting a stop loss, it's essential to trust that you've made the best choice based on the information and analysis available to you at that moment. This trust in your decisions empowers you to act confidently and stick to your trading plan, even when faced with uncertainty.

Now, let's delve deeper into the idea of uncertainty in relationships and how it applies to trading. Imagine if your partner said, "I'm not sure?" In a personal relationship, such a statement can indeed trigger feelings of unease and insecurity. It's akin to waiting for a seat at a sold-out concert or a football match, uncertain if you'll get in. Most people wouldn't hang around for their partner to make up their mind; they'd seek clarity or move on. Just like you most likely won't hang around for that sold out concert.

In trading, this concept translates to avoiding the trap of indecision. If you find yourself hesitating and constantly second-guessing your trades, it can lead to missed opportunities and heightened stress. Just as you wouldn't wait indefinitely for your partner to choose you, you shouldn't linger in a state of analysis paralysis in trading. Trust your analysis, decide, and be prepared to adjust your position if necessary. In trading, as in relationships, decisiveness can be a valuable asset, allowing you to seize opportunities and move forward with confidence.

Analysis paralysis is a common pitfall that plagues traders and decision-makers alike. It's the state of being overwhelmed by excessive information, leading to an inability to make a choice. In trading, this often manifests as a trader drowning in a sea of charts, news articles, and expert opinions, unable to pull the trigger on a trade.

Imagine being at a buffet with an endless array of dishes, each one more tempting than the last. You stand there, plate in hand, but unable to decide what to eat because you're afraid you might miss out on something better. In both trading and life, overthinking can paralyse your ability to make choices.

The Illusion of Perfection

One of the root causes of analysis paralysis is the pursuit of perfection. Traders, much like individuals in relationships, sometimes hold onto the illusion that there's a perfect decision, a flawless trade, or a flawless partner out there waiting for them. This quest for perfection can lead to endless analysis, hesitation, and missed opportunities.

Perfection is an unattainable goal. There's no such thing as a perfect trade or a perfect relationship. Every decision, whether in trading or life, comes with its share of risks and uncertainties. It's the ability to manage those risks and adapt to uncertainties that ultimately defines success.

The Role of Fear and Regret

Fear and regret are powerful emotions that often fuel analysis paralysis. In trading, the fear of losing money can lead to inaction. Traders become so focused on avoiding losses that they become paralysed, unable to make any moves. Similarly, in relationships, the fear of rejection or heartbreak can lead individuals to overanalyse their choices and hesitate to commit.

Regret also plays a significant role. Traders fear the regret of making a wrong decision, while individuals in relationships fear the regret of choosing the wrong partner. This fear of future regret can keep people stuck in a perpetual state of indecision.

Breaking Free from Analysis Paralysis

Queen's Freddie Mercury sang about wanting to break free in the hit song released in 1984, embracing his unique personality and persona, and inspiring countless individuals to do the same, even long after his passing.

The essence of Queen's "I Want to Break Free," with its theme of seeking liberation from societal norms and constraints, can be translated into the concept of analysis paralysis. In both cases, there is a common thread of yearning for freedom and a desire to break away from limitations that hinder progress.

Analysis paralysis occurs when individuals become trapped in a cycle of overthinking and excessive analysis, often driven by fear of making the wrong decision or conforming to conventional wisdom. They may feel pressured to adhere to established norms or follow the crowd, even when their instincts or unique insights suggest otherwise.

Much like the song's call for personal expression and breaking away from conformity, overcoming analysis paralysis involves embracing one's individuality and trusting in one's ability to make choices that align with their goals and values. It's about breaking free from the constraints of self-doubt, fear of failure, and the need for validation from external sources.

Just as the song's music video symbolically challenges traditional gender roles, breaking free from analysis paralysis may require challenging conventional wisdom or preconceived notions about decision-making. It encourages individuals to be bold, take calculated risks, and trust their instincts rather than feeling confined by the expectations or judgments of others.

In essence, "I Want to Break Free" captures the spirit of breaking free from the mental barriers that can lead to analysis paralysis. It encourages us to be true to ourselves, trust our intuition, and have the confidence to make decisions that reflect our unique perspectives and aspirations, whether in the realm of personal expression or in the world of trading and decision-making.

To break free from the grip of analysis paralysis, it's essential to embrace a mindset of acceptance and adaptability. Understand that there will never be a perfect choice, and that's okay. In trading, making a series of well-informed, risk-managed decisions is what leads to success over time. In relationships, it's about choosing a partner with whom you can grow and evolve together, knowing that both of you will have imperfections.

Developing a clear plan, setting predefined criteria for decision-making, and sticking to a well-defined strategy can help both traders and individuals in their personal lives overcome analysis paralysis. It's about acknowledging the presence of uncertainty, managing fear and regret, and acting with confidence.

"May your choices reflect your hopes not your fears."

Nelson Mandela

OXYGEN MASK THEORY

The "Oxygen Mask Theory" is a concept often used in discussions about self-care and personal well-being, especially in the context of helping others. It is based on the safety instructions given on airplanes before take-off, where flight attendants instruct passengers to put on their own oxygen masks before assisting others, including children or those who may need help.

The theory draws a parallel between this airplane safety instruction and taking care of oneself in everyday life. It emphasises that individuals should prioritise their own physical and emotional well-being first before attempting to help or support others.

The reasoning behind this concept is that if you neglect your own needs and well-being while trying to assist or take care of others, you may become depleted or overwhelmed, making it more difficult to provide effective help or support.

In essence, the Oxygen Mask Theory teaches us that self-care is not selfish; it's a necessary step to ensure that we are in the best position to help others. By taking care of ourselves first, we can be more present, capable, and resilient when assisting others, whether it's in personal relationships, caregiving roles, or any other situation that requires attention and care, like trading, if you are not in the right mindset, you will make silly mistakes and lose trust in yourself, it will become a never-ending loop.

This book, a reflection of my journey in helping people move toward their dreams and goals, was born from a profound realisation—a gift I have to offer the world.

The beginning of my realisation of the oxygen mask theory moment was when I sold my Modelling Casting and Promotions Agency I owned and operated for thirteen years.

It all began with my experiences in the world of acting and modelling, where I connected with individuals who had the potential to achieve greatness. Through these connections, I witnessed a spectrum of responses. Some eagerly embraced the opportunities before them, while others harboured a belief that success should be handed to them on a silver platter.

At one point in time being an actress was also my dream and I made the decision to sell the agency to pursue my own dreams and goals, and here I am. These dreams and goals changed to writing, especially about things I'm passionate about, like cryptocurrency, TheMoonMag.com was born, education GettingStartedinCrypto.com was born and changing people's lives financially ThousandtoMillions.com. And I still love the film and TV industry so write films CoinrunnersMovie.com and books CantFightFate.com with the dream and goal that one day someone will read and love them as much as I do, and they will be movies on the big or small screen.

What I noticed during the last ten years of trading cryptocurrency is that if I was stressed or in a negative frame of mind, my trading suffered greatly.

I learned over this time the principle of putting yourself first. Much like the airplane safety instruction of securing your own oxygen mask before assisting others, prioritising your well-being and personal growth is not an act of selfishness but an essential step toward achieving your dreams and goals.

As a mother of five, I often find myself reflecting on how valuable this knowledge could have been in my earlier years. It makes me ponder the possibility of being not just an amazing partner and mother, but an even more exceptional one. The thought brings a smile to my face, just as I hope it does to yours while reading this. It leads me to contemplate how nurturing my own well-being, including my mental health, might have shaped different outcomes in my past relationships.

Self-Care: The Key to Empowerment

At the heart of the Oxygen Mask Theory lies the notion that taking care of yourself is not only acceptable but crucial. It's about recognising that you are the anchor of your own life.
Just as in the world of acting and modelling, where some expected success to be handed to them and for me to do all the work while they went to auditions ill prepared wondering why they never got a call back. Life often presents us with opportunities, but it's up to us to seize them. Self-care is the foundation upon which we build the strength and resilience to navigate life's challenges and make the most of these opportunities.

I was making people's dreams a reality through my acting and modelling business and connections with all the right people and things to get them on the journey to success. Some listened and other just thought someone should do it all for you, the ones that were proactive got to where they should be, the others fell behind thinking this acting business is only for the lucky few.

"The harder I work the luckier I get."

Samuel Goldwyn

The quote the harder I work the luckier I get, it's true, and it's never been truer in the situation I'm in now. Finance is a different beast filled with greed and ignorance that someone owes you something and I'm here no say no one owes you anything it's all choice. People make choices everyday some that consider you and others that don't. Be ok with knowing all you ever really have is you, and the people that make choices to be there.

The Myth of Entitlement

It's easy to fall into the trap of entitlement—believing that someone owes you something. This mindset can be a significant barrier to progress. The truth is that no one owes you anything. Success is a matter of choice, and it starts with the choice to put yourself first. It's about embracing the fact that you are the master of your own destiny, and your choices, not entitlement, determine your path.

The Power of Choices

Every day, we are faced with choices—some that consider us and others that don't. It's essential to acknowledge that at the core of it all, you have yourself and the people who choose to be there.

Your journey to fulfilment and success begins with the choices you make for yourself. Whether it's dedicating time to self-care, pursuing your passions, or making informed financial decisions, these choices are the building blocks of your path forward.

Embracing Self-Prioritisation

In essence, the Oxygen Mask Principle teaches us that by putting ourselves first and engaging in self-care, we become better equipped to support and uplift others. It's a reminder that your well-being is the cornerstone of your ability to help those around you. As we embark on this journey of self-prioritisation, remember that it's not about selfishness but about self-empowerment—a key step toward turning your dreams and goals into reality.

Embrace the principle of putting on your own oxygen mask first and watch as it propels you toward the success and fulfilment you deserve.

"Remember, Trading is not hard, people make it hard."

Lisa N Edwards

BE YOUR OWN CHEERLEADER

Trading can be a rollercoaster, and life itself is a wild ride, especially with the day-to-day drama of the unknown.

We all know that in times of uncertainty and doubt, having someone cheering you on can make a world of difference. That's what this chapter is all about—being your own cheerleader.

For me it all started with a friend I've never met, David, who lives in Colorado. During the chaos of my trading business, COINRUNNERS, and my tumultuous personal life, with a drug addicted business and life partner, David became a guiding light, offering hope and encouragement. He was the inspiration behind the magnets on my trading charts, for those that have seen these and wondered what significance they have. They are the hope that things will be right, and everything will go as planned, they have become a symbol for those to know Bitcoin is going up, the magnets have never failed!

David's presence in my life was like a ray of sunshine breaking through the clouds. It's funny how someone you've never met in person can have such a profound impact. When everything seemed to be spiralling into chaos, he was there, sending me inspiring messages through Twitter direct messages. He was my virtual cheerleader, reminding me of my potential even when I had almost given up.

Always remember…

"You Never Fail Until You Stop Trying."

I Learned to Never Give Up on Me!

Life and trading can be tough, and there are moments when you start questioning every move, especially when setbacks hit hard. In those trying times, David, though miles away, stood as a beacon of unwavering support, a reassuring presence when I needed it most. His unwavering faith in me became my lifeline when I was on the brink of losing hope in myself. It's funny how life works, right? During all this, something incredible began to take shape—HopeaholicsAnnon.com, or simply HA for short.

Right now, it's just a domain name I own, but I've got big dreams for it. You see, I want HA to be a place where we can extend the same kind of support and encouragement that David offered me. A place where hope isn't just a word but a living, breathing force that helps us keep going, even when others might laugh or doubt us.

So, in the not-so-distant future, I envision HA becoming a beacon of hope for those who need it most. After all, just as I clung to hope in the face of doubt, I've come to understand that hope wields tremendous power in propelling us toward success. And with HA, we'll all be sharing laughter all the way to the bank—HA HA HA!

Being your own cheerleader boils down to one thing: believing in yourself. Whether you're navigating the turbulent waters of trading or dealing with life's curveballs, moments of self-doubt are bound to crop up. But here's the kicker: you have the power to be your own biggest cheerleader. It's a reminder that you possess the inner strength and resilience to overcome challenges and achieve your goals.

So, here's the deal: the concept of being your own cheerleader was inspired by the unwavering support of a friend I've never met in person, but it's most importantly, the most powerful cheerleader you'll ever have is the one staring back at you in the mirror. Remember to root for yourself, believe in your potential, and never underestimate the impact of your own encouragement as you navigate the journey to success in trading and in life.

"Be your own biggest Cheerleader."

Kevin Ngo

IS PATIENCE A VIRTUE?

Patience, often regarded as a virtue, is a quality that holds significant importance in both the realms of relationships and trading. In this chapter, we'll explore the striking similarities and nuanced differences in how patience is applied and its profound impact on these two domains.

Patience, whether in relationships or trading, shares a common thread: the ability to wait with purpose. It involves delaying immediate gratification for the promise of a greater reward or outcome. Does this tie into Trust? And the key ideas we explored there? Seems to be a common theme, don't you think?

Trading demands unwavering patience. Markets can be erratic, and impulsive decisions often lead to losses. Successful traders understand the need to wait for the right opportunities. They patiently analyse data, identify trends, and exercise restraint, even in the face of fluctuating prices. Patience in trading is about resisting the urge to chase quick gains, instead opting for well-researched, disciplined strategies that can yield substantial returns over time.

Patience in relationships is equally vital. It entails listening, empathising, and giving partners the time and space to express themselves. It involves refraining from hasty judgments or reactions during conflicts. It's about understanding that building a deep connection and trust takes time and consistent effort. Patience allows relationships to mature, and it's the foundation for enduring love and mutual growth.

Often, patience is like meeting a person where they are, understanding their unique pace, and allowing the connection to develop naturally. In the world of relationships, this concept resonates deeply. When you meet someone new, you can't rush the process of getting to know them.

You must be patient, listen, and give the relationship time to grow and evolve. Just as trying to force a connection on a dating app rarely leads

to a meaningful relationship, attempting to rush or force a relationship can be detrimental.
Now, let's dissect a trading strategy and draw a parallel. In trading, patience is akin to waiting for the right market conditions to align with your strategy. It's about recognising that the market has its own rhythm, and you must meet it where it is.

Rushing into trades without the right signals or conditions is the same as swiping right on every Tinder profile without discernment. It may yield some quick matches and likely all that happens is you get "Fucked."

In fact, I like to compare Tinder to leverage trading. Both can be tempting shortcuts to quick results, but they come with inherent risks. On Tinder, swiping right excessively may result in shallow connections that lack substance. In trading, using excessive leverage can lead to amplified gains but also magnified losses, often ending in financial heartbreak and as above… being "Fucked."

And then you have the problem of not using a stop loss or condom which often leaves you holding the baby, or the trade.

The key takeaway from this parallel is that both in relationships and trading, patience is a virtue. It's about understanding that meaningful connections and successful trades require time, effort, and a discerning approach. So, remember, just as fine wine matures with time, so do the most beautiful aspects of life, be it love or success in trading.

Key Similarities:

- In both trading and relationships, patience cultivates emotional control. It helps individuals avoid impulsive actions driven by fear, greed, anger, or frustration.

- Patience encourages a long-term perspective. In trading, it means not getting discouraged by short-term losses or gains. In relationships, it means focusing on the bigger picture rather than fixating on minor annoyances.

- Patience strengthens resilience. It allows traders to weather market fluctuations and couples to navigate challenging times without giving up prematurely.

Key Differences:

- The timeframes in trading and relationships differ significantly. In trading, patience may span minutes, hours, or days. In relationships, it often spans months, years, or a lifetime.

- Patience can lead to financial gains or losses. In relationships, it fosters emotional connection and harmony.

- Traders have more direct control over their actions, while relationships involve two individuals with their own agency. Patience in relationships often requires collaboration and mutual understanding.

To harness patience for success in both trading and relationships, consider these principles:

- Clearly define your long-term goals in both domains. Knowing what you're working toward helps maintain patience – Go back to the chapters on Visualising.

- Set Realistic Expectations as these prevent frustration and disappointment. Understand that neither trading nor relationships are free from challenges.

- Mindfulness techniques can help manage emotions and maintain patience in both trading and relationships.

- Consider seeking mentorship or guidance. In relationships, open communication and seeking professional help when needed can be invaluable.

So always remember…

"Trading is like Sex…

If you don't use a Stop Loss (Condom) you're left HODLing the baby for 9 months or more!"

Lisa N Edwards

"Trades are like relationships, if you need to chase after them, they're not worth it."

Lisa N Edwards

BECOMING YOUR BEST - YOU!

Thanks for getting this far! I appreciate you reading my thoughts, as we've explored various aspects of success, personal growth, and the intricate dance of relationships. Now, it's time to bring it all together, recognising that our approach to trading is deeply intertwined with our approach to life and the people around us.

1. **What is Your Why?** Before you embark on any Endeavour, ask yourself why you're doing it. Your "why" will be the driving force behind your actions and decisions in both trading and life.

2. **The Law of Success Philosophy.** Success isn't a random occurrence; it follows a set of principles. Embrace these principles in your trading and relationships to create a life of fulfilment.

3. **Money: What's the Big Deal?** Understand that money is a tool, not the end goal. It's a means to an end, and how you use it can shape your relationships and life.

4. **The Energy of Money** carries energy with it. Be mindful of the energy you associate with it, as it can influence your trading decisions and the way you interact with others.

5. **Understanding the Energy of Money** We delve deeper into the emotional and psychological aspects of money. Awareness of these energies can help you make better trading choices and build stronger relationships.

6. **Going with the Flow** Learning to adapt and go with the flow of life and the markets. Resistance often leads to suffering in both realms.

7. **Putting the Energy of Money into Action** Take concrete steps to align your financial actions with your values, both in trading and personal finances.
8. **Visualising Your Path to Success** Visualisation is a powerful tool. Envision your success in trading and life, and let it guide your actions.

9. **Visualising the Power of Imagination** Your imagination is your greatest asset. Use it to create the life and trading results you desire.

10. **The Sense of Success** Cultivate a sense of success within yourself, independent of external validation. This inner confidence will positively impact your trading and relationships.

11. **The Wolf You Feed** Choose to nurture positive thoughts and emotions over negative ones. This choice affects not only your trading outcomes but also your interactions with others.

12. **The Origin of Suffering** Recognise that suffering often arises from attachment and resistance. Let go of attachments to outcomes in both trading and relationships.

13. **The Green-Eyed Monster** Jealousy can poison relationships and lead to reckless trading decisions. Practice gratitude to combat envy.

14. **Am I the Problem?** In both trading and relationships, introspection is key. Sometimes, you might be your own stumbling block. Be willing to change and grow.

15. **Trusting the Trade** Trust your trading strategy, and trust in your abilities. Similarly, trust in the process of life and your ability to navigate it.

16. **The Currency of Trust** - Understand the value of trust in both trading and relationships.

17. **The Paradox of Being Irreplaceable -** We've explored this delicate balance between irreplaceability and replaceability, which influences our decisions and perspectives in trading and life.

18. **Analysis Paralysis -** Overthinking can paralyse decision-making. Keep things simple and focus on what truly matters.
19. **Oxygen Mask Theory** – Prioritise self-care and well-being in trading and life.

20. **Be Your Own Cheerleader** – Cultivate self-belief and self-motivation, propelling you toward success.

21. **Becoming Your Best – YOU!** – Achieve balance, self-awareness, and personal growth on your lifelong journey.

22. **Is Patience a Virtue?** We explore the role of patience in long-term success and personal growth in trading and relationships.

22. **Zoom Out** - Gain perspective on the bigger picture, both in trading and in life. Sometimes, taking a step back can provide valuable insights.

The key to success lies in finding balance, understanding your motivations, and being aware of the energies that surround you. Remember that your journey is a lifelong process of growth and discovery. Embrace it with an open heart and a clear mind, and you'll find that the best version of yourself emerges, both as a trader and as a person. As you continue this journey, may you find not just financial success, but also fulfilment, harmony, and deep connections with those you encounter along the way.

"Oh, the places you'll go!

You can steer yourself any direction you choose. You're on your own. And you know what you know. And YOU are the one who'll decide where to go..."

Dr. Seuss

"It's a slow process.

But quitting won't speed it up. ."

Unknown

ZOOM OUT

In this final chapter before we bridge the more technical aspects of reaching your personal goals set when you discovered what your why is, we explore why it is important to zoom out and embrace the bigger picture. This quote below and the quotes throughout the book have been carefully curated to add perspective to my words, often understanding is in clear perspective.

"I trained 4 years to run only 9 seconds.

There are people who do not see results in 2 months, give up and leave. Sometimes failure is sought by oneself."

Usain Bolt

In both the realms of relationships and trading, the ability to zoom out and view the bigger picture is an invaluable skill. It is a skill that can provide clarity, perspective, and a deeper understanding of the journey you are on. In this chapter, we will explore why this perspective is crucial, the role of trust, and why focusing on what you want, rather than getting bogged down in tiny details, can lead to more meaningful and successful outcomes.

Looking at everything through the myopic lens is a common pitfall and I'll explain why.

In our fast-paced world, it's easy to become caught up in the minutiae of daily life. This is true whether you're in the midst of a passionate relationship or navigating the turbulent waters of financial markets. It's easy to become so fixated on the immediate details that you lose sight of the bigger picture.

Imagine a trader who watches the crypto/stock market's every tick, reacting to every minor fluctuation. This trader might make hasty decisions based on fear or excitement, often to their detriment. Similarly, in a relationship, individuals can become ensnared in petty arguments or inconsequential issues, losing sight of the overarching bond they share.

How do we zoom out and what is the power and clarity gained when we do this?

Zooming out allows you to see the forest for the trees. This saying allows us to stand on a mountain top seeing the entirety of the trees coming together to make the forest full of tress and creatures while standing in the middle you only see the immediate trees in front of you.

It enables you to recognise trends, patterns, and the larger forces at play. It's about shifting your focus from the tiny details to the grand scheme of things.

In relationships, zooming out means recognising that occasional disagreements or annoyances are part of the journey. It's about understanding that trust, respect, and shared goals are more important than who left the dishes or cups in the kitchen bench or who forgot to buy milk, or leaving a computer plugged in a socket in the wrong spot.

In trading, zooming out involves considering long-term trends and market fundamentals rather than getting caught up in the day-to-day fluctuations. It's about realising that patience and a well-thought-out strategy are often more valuable than quick wins.

In both trading and relationships, the role of trust plays the fundamental bones to success. Trust is the foundation upon which both successful relationships and trading strategies are built. When you trust your partner or the fundamentals of your trading approach, you can weather the storms and uncertainties that life and the markets inevitably throw your way.
In relationships, trust allows you to give your partner the benefit of the doubt and to work through challenges together. It's the confidence that your bond can withstand adversity.

In trading, trust is placed in your chosen strategy, risk management techniques, and your ability to stay disciplined. It allows you to stick to your plan when market turbulence tempts you to deviate.

Always focusing on what you want, remember WHY you started this, and when you feel like giving up, remember who you are doing this for, and do you really want to give up on yourself again? You've come this far.

Rather than dwelling on the tiny details that can threaten to obscure your vision, focus on what you truly want to achieve. In relationships, this might mean prioritising love, connection, and growth over fleeting disagreements or minor annoyances. In trading, it means keeping your long-term financial goals in mind, not getting derailed by short-term market noise.

When you concentrate on your desired outcome, it becomes easier to make decisions that align with your objectives. This can provide clarity and resilience in the face of challenges.

Zooming out in relationships and trading allows you to see the bigger picture, recognise the importance of trust, and prioritise your true goals. It's a reminder that the journey is more significant than individual steps, and that perspective can be your greatest ally in navigating the complexities of life and financial markets. By embracing this perspective, you can move forward with confidence and purpose.

Now spread your wings and fly!

"Until you spread your wings, you'll have no idea how far you can fly."

Napoleon

"Everything you need is already within."

Unknown

SECTION 1

THE ABC OF COMPOUND TRADING

CHAPTER BREAKDOWN

Chapter A: The Compound Trading Strategy: Profits and Discipline

- Introduction
- Setting the 3% Profit and 3% Stop Loss
- Utilising Cross Supports for Minimal Losses
- The Importance of Discipline
- The Power of Compounding
- Conclusion

Chapter B: OCO Orders and Living Your Life

- Introduction
- Understanding OCO Orders
- Benefits of OCO Orders
- Implementing OCO Orders
- Conclusion

Chapter C: The Power of 3%: Achieving Consistent Results

- Introduction
- Understanding the Power of 3%
- The Mathematics of Compounding
- Risk Management and Capital Preservation
- Developing the Right Mindset
- Trading Strategies for Consistent Results
- Maintaining Focus and Adapting to Challenges
- Embracing Continuous Learning and Improvement
- Conclusion
- Recommending paper trading for beginners to gain confidence before risking capital.

This three-chapter breakdown delves into the compound trading strategy and its core principles, including setting profit and stop-loss thresholds, utilising cross supports, implementing OCO orders, balancing trading with personal life, and achieving consistent 3% profits. It also provides insights for beginners, emphasising the importance of practice (also known as paper trading) trading and gaining confidence before committing actual capital.

Achieving physical fitness or financial success requires a balanced approach and consistent effort.

While spending 9 hours a day at the gym may not be practical or effective, dedicating just 20 minutes a day to exercise, combined with a healthy diet, can yield significant results.

Similarly, in trading, it's important to engage in regular study, practice, and adhere to strict money management principles.

By following a disciplined process, it's possible to see remarkable progress, turning a modest investment of one thousand into millions within a year.

SECTION 1

THE ABC OF COMPOUND TRADING

Chapter A: The Compound Trading Strategy: Profits and Discipline

Introduction

- Overview of the compound trading strategy
- Importance of profits and discipline in trading

Setting the 3% Profit and 3% Stop Loss

- Fundamentals of the 3% Profit and 3% Stop Loss
- Understanding the significance of profit and stop-loss thresholds.
- Benefits of maintaining a favourable risk-reward ratio
- Importance of risk management and preserving capital

Utilising Cross Supports for Minimal Losses

- Explaining the concept of cross supports in diagonal lines
- Enhancing accuracy by considering wicks in drawing cross supports
- Applying cross supports in the high volatility cryptocurrency market

The Importance of Discipline

- Recognising the role of discipline in successful trading
- Avoiding emotional decision-making and impulsive trades
- Patience and long-term perspective in executing the strategy.

The Power of Compounding

- Explaining the concept of compounding in trading
- Utilising the 3% minimum bounce to achieve exponential growth.
- Example of compounding leading to substantial returns

Conclusion

- Summarising the benefits of the compound trading strategy
- Emphasising the importance of practice, learning, and dedication in trading success

---

"Compound interest is the eighth wonder of the world. He who understands it, earns it, he who doesn't pays it."

Albert Einstein

Chapter A

THE COMPOUND TRADING STRATEGY: PROFITS AND DISCIPLINE

Introduction

"Nothing will work unless you do."
Maya Angelou

This is where the work begins, it's time to learn and understand how compound trading works. Having a well-defined and robust strategy is crucial. In this book the main aim is to make this simple!

Traders are constantly on the lookout for approaches that offer consistent profits and a disciplined approach to trading. One such strategy that has gained significant popularity in recent years is the compound trading strategy.

The compound trading strategy focuses on the principles of consistent profits and disciplined trading to achieve long-term wealth accumulation in the financial markets. It provides traders with a systematic and structured approach to building their portfolios and achieving their financial goals. In this book, we will delve deep into the intricacies of the compound trading strategy and equip traders with the necessary tools and knowledge to implement it effectively.

One of the fundamental aspects of the compound trading strategy is setting profit and stop-loss thresholds. By carefully determining the minimum profit percentage that traders aim to achieve on each trade, they establish a clear target that aligns with their long-term financial objectives. This approach helps traders avoid the pitfalls of greed and impulsive decision-making that can often lead to significant losses.

Similarly, incorporating a strict stop-loss mechanism is crucial for risk management and capital preservation. Setting a maximum stop-loss percentage allows traders to limit their potential losses and protect their trading capital. This disciplined approach ensures that no single trade has the power to wipe out a significant portion of the portfolio, enabling traders to stay in the game and continue their journey towards wealth accumulation.

One key component of the compound trading strategy is the utilisation of cross supports. By drawing diagonal cross supports on charts, traders identify strong support zones that can enhance the probability of successful trades. It is imperative to include the wicks when drawing these cross supports, as they provide valuable information about market volatility and can influence trading decisions.

However, implementing the compound trading strategy goes beyond technical analysis and chart patterns. It requires a disciplined mindset and a commitment to adhering to the strategy's principles. Traders must resist the temptation to deviate from the plan or chase trades that do not meet the predefined criteria.

Patience and emotional control are vital for success, as they allow traders to wait for high-quality trade setups and avoid impulsive decisions driven by fear or greed.

Throughout this book, we will explore various techniques and best practices for implementing the compound trading strategy effectively. We will delve into topics such as position sizing, risk-reward ratios, and adapting to different market conditions. By equipping traders with these essential tools and knowledge, we aim to empower them to make informed trading decisions and increase their potential for long-term success.

The compound trading strategy is not a get-rich-quick scheme; it is a disciplined and systematic approach to wealth accumulation. It requires dedication, continuous learning, and a commitment to self-improvement. Traders who embrace the principles of the compound trading strategy have the opportunity to navigate the dynamic and unpredictable financial markets with confidence and increase their chances of achieving their long-term financial goals.

In the following chapters, we will delve into the specific components, exploring topics such as risk management, technical analysis, trade planning, and portfolio management. By understanding and implementing these key concepts, traders will be equipped with a comprehensive framework for achieving consistent profits and long-term success in their trading endeavours.

"Play long term games with long term people. All returns in life, whether in wealth, relationships, or knowledge, come from compound interest."

Naval Ravikant

Quote from COINRUNNERSMOVIE.COM Award winning Script.

Image from COINRUNNERSMOVIE.COM NFT Collection

SETTING THE 3% PROFIT AND 3% STOP LOSS

At the core of the compound trading strategy lies the concept of setting a 3% minimum profit and a strict 3% maximum stop loss. This approach ensures that trades are entered with a favourable risk-reward ratio and seeks to capitalise on profitable opportunities while limiting potential losses. While some traders may scoff at the notion of a small stop loss, it is essential to embrace the principle of risk management. By keeping losses contained, traders can preserve their capital and maintain a healthy trading account. It's important to also note these are SPOT trades and not margin or leverage.

Fundamentals of the 3% Profit and 3% Stop Loss

One of the fundamental principles of trading is establishing clear profit and stop-loss thresholds. Setting a 3% profit target and a corresponding 3% stop-loss level ensures that trades are exited at predetermined points, regardless of emotional bias. These thresholds act as objective benchmarks, limiting potential losses and securing profits. By consistently adhering to these thresholds, traders can avoid emotional decision-making, which often leads to impulsive and irrational choices.

Understanding the Significance of Profit and Stop-Loss Threshold

Profit and stop-loss thresholds provide traders with a structured approach to trading. The profit target ensures that traders exit trades when the anticipated profit has been achieved, preventing greed from driving them to hold positions for too long. Conversely, the stop-loss level serves as a safety net, protecting traders from excessive losses by automatically closing positions when the market moves against their expectations. Understanding the significance of these thresholds instils discipline and prevents trades from turning into long-term losses.

Benefits of Maintaining a Favourable Risk-Reward Ratio

Maintaining a favourable risk-reward ratio is a vital aspect of successful trading. By aiming for trades that offer a higher potential reward compared to the risk taken, traders can stack the odds in their favour. A common rule of thumb is to target a risk-reward ratio of at least 1:2 or higher. This means that for every dollar risked, the trader aims to make at least two dollars in potential profit. A favourable risk-reward ratio allows traders to be profitable even if they have a win rate of less than 50%. It is essential to analyse potential trades based on this ratio to identify favourable opportunities and minimise the impact of losing trades.

Importance of Risk Management and Preserving Capital

Risk management is the backbone of successful trading. It involves implementing strategies to protect capital and minimise losses. By allocating a predetermined percentage of their capital to each trade and adhering to strict risk management rules, traders can shield themselves from substantial drawdowns and prevent catastrophic losses. Preserving capital is crucial because it allows traders to remain in the game and capitalise on future opportunities. A well-defined risk management strategy includes position sizing, diversification, and utilising tools such as trailing stops to lock in profits and manage risk effectively.

"Risk comes from not knowing what you are doing."

Warren Buffet

UTILISING CROSS SUPPORTS FOR MINIMAL LOSSES

To implement the compound trading strategy effectively, it is crucial to incorporate cross supports when drawing diagonal lines on charts. Cross supports refer to the intersection of diagonal support lines, creating a stronger support zone. This technique helps minimise potential losses by identifying key levels where a bounce is more likely to occur.

For a trader with little to no knowledge, drawing support lines on a chart is the easiest way to start. By also considering the wicks when drawing these diagonal cross supports, traders can enhance their accuracy in identifying optimal entry points. This method is particularly relevant in the high volatility cryptocurrency market, where precise entries can significantly impact trading outcomes.

Explaining the Concept of Cross Supports in Diagonal Lines

Cross supports refer to the points where diagonal lines intersect, forming a confluence of support levels. These intersecting points provide traders with a powerful tool for identifying potential areas of price reversal or continuation. By connecting lows or highs using diagonal lines and observing where they intersect, traders can pinpoint critical levels of support or resistance. The concept of cross supports adds an additional layer of confirmation to trading decisions, helping traders make more informed choices based on multiple confluences of support.

Enhancing Accuracy by Considering Wicks in Drawing Cross Supports

When drawing cross supports, it is important to consider the presence of wicks, also known as shadows or tails, on price candles. Wicks represent intraday price fluctuations beyond the opening and closing prices. By incorporating wicks into the analysis of cross supports, traders gain a more comprehensive understanding of price action and market sentiment. Paying attention to wicks can help identify false breakouts or breakdowns, as they reflect temporary market noise or liquidity imbalances. Incorporating wicks in drawing cross supports helps traders filter out noise and focus on more reliable support and resistance levels.

Applying Cross Supports in the Cryptocurrency Market

The cryptocurrency market is notorious for its high volatility, presenting both significant opportunities and risks. Utilising cross supports becomes even more valuable in such a market environment. The intersecting points of diagonal lines act as potential levels where price reversals or continuations may occur, allowing traders to enter or exit positions with better precision.
Cryptocurrencies often exhibit rapid price movements, making the identification of reliable support and resistance levels essential. Cross supports provide traders with a technical framework to navigate the dynamic cryptocurrency market, reducing the risk of losses and improving trading accuracy.

In the pursuit of profitability, traders must embrace techniques that minimise losses and increase accuracy. Utilising cross supports is a powerful strategy to achieve these goals.

"Trading is mindset. You never miss anything. Everything that is meant for you will find a way! Trading is PATIENCE and when I say that I really mean – Trading is PAY-ience! Because it's the patience to wait for anything in life pays off. "

Lisa N Edwards

THE IMPORTANCE OF DISCIPLINE

Discipline plays a pivotal role in the success of any trading strategy, and the compound trading strategy is no exception. Parts of this book may be repetitive because it is vital you adhere to them. Being strict with predetermined profit and stop-loss thresholds without succumbing to emotional decision-making. The ability to stay disciplined helps to avoid impulsive trading, chasing trades midwave, or deviating from the defined plan. Patience is a virtue in this strategy, as traders wait for favourable entries that align with their set parameters. It is essential to maintain a long-term perspective and focus on the bigger picture, rather than being swayed by short-term market fluctuations.

Recognising the Role of Discipline in Successful Trading

The foundation upon which successful trading is built is discipline. It encompasses a wide range of traits, including consistency, self-control, and adherence to a well-defined trading plan. Without discipline, traders are susceptible to making impulsive decisions driven by emotions, which can lead to significant losses. Recognising the crucial role of discipline in trading is the first step towards developing the necessary mindset to achieve consistent profitability.

Avoiding Emotional Decision-Making and Impulsive Trades

Emotions have the potential to cloud judgment and disrupt the rational decision-making process. Fear and greed are two primary emotions that often influence trading decisions, leading to impulsive and ill-advised trades. Successful traders understand the importance of keeping emotions in check and avoiding impulsive behaviour. By sticking to a predetermined trading plan and maintaining discipline, traders can overcome emotional biases and make objective decisions based on analysis and strategy.

Patience and Long-Term Perspective in Executing the Strategy

Patience is a virtue that pays off in trading. Markets can be volatile and unpredictable, often testing the patience of traders. It is essential to remain calm and composed, even during periods of market turbulence or prolonged periods of no activity. By staying patient and not succumbing to the temptation of deviating from the trading plan, traders allow their strategies to unfold over time. A long-term perspective helps traders avoid chasing short-term gains and instead focus on consistent profitability and capital preservation.

Discipline is crucial for successful trading. It's vital to recognise its importance and integrate it into your approach for consistent profitability. By avoiding emotions and impulsive trades, you can maintain an objective mindset, leading to better outcomes. Patience and a long-term perspective help navigate market fluctuations. Embracing discipline enhances trading performance and fosters a disciplined mindset in all aspects of life. Remember, discipline is a skill that can be developed over time. Prioritise it in your trading journey for long-term success.

"Have patience with all things, but first of all with yourself."

Saint Francis de Sales

THE POWER OF COMPOUNDING

One of the key advantages of the compound trading strategy is its potential for exponential growth through compounding. By aiming for a minimum bounce of 3% per trade and consistently reinvesting profits, traders can harness the power of compounding. Compounding refers to the process of reinvesting profits to generate additional gains, resulting in accelerated wealth accumulation over time. In the case of the compound trading strategy, achieving a 3% compounded profit per day can lead to substantial returns. For instance, starting with $1,000 and compounding at 3% daily, a trader could potentially reach one million dollars in approximately a year, even with occasional 3% losses.

Recognising the Role of Discipline in Successful Trading

Discipline is the foundation upon which successful trading is built. It encompasses a wide range of traits, including consistency, self-control, and adherence to a well-defined trading plan. Without discipline, traders are susceptible to making impulsive decisions driven by emotions, which can lead to significant losses. Recognising the crucial role of discipline in trading is the first step towards developing the necessary mindset to achieve consistent profitability.

Avoiding Emotional Decision-Making and Impulsive Trades

Emotions have the potential to cloud judgment and disrupt the rational decision-making process. Fear and greed are two primary emotions that often influence trading decisions, leading to impulsive and ill-advised trades. Successful traders understand the importance of keeping emotions in check and avoiding impulsive behaviour. By sticking to a predetermined trading plan and maintaining discipline, traders can overcome emotional biases and make objective decisions based on analysis and strategy.

Patience and Long-Term Perspective in Executing the Strategy

Patience is a virtue that pays off in trading. Markets can be volatile and unpredictable, often testing the patience of traders. It is essential to remain calm and composed, even during periods of market turbulence or prolonged periods of no activity. By staying patient and not succumbing to the temptation of deviating from the trading plan, traders allow their strategies to unfold over time. A long-term perspective helps traders avoid chasing short-term gains and instead focus on consistent profitability and capital preservation.

EFFORT AND SOME MORE EFFORT!

Trading success is not an overnight achievement but a result of consistent effort, dedication, and employing effective strategies. I wish I could say it was as easy as having a bit of luck on the roulette table, believe me some people do get lucky, but if you do the work in this book, you will be on the path to success!

"Strength and growth come only through continuous effort and struggle."

Napoleon Hill

CONCLUSION

Summarising the Benefits of the Compound Trading Strategy

The compound trading strategy offers numerous advantages that can propel traders towards their financial goals. Firstly, compounding allows traders to reinvest profits and maximise their potential returns over time. By consistently reinvesting gains, traders benefit from the exponential growth of their trading capital, resulting in accelerated returns and increased account value.
Additionally, compound trading helps mitigate the risks associated with relying solely on large single trades, promoting a more balanced and sustainable approach to trading. It also instils discipline, as traders are motivated to maintain consistent performance and avoid unnecessary risks.

Emphasising the Importance of Practice, Learning, and Dedication

While the compound trading strategy is a powerful tool, achieving success in trading requires more than just employing the right strategies. It demands a continuous commitment to learning, practicing, and honing trading skills. By dedicating time to understand market dynamics, learning technical and fundamental analysis, and staying updated with the latest trends, traders can make informed decisions and adapt to changing market conditions. Consistent practice through simulated trading or paper trading can also help traders refine their strategies, identify weaknesses, and develop the necessary discipline to execute their trades effectively.

Furthermore, dedication plays a crucial role in trading success. Trading is a competitive field that demands perseverance and resilience. Traders need to approach their craft with a growth mindset, embracing challenges as opportunities for learning and improvement. The ability to adapt to market fluctuations, manage emotions, and stay committed to their trading plans during both favourable and challenging times is paramount.

By staying curious, dedicated, and open to new information and strategies, traders can enhance their skills, adapt to changing market conditions, and increase their chances of long-term success.

The compound trading strategy offers a systematic approach to trading, emphasising consistent profits and disciplined decision-making. By setting profit and stop-loss thresholds, utilising cross supports, and maintaining a disciplined mindset, traders can position themselves for long-term success.

One thing to remember is that people can study for years to become successful, in this book you are given tools and strategies that have been proven to work successfully, time and time again!

"Curiosity is the most powerful thing you own."

James Cameron

SECTION 1 - THE ABC OF COMPOUND TRADING

Chapter B: OCO Orders and Living Your Life:

Introduction

- Balancing trading and personal life
- Introduction to OCO (One Cancels the Other) orders and their benefits.

Understanding OCO Orders

- Definition and functionality of OCO orders
- Simultaneously setting stop-loss and profit target orders
- Automation of trade management and exit points.

Benefits of OCO Orders

- Efficient trade management
- Emotion-Free Execution
- Enhancing work-life balance and personal well-being
- Reducing stress levels in trading

Implementing OCO Orders

- Defining trade parameters and risk tolerance
- Setting up OCO orders on trading platforms
- Monitoring trade progress and adjusting exit points if needed.
- Emphasising the importance of discipline and sticking to the plan

Conclusion

- Recap of the benefits of OCO orders
- Reminding traders of the need for risk management and strategy development
- Encouraging a healthy balance between trading and personal life

"If you can learn to create a state of mind that is not affected by the market's behaviour, the struggle will cease to exist."

Mark Douglas

Chapter B

OCO ORDERS AND LIVING YOUR LIFE

"A One-Cancels-the-Other (OCO) order is a set of two pending orders, where the execution of one order automatically cancels the other.

This type of order is designed to provide traders with increased flexibility and risk management capabilities in the financial markets (and allow you to live your life!"

Introduction

Riding the waves of trading can be exhilarating and addictive, so, finding the right balance between actively managing your trades and enjoying a fulfilling life outside of the markets can be a challenge. The allure of financial markets often draws individuals into a world of numbers, charts, and constant market analysis, where the pursuit of profits becomes an all-consuming passion.

Traders, especially when they first start, can be easily consumed by their desire to succeed, often exhibiting obsessive tendencies in their relentless pursuit of wealth. While this passion and dedication are admirable, it is crucial for traders to recognise the importance of finding balance in their lives.

Those new to the market, often find themselves immersed in a whirlwind of information, constantly monitoring charts, analysing market trends, and executing trades. The desire to stay ahead of the game and capitalise on every opportunity can lead to an unrelenting dedication that consumes their time and energy.

This single-minded focus on trading can have detrimental effects on other aspects of life, such as relationships, physical and mental well-being, and personal fulfilment.

Balancing Trading and Personal Life

Finding balance is essential. A trader's journey is not just about making profits but also about creating a harmonious and well-rounded life. Recognising the need to strike a balance between work and personal life is a crucial step towards long-term success and happiness.

In this chapter, we will explore a powerful tool that can help new traders achieve this delicate balance - the concept of OCO (One Cancels the Other) orders. OCO orders provide traders with the convenience of setting both a stop-loss order and a profit target simultaneously, allowing them to automate their trade management while freeing up time for other activities. By leveraging the power of OCO orders, traders can protect their investments, reduce stress, and enjoy the benefits of living a well-rounded life.

We will delve into the mechanics of OCO orders, understanding how they work, and how traders can effectively implement them into their trading strategies. We will also explore real-life examples and case studies to illustrate the impact of OCO orders on traders' lives.

Ultimately, the goal of this chapter is to shed light on the significance of finding balance in the world of trading. By integrating OCO orders into their trading routines, traders can automate their risk management and profit-taking processes, allowing them to regain control over their time and create a healthier work-life balance. The ability to step away from the screens, enjoy personal relationships, pursue hobbies, and engage in self-care activities is essential for long-term success in both trading and life as a whole and once you understand how OCO orders work, you can get on with your life!

Introduction to OCO Orders and Their Benefits

OCO orders are a pair of pending orders in which the execution of one order automatically cancels the other. They offer traders a range of benefits that enhance trade management efficiency, mitigate emotional bias, and promote overall well-being. Here are some key advantages of OCO orders:

Efficient Trade Management: OCO orders streamline the process of managing trades by automating the execution of predetermined exit points. Traders can set stop-loss levels to protect against potential losses and establish profit targets to secure gains. This automation eliminates the need for continuous monitoring, allowing traders to focus on other aspects of their lives while still actively participating in the market.

Emotion-Free Execution: Emotional biases can cloud judgment and lead to irrational decision-making, which can be detrimental to trading performance. OCO orders help eliminate emotional interference by setting predefined exit points based on a trading plan. By executing trades based on predetermined criteria, traders can reduce impulsive and emotionally driven decisions, leading to more rational and objective trading strategies.

Stress Reduction: The constant monitoring of trades and the pressure to make quick decisions can lead to high levels of stress and anxiety. OCO orders alleviate this burden by providing a sense of control and peace of mind. Traders can trust that their predetermined exit points will be executed, reducing stress, and promoting a calmer trading experience.

Risk Management: OCO orders are instrumental in implementing effective risk management strategies. Traders can set stop-loss orders to limit potential losses by automatically exiting a trade if it reaches a predetermined price level. Simultaneously, profit target orders ensure that traders secure gains by automatically closing the trade when the desired profit level is achieved. These risk management measures protect traders' capital and allow for better control over potential losses.

Flexibility and Adaptability: OCO orders offer traders flexibility and adaptability in responding to market volatility and changing conditions. As market dynamics shift, traders can modify their OCO orders to adjust stop-loss and profit target levels accordingly. This adaptability enables traders to optimise their risk-reward ratio and adapt to evolving market trends, ultimately increasing their chances of success.

Understanding OCO Orders

OCO orders are a powerful tool in the trading arsenal, enabling traders to set both stop-loss and profit target orders simultaneously. When one of the orders is triggered, the other is automatically cancelled, ensuring that only one scenario is executed. This functionality provides traders with a sense of security and control over their trades without the need for constant monitoring.

By utilising OCO orders, traders can establish predetermined exit points, safeguarding their capital and eliminating the need for constant manual intervention.

Definition and Functionality of OCO Orders

The functionality of OCO orders lies in their ability to automate trade management and simplify the process of setting stop-loss and profit target orders. Traders can define two orders within an OCO order: a stop-loss order to limit potential losses and a profit target order to secure gains. These orders are linked together, with the execution of one order triggering the cancellation of the other.

Simultaneously Setting Stop-Loss and Profit Target Orders

One of the key advantages of OCO orders is the ability to set stop-loss and profit target orders simultaneously. Traditionally, traders would have to manually monitor their positions and execute trades to close them once a specific profit level or stop-loss level was reached. With OCO orders, traders can define their desired stop-loss and profit target levels upfront, eliminating the need for constant monitoring. This not only saves time but also reduces the risk of missing exit points due to distractions or delayed execution.

Automation of Trade Management and Exit Points

OCO orders bring automation to trade management by ensuring that exit points are executed automatically. Once either the stop-loss or profit target level is reached, the corresponding order is triggered, and the other order is cancelled. This automation removes the burden of manual trade execution and allows traders to focus on market analysis, strategy development, and other aspects of trading.

"One of the best ways to reduce trading stress is to set an OCO.

This automates your trades allowing you to live life."

Lisa N Edwards

"If I have positions going against me, I get right out: if they are going for me, I keep them.

Risk control is the most important thing in trading. If you have a losing position that is making you uncomfortable, the solution is very simple:

GET OUT!

Because you can always get back in. ."

Paul Tudor Jones

BENEFITS OF OCO ORDERS

It's important to keep in mind two significant aspects when dealing with these orders. Firstly, when one order is executed, the other order is automatically cancelled.

Secondly, if either of the orders is cancelled, the second order is also deleted.

Efficient Trade Management

By automating the execution of predetermined exit points, OCO orders make for more efficient trading, streamlining the trade management process. Traders can set their stop-loss level to protect against potential losses and establish a profit target to secure gains. This eliminates the need for continuous monitoring and allows traders to focus on other aspects of their lives.

Emotion-Free Execution

Emotions can often cloud judgment and lead to irrational decision-making in the heat of trading. OCO orders help traders eliminate emotional bias by setting predefined exit points based on their trading plan. This reduces the chances of making impulsive and emotionally driven decisions that may result in negative outcomes.

Why are men emotional about money?

The idea that men are emotional about money is a generalisation and can vary from person to person.

However, it is worth noting that emotions regarding money are not exclusive to any specific gender. Both men and women can experience a wide range of emotions when it comes to financial matters.

Enhancing work-life balance and personal well-being

Work-Life Balance: OCO orders enable traders to strike a healthy balance between their trading activities and personal life. By automating trade management, traders can step away from the computer and engage in other activities, whether it's spending time with family, pursuing hobbies, or taking care of personal well-being. This freedom allows for a more well-rounded and fulfilling life outside of trading.

Stress Reduction: Constantly monitoring trades and making split-second decisions can be mentally exhausting and contribute to high levels of stress. OCO orders alleviate this burden by providing a sense of control and peace of mind. Traders can trust that their predetermined exit points will be executed, reducing anxiety, and allowing for a more relaxed trading experience.

Have you heard Men are from Mars and Women from Venus? Women love to love and nurture, while Men love money? Right? No! Emotional attachment to money is not exclusive to men; it's a common human trait that can be observed in individuals of all genders. However, it is worth noting that people's emotional responses to money can vary based on various factors, including cultural, societal, and personal influences. While it is not accurate to generalise and claim that all men are emotional about money, there are a few reasons

why some individuals, including men, may exhibit emotional reactions when it comes to financial matters:
Societal Expectations: Societal norms and expectations can influence how individuals perceive and handle money. Cultural conditioning may place a greater emphasis on financial success and providing for oneself and others, leading to heightened emotional responses when financial stability or goals are compromised.

Sense of Security: Money often represents a sense of security and stability. Men, like anyone else, may feel emotionally attached to money because they associate it with meeting their basic needs, supporting their loved ones, or achieving long-term goals. Financial uncertainty or loss can evoke feelings of anxiety, stress, or fear, leading to emotional responses.

Identity and Self-Worth: For some individuals, particularly in societies where financial success is highly valued, money can become closely tied to their sense of self-worth and identity. When financial setbacks occur, it can impact their self-esteem and trigger emotional reactions such as frustration, disappointment, or a sense of failure.

Future Planning and Goals: All genders, may have specific financial aspirations, such as saving for retirement, providing for their families, or achieving certain milestones. When faced with challenges or setbacks that hinder progress towards these goals, individuals may experience emotions such as frustration, impatience, or concern about the future.

Personal Experiences and Beliefs: Past experiences with money, both positive and negative, can shape emotional responses. For example, individuals who have experienced financial hardships or grew up in financially unstable environments may develop a heightened emotional attachment to money as a means of safeguarding themselves from similar situations in the future.

It is important to recognise that emotional responses to money are not solely determined by gender, but rather by a complex interplay of various personal, social, and psychological factors. Individual experiences, values, and societal expectations all contribute to the diverse range of emotional attitudes towards money that can be observed in both men and women.

Reducing stress levels in trading

Money holds significant meaning for many individuals as it is intricately linked to dreams, goals, and personal achievements. The pursuit of financial stability and success can introduce a considerable amount of stress and pressure. However, the implementation of strategies such as One Cancels the Other (OCO) orders can provide a sense of peace of mind and protection in the face of uncertainty.

OCO orders serve as a risk management tool, allowing traders to set predefined exit points for their trades. By simultaneously setting stop-loss and profit target orders, traders can protect themselves from significant losses while also ensuring that they secure profits when favourable market conditions arise. This automated approach to trade management offers a degree of reassurance and security, reducing the stress associated with constantly monitoring and making split-second decisions.

We will embark on a journey to explore the intricacies of OCO orders, unravelling their potential to simplify trade execution and enhance risk management.

"There will always be people who can do it better than you, but that's a good thing!

Start to see competition as inspiration – without envy."

Kathyn Budig

IMPLEMENTING OCO ORDERS

Defining Trade Parameters and Risk Tolerance

To begin our journey, let's first delve into the importance of defining trade parameters and understanding risk tolerance. Successful traders know that clarity in trade parameters is the foundation of a well-executed plan. Identifying entry points, profit targets, and stop-loss levels ensures a clear roadmap for each trade. Simultaneously, assessing risk tolerance helps traders determine the amount of potential loss they are willing to accept in a trade. By aligning trade parameters with risk tolerance, traders can strike a balance that sets the stage for success.

Setting Up OCO Orders on Trading Platforms

Now that we have a clear understanding of trade parameters, it's time to put them into action through the implementation of OCO orders on trading platforms. Picture yourself sitting at your trading desk, armed with knowledge and ready to execute trades efficiently. With step-by-step guidance, we will navigate through popular trading platforms, uncovering the intricacies of setting up OCO orders. Customising order parameters allows traders to fine-tune their OCO orders to match their trade objectives and risk management strategies, putting them in full control of their trades.

Monitoring Trade Progress and Adjusting Exit Points (if needed)

As our trades unfold, it is essential to monitor their progress and adapt accordingly. Markets are dynamic, and conditions can change in an instant. By actively managing our trades, we can assess performance, consider market conditions, and adjust profit targets and stop-loss levels when necessary. Embracing tools like trailing stop orders enables us to maximise profits while safeguarding against potential reversals. It's a dance between vigilance and flexibility, ensuring our trades stay on the right track.

Emphasising the Importance of Discipline: Staying True to the Plan

To implement OCO – KEY STEPS:

Define Trade Parameters: Establish clear stop-loss and profit target levels based on your trading strategy and risk tolerance. Consider factors such as support and resistance levels, including cross support/resistance regions, volatility, and market conditions.

***Set Up OCO Orders*:** Depending on the trading platform, locate the OCO order functionality and input the desired stop-loss and profit target values. Ensure that the order is placed correctly and is active.

***Monitor Trade Progress**:* Keep a watchful eye on your trades to gauge whether the stop-loss or profit target levels are triggered. Be prepared to adjust your exit points if market conditions change or new information arises. As you become more experienced, moving the sell order higher in the right market conditions will help to gain more profit. And alternatively raise the stop loss into the profit as the trade progresses to protect this for a higher return.

Maintain Discipline: When starting stick to your trading plan and avoid the temptation to manually override or adjust the OCO orders based on short-term market fluctuations or emotional impulses. Working with the market trend is essential, and when starting it can be hard to know and understand the market changes. Consistency and discipline are key to the success of this strategy.

Trading often involves split-second decisions that can make all the difference; implementing effective order types is crucial. Discipline is the guiding force that separates the successful from the struggling. It is crucial to resist the temptations of impulsive decision-making and the urge to deviate from our predefined trade parameters and exit points. Our story emphasises the significance of discipline, urging traders to maintain a consistent approach. Both winning and losing trades provide valuable lessons for continuous improvement. By embracing discipline, we can navigate the unpredictable waters of the market with confidence.

Conclusion

Our journey into the world of OCO orders has shed light on their potential to streamline trade execution and enhance risk management. By defining trade parameters, setting up OCO orders on trading platforms, monitoring trade progress, and embracing discipline, traders can unlock the power to execute trades efficiently while effectively managing risk.

OCO orders are not a guarantee of success. Traders must still adhere to sound risk management principles, develop a robust trading strategy, and continuously monitor market conditions. By striking the right balance between trading and living a fulfilling life, traders can enhance their overall well-being and long-term success in the financial markets.

The story of OCO orders is one of empowerment, where traders take control of their trading journey, harnessing the tools and strategies that pave the path to success. The ability to step away from the computer and enjoy personal endeavours while knowing that trades are being managed effectively brings peace of mind. So, take the first step, embrace the possibilities, and embark on your own journey of mastering OCO orders. The world of trading awaits, ready to reward those who are prepared.

Only YOU can create the life you want so what are you waiting for?

"Before starting the next chapter!

Remember…

You can't start the next chapter of your life if you keep re-reading the last one.

Although I recommend this for the book, not for life!"

Chapter C

THE POWER OF 3%-ACHIEVING CONSISTENT RESULTS

Introduction

- Importance of consistency in trading
- Introduction to targeting 3% gains.

Understanding the Power of 3%

- The Mathematics of Compounding
- Exploring the exponential growth potential
- Examples of compounding with 3% gains

Risk Management and Capital Preservation

- Developing The Right Mindset
- Trading Strategies For Consistent Results
- Maintaining Focus and Adapting to Challenges
- Embracing Continuous Learning and Improvement
- Conclusion

"Success isn't always about greatness.

It's about consistency.

Consistent hard work leads to success.

Greatness will come."

Dwayne Johnson (The Rock)

Chapter C

THE POWER OF 3%-ACHIEVING CONSISTENT RESULTS

The number 3 has always held a special significance throughout history. It represents harmony, wisdom, and understanding. In fairy tales like the Three Little Pigs and Goldilocks and the Three Bears, the power of three is clear. These stories teach us about diligence, finding balance, and the importance of discipline. When it comes to trading, we can apply these lessons by defining our parameters, using OCO orders, monitoring trades, and staying disciplined. Let the magic of three guide us in our journey to success.

Introduction

To unlock the success of trading, consistency is key. It's not about hitting home runs with every trade but rather about achieving steady and consistent results over time. One powerful strategy that can help traders accomplish this is the concept of targeting a 3% gain on each trade.

This chapter explores the power of 3 – aiming for 3% returns and how it can lead to long-term success in the financial markets. We will delve into the benefits of consistent growth, the mathematics behind compounding, and the mindset required to achieve this goal. By embracing the power of 3% gains, traders can build a solid foundation for their trading journey and pave the way for financial success.

Importance of Consistency in Trading

Consistency is key when it comes to trading in the financial markets. Many points in the book are repeated, as the old saying goes, *"In the quest for learning, repetition becomes the nurturing soil from which mastery blossoms."* Whether you're a seasoned trader or just starting out, maintaining consistency in your trading approach can make a significant difference in your overall success. But how can we achieve this consistency? One effective strategy is targeting 3% gains. Setting a specific target, such as a 3% gain, provides a clear focus and allows for better risk management. It helps traders avoid the common pitfall of aiming for unrealistic profits and taking unnecessary risks. By aiming for smaller, more achievable gains, traders can build their confidence, develop a disciplined mindset, and gradually grow their trading accounts over time.

Introduction to Targeting 3% Gains

The concept of targeting 3% gains aligns with the principle of compounding is not new. Even though 3% may seem like a modest figure, consistent 3% gains can compound into significant returns over the long term. As Albert Einstein famously said, "Compound interest is the eighth wonder of the world. He who understands it, earns it; he who doesn't pays it."

Consistency is not just about making profits; it also involves managing losses. By implementing a maximum stop-loss threshold, such as 3%, traders can limit their potential losses and protect their capital. This disciplined approach ensures that no single trade has the power to impact their overall trading performance significantly.

Targeting 3% gains also helps traders develop patience and discipline. It encourages them to wait for high-quality trade setups and avoid impulsive decisions driven by fear or greed. Instead of constantly chasing big gains, traders can focus on taking small, consistent profits, which can ultimately lead to long-term success.

It's important to note that targeting 3% gains does not mean winning every trade. Losses are an inevitable part of trading, but with a disciplined approach, the impact of losses can be minimised.

As legendary trader Paul Tudor Jones once said,

"The secret to being successful from a trading perspective is to have an indefatigable, undying, unquenchable thirst for information and knowledge."

To target 3% gains consistently, traders need to develop a robust trading plan. This includes conducting thorough market analysis, identifying high-probability trade setups, and implementing proper risk management techniques. It's also crucial to continually educate oneself and adapt to changing market conditions.

As the saying goes, "Consistency is the key to unlocking the door of success."

"Goals on the road to achievement cannot be achieved without discipline and consistency."

Denzel Washington

UNDERSTANDING THE POWER OF 3%

You might be wondering, why focus on just 3% gains? Well, consistency is the name of the game. It's not about hitting it big on one trade and then losing it all on the next. By aiming for consistent 3% gains, you create a solid foundation for your trading success. It's like building a staircase, one step at a time, steadily progressing towards your financial goals.

These incremental gains may not seem like much at first, but they add up over time and can lead to significant wealth accumulation. In fact, if you were able to trade 3% compounding from a starting balance of one thousand dollars, you could reach the magic million in just 236 successful trades.

Consistency vs. Big Winners

In the world of trading, there is often a misconception that big winners are the key to success. While it's true that hitting a jackpot trade can be exhilarating, relying solely on big wins is a risky strategy. The truth is, consistent gains, no matter how small, can outperform the occasional big winners in the long run.

By focusing on consistent 3% gains, you minimise the risk of experiencing significant losses. It's about preserving your trading capital and avoiding the emotional rollercoaster that comes with chasing after big wins.

As Warren Buffett once said, "Rule No. 1: Never lose money. Rule No. 2: Never forget rule No. 1."

Benefits of Incremental Gains and Minimising Losses

Trading is a game of probabilities and targeting 3% gains aligns with a prudent risk management approach. By consistently booking small profits, you not only grow your trading account but also build confidence in your trading strategy. Each successful trade reinforces your belief in your approach and helps you stay disciplined even during challenging market conditions.

Moreover, by aiming for smaller gains, you protect yourself from significant losses that can have a devastating impact on your trading capital. It's much easier to recover from a 3% loss than a 30% loss. Remember, it's not just about making profits; it's about minimising losses and preserving your capital for future trades.

The Power of Compounding

The real power of targeting 3% gains lies in the principle of compounding. As you consistently accumulate small gains, your trading capital grows, and so does the potential for larger gains. Albert Einstein called compounding the eighth wonder of the world for a reason.

The magic of compounding occurs when you reinvest your profits back into your trades, allowing your account balance to snowball over time. The more trades you make and the longer you stay consistent with your 3% gains, the greater the compounding effect. It's the exponential growth that can turn a modest starting balance into substantial wealth.

Understanding the power of 3% gains is about these 3 things:

- Embracing consistency
- Risk management
- The magic of compounding.

By focusing on incremental gains, you build a solid foundation for long-term trading success. It's not about chasing after big winners or taking unnecessary risks; it's about steadily progressing towards your financial goals, one small step at a time. As the saying goes…

"Rome wasn't built in a day." Similarly, your trading success will be built on the power of consistent 3% gains.

Remember these 3 Key Points:

- Targeting just 3% gain on a trade takes 236 trades from one thousand to a Million (and beyond)
- Consistency matters more than hitting big winners.
- The advantages of incremental gains and reducing the impact of losses by using 3% each way

The Mathematics of Compounding

Compounding is a powerful force in the world of finance, and it plays a significant role in the 3% strategy. The concept is simple yet profound. When you consistently achieve 3% gains, these gains compound over time, multiplying your wealth exponentially. It's like a snowball rolling down a hill, gaining momentum and size as it goes. The more consistent you are with your 3% gains, the faster your wealth grows. It's a remarkable phenomenon that showcases the power of compounding in action.

Exploring the Exponential Growth Potential

To truly grasp the magnitude of compounding, let's delve into the mathematics behind it. Imagine starting with an initial investment of $1,000 and consistently achieving 3% gains on each trade. The power of compounding becomes evident as these gains accumulate over time.

In less than a year, with compounding at a 3% gain on each trade, your initial $1,000 investment can grow to a staggering $1 million. It may sound incredible, but the mathematics proves its feasibility.

If you were to trade 3% compounding from a starting balance of $1,000, with each successful trade, your account balance would increase by $30 (3% of $1,000). By repeating this process consistently, you can witness the exponential growth of your wealth.

To put it into perspective, it would take just 234 successful trades, compounding at 3% each time, to reach the magic million-dollar mark. That's less than one trade per day for a year. It's an astonishing revelation that demonstrates the extraordinary potential of compounding when harnessed effectively.

Examples of Compounding with 3% Gains

Let's consider the practical application of compounding with 3% gains. Starting with a modest $1,000, let's explore how your wealth can grow over time.

After one winning trade of achieving 3% gains, your account balance would increase by $30, bringing your total to $1,030. In the second trade, your gain is not just 3% of the initial $1,000, but also 3% of the additional $30 from the previous trade. This translates to a gain of $31 (3% of $1,030), raising your balance to $1,061.

As you continue this pattern of consistent 3% gains trade after trade, your wealth starts compounding exponentially. After six trades, your account balance would reach $1,197.83. And within a year, your initial $1,000 investment would have grown to an impressive one million dollars.

These examples highlight the power of compounding and the remarkable growth potential of consistently achieving 3% gains. By staying focused, disciplined, and committed to the strategy, you can witness the snowball effect of compounding on your wealth.

Key Points:

- Exploring the exponential growth potential of compounding
- How consistent 3% gains can lead to significant wealth accumulation.
- Demonstrating the long-term impact of compounding with examples

The compounding gains are clearly seen on the tables over the following pages. From first trade and beyond.

Risk comes from not knowing what you are doing.

Warren Buffet

1	TRADE	BALANCE	PROJECTION
4	1	1000.00	1030.00
5	2	1030.00	1060.90
6	3	1060.90	1092.73
7	4	1092.73	1125.51
8	5	1125.51	1159.27
9	6	1159.27	1194.05
10	7	1194.05	1229.87
11	8	1229.87	1266.77
12	9	1266.77	1304.77
13	10	1304.77	1343.92
14	11	1343.92	1384.23
15	12	1384.23	1425.76
16	13	1425.76	1468.53
17	14	1468.53	1512.59
18	15	1512.59	1557.97
19	16	1557.97	1604.71
20	17	1604.71	1652.85
21	18	1652.85	1702.43
22	19	1702.43	1753.51
23	20	1753.51	1806.11
24	21	1806.11	1860.29
25	22	1860.29	1916.10
26	23	1916.10	1973.59
27	24	1973.59	2032.79
28	25	2032.79	2093.78
29	26	2093.78	2156.59
30	27	2156.59	2221.29
31	28	2221.29	2287.93
32	29	2287.93	2356.57
33	30	2356.57	2427.26

1	TRADE	BALANCE	PROJECTION
34	31	2427.26	2500.08
35	32	2500.08	2575.08
36	33	2575.08	2652.34
37	34	2652.34	2731.91
38	35	2731.91	2813.86
39	36	2813.86	2898.28
40	37	2898.28	2985.23
41	38	2985.23	3074.78
42	39	3074.78	3167.03
43	40	3167.03	3262.04
44	41	3262.04	3359.90
45	42	3359.90	3460.70
46	43	3460.70	3564.52
47	44	3564.52	3671.45
48	45	3671.45	3781.60
49	46	3781.60	3895.04
50	47	3895.04	4011.90
51	48	4011.90	4132.25
52	49	4132.25	4256.22
53	50	4256.22	4383.91
54	51	4383.91	4515.42
55	52	4515.42	4650.89
56	53	4650.89	4790.41
57	54	4790.41	4934.12
58	55	4934.12	5082.15
59	56	5082.15	5234.61
60	57	5234.61	5391.65
61	58	5391.65	5553.40
62	59	5553.40	5720.00
63	60	5720.00	5891.60

1	TRADE	BALANCE	PROJECTION
64	61	5891.60	6068.35
65	62	6068.35	6250.40
66	63	6250.40	6437.91
67	64	6437.91	6631.05
68	65	6631.05	6829.98
69	66	6829.98	7034.88
70	67	7034.88	7245.93
71	68	7245.93	7463.31
72	69	7463.31	7687.21
73	70	7687.21	7917.82
74	71	7917.82	8155.36
75	72	8155.36	8400.02
76	73	8400.02	8652.02
77	74	8652.02	8911.58
78	75	8911.58	9178.93
79	76	9178.93	9454.29
80	77	9454.29	9737.92
81	78	9737.92	10030.06
82	79	10030.06	10330.96
83	80	10330.96	10640.89
84	81	10640.89	10960.12
85	82	10960.12	11288.92
86	83	11288.92	11627.59
87	84	11627.59	11976.42
88	85	11976.42	12335.71
89	86	12335.71	12705.78
90	87	12705.78	13086.95
91	88	13086.95	13479.56
92	89	13479.56	13883.95
93	90	13883.95	14300.47

1	TRADE	BALANCE	PROJECTION
94	91	14300.47	14729.48
95	92	14729.48	15171.37
96	93	15171.37	15626.51
97	94	15626.51	16095.30
98	95	16095.30	16578.16
99	96	16578.16	17075.51
100	97	17075.51	17587.77
101	98	17587.77	18115.40
102	99	18115.40	18658.87
103	100	18658.87	19218.63
104	101	19218.63	19795.19
105	102	19795.19	20389.05
106	103	20389.05	21000.72
107	104	21000.72	21630.74
108	105	21630.74	22279.66
109	106	22279.66	22948.05
110	107	22948.05	23636.49
111	108	23636.49	24345.59
112	109	24345.59	25075.96
113	110	25075.96	25828.23
114	111	25828.23	26603.08
115	112	26603.08	27401.17
116	113	27401.17	28223.21
117	114	28223.21	29069.91
118	115	29069.91	29942.00
119	116	29942.00	30840.26
120	117	30840.26	31765.47
121	118	31765.47	32718.43
122	119	32718.43	33699.99
123	120	33699.99	34710.99

1	TRADE	BALANCE	PROJECTION
124	121	34710.99	35752.32
125	122	35752.32	36824.89
126	123	36824.89	37929.63
127	124	37929.63	39067.52
128	125	39067.52	40239.55
129	126	40239.55	41446.73
130	127	41446.73	42690.14
131	128	42690.14	43970.84
132	129	43970.84	45289.97
133	130	45289.97	46648.66
134	131	46648.66	48048.12
135	132	48048.12	49489.57
136	133	49489.57	50974.25
137	134	50974.25	52503.48
138	135	52503.48	54078.59
139	136	54078.59	55700.94
140	137	55700.94	57371.97
141	138	57371.97	59093.13
142	139	59093.13	60865.93
143	140	60865.93	62691.90
144	141	62691.90	64572.66
145	142	64572.66	66509.84
146	143	66509.84	68505.14
147	144	68505.14	70560.29
148	145	70560.29	72677.10
149	146	72677.10	74857.41
150	147	74857.41	77103.13
151	148	77103.13	79416.23
152	149	79416.23	81798.71
153	150	81798.71	84252.68

1	TRADE	BALANCE	PROJECTION
154	151	84252.68	86780.26
155	152	86780.26	89383.66
156	153	89383.66	92065.17
157	154	92065.17	94827.13
158	155	94827.13	97671.94
159	156	97671.94	100602.10
160	157	100602.10	103620.16
161	158	103620.16	106728.77
162	159	106728.77	109930.63
163	160	109930.63	113228.55
164	161	113228.55	116625.41
165	162	116625.41	120124.17
166	163	120124.17	123727.90
167	164	123727.90	127439.73
168	165	127439.73	131262.92
169	166	131262.92	135200.81
170	167	135200.81	139256.84
171	168	139256.84	143434.54
172	169	143434.54	147737.58
173	170	147737.58	152169.71
174	171	152169.71	156734.80
175	172	156734.80	161436.84
176	173	161436.84	166279.95
177	174	166279.95	171268.34
178	175	171268.34	176406.39
179	176	176406.39	181698.59
180	177	181698.59	187149.54
181	178	187149.54	192764.03
182	179	192764.03	198546.95
183	180	198546.95	204503.36

1	TRADE	BALANCE	PROJECTION
184	181	204503.36	210638.46
185	182	210638.46	216957.61
186	183	216957.61	223466.34
187	184	223466.34	230170.33
188	185	230170.33	237075.44
189	186	237075.44	244187.71
190	187	244187.71	251513.34
191	188	251513.34	259058.74
192	189	259058.74	266830.50
193	190	266830.50	274835.41
194	191	274835.41	283080.48
195	192	283080.48	291572.89
196	193	291572.89	300320.08
197	194	300320.08	309329.68
198	195	309329.68	318609.57
199	196	318609.57	328167.86
200	197	328167.86	338012.89
201	198	338012.89	348153.28
202	199	348153.28	358597.88
203	200	358597.88	369355.82
204	201	369355.82	380436.49
205	202	380436.49	391849.58
206	203	391849.58	403605.07
207	204	403605.07	415713.22
208	205	415713.22	428184.62
209	206	428184.62	441030.16
210	207	441030.16	454261.06
211	208	454261.06	467888.90
212	209	467888.90	481925.56
213	210	481925.56	496383.33

1	TRADE	BALANCE	PROJECTION
214	211	496383.33	511274.83
215	212	511274.83	526613.07
216	213	526613.07	542411.47
217	214	542411.47	558683.81
218	215	558683.81	575444.33
219	216	575444.33	592707.65
220	217	592707.65	610488.88
221	218	610488.88	628803.55
222	219	628803.55	647667.66
223	220	647667.66	667097.69
224	221	667097.69	687110.62
225	222	687110.62	707723.94
226	223	707723.94	728955.65
227	224	728955.65	750824.32
228	225	750824.32	773349.05
229	226	773349.05	796549.53
230	227	796549.53	820446.01
231	228	820446.01	845059.39
232	229	845059.39	870411.17
233	230	870411.17	896523.51
234	231	896523.51	923419.21
235	232	923419.21	951121.79
236	233	951121.79	979655.44
237	234	979655.44	1009045.11
238	235	1009045.11	1039316.46
239	236	1039316.46	1070495.95
240	237	1070495.95	1102610.83
241	238	1102610.83	1135689.16
242	239	1135689.16	1169759.83
243	240	1169759.83	1204852.63

Risk Management and Capital Preservation

While targeting 3% gains is exciting, it's crucial to remember the importance of risk management. Preserving your capital is essential for long-term success. One way to protect yourself is by setting appropriate stop-loss levels. This ensures that if a trade goes against you, your losses are limited, and you can live to trade another day. By effectively managing risk, you safeguard your trading capital and maintain an edge in the markets.

Key Points

- The importance of proper risk management in achieving consistent results
- Setting appropriate stop-loss levels to protect against losses.
- Preserving capital for future trades and maintaining a trading edge

Developing the Right Mindset

Consistency requires discipline and the right mindset. It's about sticking to your plan, even when faced with tempting opportunities or market fluctuations. Avoid the temptation to chase trades or take unnecessary risks. Patience is key. Wait for the right setups and let the trades come to you. By cultivating a disciplined and patient mindset, you set yourself up for success in achieving consistent 3% gains.

Key Points:

- Cultivating discipline and patience in the pursuit of consistent gains
- Overcoming the urge to chase trades or take unnecessary risks.
- The role of emotional intelligence in maintaining a steady approach

Trading Strategies for Consistent Results

To achieve consistent results, it's essential to align your trading strategies with the 3% gain target. Position sizing and risk-reward ratios play a crucial role in this process. You want to ensure that your potential gains outweigh your potential losses. Additionally, adaptability is key. Markets change, and you need to be able to adjust your strategies accordingly. By staying adaptable and employing strategies that fit different market conditions, you increase your chances of maintaining consistent growth.

Key Points:

- Exploring strategies that align with the 3% gain target.
- Position sizing and risk-reward ratios for consistent growth
- Diversification and adapting strategies to different market conditions.

Maintaining Focus and Adapting to Challenges

Staying focused on your long-term goal of consistent gains is crucial. The market can be volatile, and there will be challenges along the way. But by keeping your eye on the prize and not getting caught up in short-term fluctuations, you can navigate through the ups and downs with confidence. Learn from your losses and use them as opportunities for growth. Remember, it's not about winning every trade but about consistently progressing towards your financial objectives.

Key Points:

- Strategies for staying focused on the long-term goal of consistent gains.
- Dealing with market volatility and adapting to changing market conditions
- Learning from losses and using them as opportunities for growth

Embracing Continuous Learning and Improvement

The journey towards consistent results is a continuous learning process. Education is a vital component of trading success. Stay hungry for knowledge, seek feedback, and continuously improve your skills. Keep up with the latest tools, techniques, and market developments. Adaptation is the key to staying ahead in the ever-evolving world of trading. By embracing continuous learning and improvement, you position yourself for long-term success in achieving consistent 3% gains.

Key Points:

- The role of education and continuous learning in achieving consistent results
- Seeking feedback and adapting trading strategies accordingly
- Incorporating new tools and techniques to improve trading performance.

Conclusion

Consistency is the key to unlocking the doors of financial success in trading. By targeting 3% gains, you establish a solid foundation for steady growth and compounding. With effective risk management, the right mindset, and adaptable strategies, achieving consistent results becomes attainable. Remember, it's the journey of incremental gains that will lead you to your financial goals. So, embrace the power of 3%, stay focused, and never stop learning. With determination and discipline, you can achieve remarkable results and build the future you desire through consistent 3% gains.

Key Points:

Recap of the power of targeting 3% gains for consistent results

- Emphasising the importance of risk management and capital preservation

- Encouraging traders to develop the right mindset and embrace continuous learning.
- The path to long-term success lies in consistent growth and a disciplined approach to trading. By targeting 3% gains, traders can harness the power of compounding and build a strong foundation for their financial future. With proper risk management, a focused mindset, and a commitment to continuous improvement, achieving consistent results becomes an attainable goal.

"Life is inherently risky. There is only one big risk you should avoid at all costs, and that is the risk of doing nothing."

Denis Waitley

"Life is all about taking risks. If you never take risks, then you'll never know what you are truly capable of."

Unknown

SECTION 2

THE MARKETS - ALL MARKETS NOT JUST CRYPTO

SECTION 2 - CHAPTER BREAKDOWN

" Never stand begging for that which you have the power to earn."

Miguel de Cervantes

THE POWER OF COMPOUND TRADING

Introduction

"Because nobody wants to get rich slow."

Warren Buffet

Few concepts in wealth creation are as powerful and transformative as compound trading. This chapter unveils the awe-inspiring potential that lies within this financial phenomenon. By understanding and harnessing the power of compounding, you will unlock the key to exponential growth on your journey from $1,000 to $1,000,000.

The Compound Effect

At its core, compound trading is based on the principle of the compound effect, where your initial investment grows exponentially over time. This section delves into the mathematical magic that occurs when returns are reinvested, emphasising how even small gains can snowball into substantial wealth given enough time.

The Compound Effect, when applied to trading, operates on the fundamental principle of compounding, highlighting the remarkable power of incremental growth over an extended period. This phenomenon is not just a financial concept; it is a mathematical magic that can turn modest gains into significant wealth through the process of reinvesting returns.

Imagine you start with an initial investment, for us, it's one thousand dollars, and instead of withdrawing your profits, you reinvest them. The magic begins to happen as each reinvested gain contributes to the overall investment, creating a compounding effect. This compounding effect is akin to a snowball rolling down a hill, gradually picking up more snow and momentum as it goes.

The mathematics behind compounding is deceptively simple yet extraordinarily powerful. Consider this scenario where you trade for a consistent percentage return on your investment. As this return is reinvested, the next round of gains is not just calculated on the initial investment but on the accumulated total, including the previously earned returns. This continuous cycle of reinvesting creates a compounding snowball effect.

Over time, the impact of compounding becomes increasingly significant. Small gains, when consistently reinvested, accumulate at an accelerating rate. The compounding effect magnifies the growth, leading to exponential increases in wealth.

This concept underscores the importance of a long-term perspective in compound trading, we are looking at a year or two, but in the entire scheme of things, when we think of traders like Warren Buffet, two years is not much in comparison to his YEARS of compounding, we've just sped up the process. Remember, it's not about making massive gains overnight; rather, it's about the sustained, disciplined approach of allowing your trades to grow trade by trade over time. The patience to let the compounding process work its magic is a key aspect of successful compound trading.

Moreover, the Compound Effect teaches us that consistency in performance is crucial. Even if the returns are modest, the regularity of positive gains, when compounded, can result in substantial financial growth.

It's not just about hitting the jackpot with one big trade but about steadily building wealth through a series of well-thought-out, consistent trading decisions.

The Compound Effect in trading is a testament to the power of time, consistency, and reinvestment. By understanding and harnessing this mathematical magic, traders can unlock the potential for their initial investments to grow into significant wealth over the long haul.

Time: The Investor's Greatest Ally

Time is an investor's most valuable asset when it comes to compound trading. This segment explores the concept of compounding over 72 successful trades, yes, we've changed how the RULE of 72 is implemented into trading, highlighting the astonishing results that can be achieved by compounding 10% profit starting from one thousand.

The Rule of 72 Reimagined

An essential tool in the compound trader's arsenal is the Rule of 72 Reimagined. This rule provides a quick and handy way to estimate how long it takes for your investment to go from one thousand to one million and the rate of return. We will delve into this concept a little deeper, empowering you to make informed decisions about taking slightly larger profits than 3%.

Time stands out as the investor's most invaluable asset for compound trading. This critical component is the catalyst that propels the magic of compounding, turning incremental gains into significant wealth. The significance of time becomes even more apparent when we explore the concept of compounding over a series of successful trades and reimagine the Rule of 72 as a powerful tool in the compound trader's toolkit.

The Rule of 72 Reimagined transforms the way investors perceive the journey from one financial milestone to another. Traditionally, the Rule of 72 has been a rule of thumb for estimating the number of years it takes for an investment to double based on a fixed annual rate of return. However, in the context of compound trading, we take this concept to new heights by applying it to a series of trades.

Imagine compounding a 10% profit starting from an initial investment of one thousand dollars over the course of 72 successful trades. This reimagined application of the Rule of 72 opens up a world of possibilities, showcasing the astonishing results that can be achieved through disciplined and strategic compounding.

This innovative approach empowers investors to project not only the time it takes for their investment to multiply but also to estimate the potential final value of their portfolio. By compounding profits at a rate higher than the traditional 3%, investors can expedite their journey from a modest initial investment to a substantial financial milestone.

Delving deeper into the Rule of 72 Reimagined allows investors to make more informed decisions about their trading strategy. It encourages them to consider taking slightly larger profits than the conventional 3%, understanding that a marginally higher rate of return can significantly impact the speed at which their investment grows, in fact, in under 72 successful trades.

In essence, this segment underscores the symbiotic relationship between time and compounding AND the percentages needed to achieve differing results. By leveraging the Rule of 72 Reimagined and recognising the potential of compounding over a series of successful trades, investors can harness the power of time to propel their financial growth and achieve remarkable results in their compound trading endeavours.

Harnessing the Power of Reinvestment

Reinvestment is a key driver of compounding success. The key to this theory working effectively.
Reinvestment stands as a pivotal and dynamic force in the realm of compounding success. The core principle underlying the efficacy of this concept lies in its ability to amplify returns and accelerate the growth of an investment portfolio over time. To truly grasp the significance of reinvestment, it is essential to delve into the mechanisms that make this theory a linchpin of compounding success.

At its essence, reinvestment involves taking the returns generated from a trade and channelling them back into the next trade, compounding the gains. This process sets in motion a compounding cycle where each reinvested gain contributes not only to the principal amount but also to the overall cumulative returns.

The magic happens as these compounded returns become the foundation for calculating subsequent gains, creating a financial snowball effect. You'll hear this a lot, I am really trying to drill this in.

The key to making this theory work effectively lies in the continuity and consistency of the reinvestment strategy. Regularly reinvesting returns, regardless of their size, ensures a continuous compounding process that gradually builds momentum. It's not merely about the magnitude of the individual returns but the sustained commitment to plough those returns into the investment vehicle, allowing the compounding effect to flourish.

Moreover, reinvestment aligns seamlessly with the concept of a long-term investment horizon. By resisting the temptation to withdraw profits and instead reinvesting them, traders position themselves to reap the full benefits of compounding over an extended period. This patient and disciplined approach is a distinguishing factor between short-term gains and the creation of substantial wealth through compounding.

The power of reinvestment is magnified when coupled with a well-thought-out strategy that aims to capitalise on compounding opportunities. This strategy involves identifying investments that offer a balance between risk and return, allowing for sustainable and consistent gains that can be systematically reinvested to fuel the compounding engine.

Reinvestment in each trade is the linchpin of compounding success, unlocking the true potential of incremental gains. By understanding and actively harnessing the power of reinvestment, investors can embark on a journey where the sum becomes greater than its parts, and the compounding effect transforms a modest investment into a source of substantial wealth over time.

The Impact of Consistent Contributions to Learning

Regular education plays a pivotal role in the growth of your portfolio. We explore the impact of consistent learning, emphasising how even a few hours a month can contribute to yielding extraordinary results over time. Learn strategies to ensure a disciplined approach to building your investments.

The value of continuous education cannot be overstated. Regular learning becomes a driving force behind the growth of your investment portfolio, shaping your understanding of market trends, risk management, and strategic decision-making. This exploration delves into the profound impact of consistent learning, highlighting how dedicating even a few hours a month to expanding your financial knowledge can yield extraordinary results over time. Moreover, it provides insights into strategies that ensure a disciplined approach to building and nurturing your longer-term investments.

The financial markets are ever evolving, influenced by a myriad of factors such as economic trends, geopolitical events, and technological advancements. In this environment, the adage "knowledge is power" holds true, emphasising the critical role of continuous learning in navigating the complexities of the investment landscape. Consistent contributions to your learning journey serve as a compass, guiding you through the nuances of the market and helping you make informed decisions.

The impact of consistent learning is not confined to short-term gains; rather, it sets the stage for long-term success. By dedicating even a few hours a month to staying informed about market dynamics, investment strategies, and emerging opportunities, you position yourself to adapt to changing conditions and capitalise on trends that may shape the future of your portfolio.

One of the key benefits of ongoing education is the empowerment it provides in risk management. Understanding the intricacies of various investment tools, market behaviours, and financial instruments enables you to make more informed and calculated decisions. This knowledge acts as a shield, helping you mitigate potential risks and navigate through volatile market conditions with a greater degree of confidence.

To ensure a disciplined approach to building your investments, consider implementing strategies that integrate learning into your routine. This might involve setting aside dedicated time each month for reading financial publications, attending webinars or workshops, and engaging with reputable investment forums. Additionally, actively seeking mentorship or networking with seasoned investors can provide valuable insights and perspectives that contribute to your learning journey.

The impact of consistent contributions to learning is transformative just like compound trading money, you are compound trading your belief in yourself and your future. By recognising the value of continuous education and committing to expanding your financial knowledge, you not only enhance your decision-making capabilities but also lay the groundwork for sustained success and extraordinary results in the growth of your investment portfolio over time.

Compound Trading and Risk Management

While compound trading offers immense growth potential, it is crucial to understand the role of risk management in maximising long-term success. We will discuss strategies to protect your investments, diversify your portfolio, and minimise potential losses, ensuring that the power of compound trading is harnessed responsibly.

Where the potential for substantial growth is ever-present, a critical counterpart that cannot be overlooked is the role of effective risk management. This symbiotic relationship between compound trading and risk management is fundamental to maximising long-term success and ensuring that the journey towards financial growth is both rewarding and sustainable. In this exploration, we delve into strategies that safeguard your investments, promote portfolio diversification, and minimise potential losses, thereby ensuring that the power of compound trading is harnessed responsibly.

At its core, risk management in compound trading is the art of striking a delicate balance between seizing opportunities for growth and protecting your capital from potential downturns. One fundamental strategy involves setting clear risk tolerance levels defining the maximum amount of capital that one is willing to expose to any given trade or investment. This disciplined approach acts as a shield, preventing impulsive decisions that could jeopardise the cumulative gains accrued through compounding.

Diversification emerges as another key pillar in risk management for compound traders. As your balance grows you must spread your risk. By spreading trades across different coins, tokens or even asset classes, traders and investors can limit risks. Diversification acts as a safety net, mitigating the risk associated with the underperformance of a single investment and promoting a more resilient and stable portfolio.

Additionally, adopting a systematic and analytical approach to market research is integral to effective risk management in compound trading. Thoroughly understanding the factors that influence market trends, potential catalysts, and the overall economic landscape empowers traders to make informed decisions.

This knowledge enhances the likelihood of successful trades and enables quick and strategic responses to unforeseen market developments.

Implementing risk management tools, we have spoken about, such as OCO or stop-loss orders and position sizing, is paramount in protecting investments during volatile market conditions. Stop-loss orders, for instance, automatically trigger a sell order when an investment reaches a predetermined price, limiting potential losses. Position sizing involves carefully determining the amount of capital allocated to each trade, aligning with risk tolerance levels and overall portfolio objectives.

Furthermore, embracing the concept of continuous learning, as discussed earlier, extends to understanding risk management strategies. Staying informed about evolving risk factors and adapting your risk

management approach accordingly is crucial in the ever-changing landscape of financial markets.
While compound trading holds the promise of remarkable wealth accumulation, responsible risk management is the linchpin that ensures the sustainability of this growth. By implementing strategies to protect investments, diversify portfolios, and minimise potential losses, compound traders not only navigate the inherent uncertainties of the market but also cultivate a disciplined and resilient approach to long-term success.

Case Studies of Compound Trading Success

To inspire and motivate, this chapter concludes with real-life case studies of individuals who have leveraged the power of compound trading to transform their financial lives. These stories exemplify the principles and strategies discussed earlier and serve as a testament to the life-changing potential that awaits those who embark on the compound trading journey.

Case Study 1: The Patient Investor

John, a seasoned investor, exemplifies the power of patience and long-term commitment in compound trading. Starting with a modest initial investment, John consistently applied the principles of compounding, reinvesting his returns and adhering to a disciplined approach. Over a span of several months and now to years, the compounding effect took hold, and John's portfolio grew exponentially.

What started as a small investment became a substantial source of wealth, highlighting how the patient application of compound trading principles can yield remarkable success.

Case Study 2: Diversification Mastery

Sarah, an astute investor, understood the importance of diversification in risk management. By carefully spreading her investments across various asset classes and sectors, she created a robust and resilient portfolio. This diversification strategy protected her from the impact of market volatility and allowed her to capture opportunities in different market segments. Sarah's case highlights how a well-executed diversification strategy can contribute to sustained success in compound trading.

Case Study 3: Adaptive Learning in Action

Michael, a dynamic trader, recognised the changing nature of financial markets. He embraced a continuous learning mindset, staying informed about market trends, emerging technologies, and global events. This commitment to adaptive learning allowed Michael to adjust his trading strategies in response to changing market conditions. His ability to evolve with the market contributed to consistent gains and highlighted the importance of staying educated and agile in the world of compound trading.

These case studies illuminate the diversity of approaches that can lead to success in compound trading. Whether it's through patient and consistent application, strategic diversification, or adaptive learning, everyone found a path that resonated with their financial goals and risk tolerance.

By presenting these real-life stories, the aim is to inspire and motivate aspiring compound traders. I have seen many reach the magic 1 million!

These individuals started with various backgrounds, initial investments, and risk appetites, yet they all shared a commitment to the principles discussed in this chapter. Their success stories underscore the transformative potential of compound trading and serve as beacons of encouragement for those looking to navigate the complexities of the financial markets, especially the cryptocurrency market, with a strategic and disciplined approach.

CULTIVATING A WEALTH MINDSET

A quick recap of what we have already learned. Before embarking on the journey of turning $1,000 into $1,000,000, it is essential to cultivate a wealth mindset. This chapter explores the powerful role that beliefs and attitudes play in achieving financial success. By adopting the right mindset, you will set the foundation for your wealth-building journey and overcome any mental barriers that may hinder your progress.

The Power of Beliefs

Beliefs shape our reality and influence our actions. This section delves into the importance of examining and reshaping your beliefs about money, wealth, and success. You will learn how to identify and challenge limiting beliefs, replacing them with empowering beliefs that align with your financial aspirations.

Understanding the profound impact of beliefs on our lives is crucial for personal development, particularly in the realms of money, wealth, and success. Beliefs are like lenses through which we perceive the world, shaping our thoughts, emotions, and behaviours. In the context of finances, these beliefs can either propel us towards prosperity or hold us back from realising our full potential.

Firstly, it's essential to recognise that beliefs are not absolute truths, but rather subjective interpretations formed through experiences, upbringing, and societal influences. By delving into the origins of your beliefs about money, wealth, and success, you gain insight into the factors that have shaped your financial mindset. This self-awareness is the first step toward transforming limiting beliefs into powerful catalysts for positive change.

Identifying limiting beliefs involves scrutinising thoughts that may be hindering your financial progress. Common limiting beliefs include "money is the root of all evil," "I'm not good with finances," or "success is only for the lucky few." These beliefs create mental barriers and contribute to self-sabotaging behaviours. The process of challenging these beliefs involves questioning their validity and seeking evidence to the contrary.

Once you've pinpointed limiting beliefs, the next step is replacing them with empowering ones. For instance, reframing "money is the root of all evil" to "money is a tool for positive change" shifts the perspective from a negative association to a more constructive view. Similarly, changing "I'm not good with finances" to "I am continuously improving my financial literacy and skills" opens the door to growth and learning.

Cultivating empowering beliefs aligns your mindset with your financial aspirations. This alignment fosters a positive attitude towards wealth creation and success, influencing your actions and decisions. Instead of being paralysed by fear or doubt, you become more proactive in pursuing opportunities, making informed financial choices, and persisting in the face of challenges.

Moreover, the power of beliefs extends beyond individual impact to interpersonal relationships and societal dynamics. As individuals challenge and reshape their beliefs about money, a collective shift towards a more positive and abundance-focused mindset can occur. This shift not only benefits individuals but contributes to a healthier and more prosperous community at large.

The power of beliefs will change your world, you are what you think has never been truer, especially in the realms of money, wealth, and success. By examining and reshaping your beliefs, you unlock the potential for personal and financial growth. This journey involves self-reflection, questioning ingrained beliefs, and consciously cultivating a mindset that aligns with your financial goals. As you embrace empowering beliefs, you set the stage for positive change, not only in your financial life but also in the broader context of the communities you are a part of.

Embracing an Abundance Mentality

An abundance mentality is a fundamental pillar of a wealth mindset. We explore the mindset of abundance versus scarcity, helping you shift from a scarcity-driven mindset to one that embraces abundance and opportunity. Discover how to attract wealth and create a mindset conducive to financial success.

Cultivating an abundance mentality is a transformative journey that goes beyond financial strategies; it is a fundamental shift in mindset that can profoundly impact various aspects of life. At its core, an abundance mentality revolves around the belief that there is more than enough for everyone and that opportunities for growth, success, and wealth are limitless.

One of the key distinctions lies in the comparison between an abundance mentality and a scarcity mindset. A scarcity mindset is characterised by a fear of lack – the belief that resources, opportunities, and success are limited. This perspective can breed feelings of competition, jealousy, and a reluctance to share knowledge or collaborate. On the other hand, an abundance mentality operates from the premise that there is an abundance of resources, opportunities, and success to go around. This mindset fosters collaboration, gratitude, and a willingness to uplift others.

Shifting from a scarcity-driven mindset to one of abundance involves rewiring your thought patterns and reframing your perceptions. Instead of viewing success as a zero-sum game where one person's gain is another's loss, an abundance mentality encourages the recognition that success is not finite. The success of others does not diminish your potential for success; in fact, it can create a conducive environment for collective growth.

An essential aspect of embracing an abundance mentality is gratitude. By acknowledging and appreciating the resources and opportunities already present in your life, you create a positive foundation for attracting more. Gratitude acts as a magnet for abundance, drawing in positivity and opportunities that align with your financial goals.

Furthermore, an abundance mentality involves taking a proactive approach to life. Rather than being reactive to challenges, individuals with an abundance mindset see obstacles as opportunities for growth. They approach setbacks with resilience and use them as stepping stones toward success. This proactive stance enables them to learn from failures, adapt to changes, and maintain a long-term vision for financial prosperity.

Attracting wealth is not solely about financial strategies or external factors; it begins with a mindset that magnetises opportunities. An abundance mentality creates a mental space where creativity flourishes, enabling you to see possibilities that may have been obscured by a scarcity mindset. This shift in perspective can lead to innovative solutions, entrepreneurial ventures, and a greater willingness to take calculated risks.

Embracing an abundance mentality is a fundamental pillar of a wealth mindset. It involves transcending the limitations of a scarcity-driven mindset, cultivating gratitude, and adopting a proactive approach to life. As you shift your focus from scarcity to abundance, you open yourself up to a world of possibilities and position yourself to attract wealth and success. This mindset not only transforms your relationship with money but also influences your interactions with others, fostering a collaborative and supportive community where everyone can thrive.

Developing Financial Confidence

Confidence is key to navigating the unpredictable aspects of life, especially trading. By learning techniques to build financial confidence, including gaining knowledge, developing a strong financial plan, and surrounding yourself with a supportive network, you will bolster your confidence, you will make more informed decisions and overcome obstacles on your path to $1,000,000.

Developing financial confidence is a crucial component of achieving success in the arena of finance. Confidence not only empowers you to make informed decisions but also provides the resilience needed to overcome obstacles on your journey to financial milestones, such as reaching $1,000,000. Here are key strategies to cultivate and strengthen your financial confidence:

Educate Yourself: Knowledge is a powerful tool for building confidence. Take the time to educate yourself about various aspects of finance, including investment strategies, budgeting, and risk management. Attend workshops, read books, follow reputable financial news sources, and consider seeking advice from financial professionals. As your understanding deepens, you'll feel more capable of navigating the intricacies of the financial landscape. The more you know, the more you will grow… your balance!

Set Clear Financial Goals: Establishing clear and realistic financial goals provides a roadmap for your journey. Break down your goals into smaller, manageable milestones, creating a step-by-step plan to reach the $1,000,000 target. Having a well-defined plan gives you a sense of direction and purpose, reinforcing your confidence in your ability to achieve financial success. Go back to the chapters on visualisation and reinforce this!

Create a Strong Financial Plan: Building confidence involves having a solid foundation, and a comprehensive financial plan serves as just that. Develop a budget that aligns with your goals, outlines your income, and expenses, and includes strategies for saving and investing. Regularly review and adjust your plan as needed, ensuring it remains relevant to your evolving financial situation.

Build a Supportive Network: Surround yourself with a network of individuals who share similar financial goals or have expertise in relevant areas. This could include mentors, financial advisors, or peers who can provide guidance, share experiences, and offer support during challenging times. Collaborating with others can boost your confidence and provide valuable insights.

Take Calculated Risks: Financial growth often requires taking calculated risks. Embrace a mindset that acknowledges risk as an inherent part of financial endeavours and learn to evaluate and manage risks effectively. By understanding that not all risks are detrimental and that some are necessary for growth, you'll develop the confidence to make strategic decisions that propel you towards your financial goals.

Track Your Progress: Regularly monitor and celebrate your financial progress. Documenting achievements, no matter how small reinforces your confidence and motivates you to continue working towards your goals. Reflecting on past successes can also serve as a reminder of your capability to overcome challenges and adapt to changing circumstances.

Download my **TRADE TRACKER** - https://gettingstartedincrypto.com/start-up-kit/

Embrace a Positive Mindset: Confidence is closely linked to mindset. Cultivate a positive attitude towards your financial journey, viewing challenges as opportunities for growth rather than insurmountable obstacles. Adopting a growth mindset allows you to approach setbacks with resilience and learn from experiences, further strengthening your financial confidence.

Continuous Learning and Adaptation: Stay informed about market trends, economic developments, and changes in financial regulations. The commitment to continuous learning not only enhances your knowledge but also instils confidence in your ability to adapt to a dynamic financial environment.

By implementing these strategies, you can systematically build and reinforce your financial confidence. As you navigate the unpredictable world of finance on your path to $1,000,000, this confidence will serve as a guiding force, empowering you to make informed decisions and persevere in the face of challenges.

SMART – GOAL SETTING AND VISUALISATION

Setting clear goals is crucial for achieving financial success.

This segment guides you through the process of setting:

SPECIFIC

MEASURABLE

ACHIEVABLE

RELEVANT

TIME-BOUND

***SMART** goals.*

Through learning visualisation techniques to align your subconscious mind with your desired financial outcomes, reinforcing your commitment and motivation, you will reach your goals.

Goal setting and visualisation are powerful tools that can significantly enhance your journey toward financial success. This segment emphasises the importance of setting SMART goals and utilising visualisation techniques to align your subconscious mind with your financial aspirations.

Setting SMART Goals

Specific: Clearly define your financial objectives. Instead of a vague goal like "save money," specify a precise amount or a particular financial milestone, such as "Trade to $10,000 for a holiday."

Measurable: Establish criteria to track your progress. Assign numerical values to your goals, making it easier to evaluate your success. For example, if your goal is to trade to reduce debt, set a measurable target like "pay off $5,000 in credit card debt within three to six months." (Allowing for your skill levels.)

Achievable: Ensure that your goals are realistic and attainable. While our ambitious goals to reach one million are admirable, setting objectives that are within your reach boosts your confidence and motivates consistent efforts to get you eventually to the million-dollar mark. For instance, if you aim to double your thousand dollars within a short period to prove this is possible.

Relevant: Align your goals with your overall financial objectives. Consider how each goal contributes to your larger financial plan. If your primary focus is building wealth or generational wealth, set goals related to reaching pivotal points on your journey to one million!

Time-Bound: Establish a timeline for each goal. This adds a sense of urgency and prevents procrastination. For example, if you aim to save for a down payment on a house, set a specific timeframe, such as "save $20,000 in three to six months." Depending on your trading skill level, this allows for errors and setbacks along the back, without loss of hope to the final destination.

By combining **SMART** goal setting with visualisation techniques, you create a powerful synergy between conscious planning and subconscious alignment. This holistic approach enhances your commitment, motivation, and belief in your ability to achieve your financial aspirations. As you consistently apply these practices, you'll find that your goals become more tangible, and your path to financial success becomes clearer and more achievable.

Visualisation Techniques

Create a Mental Image: Visualise your financial success by creating a vivid mental image of achieving your goals. Imagine the positive emotions, the sense of accomplishment, and the improved financial situation. This mental rehearsal helps align your subconscious mind with your desired outcomes.

Vision Board: Develop a vision board that visually represents your financial goals. Include images, words, and symbols that resonate with your aspirations. Place the vision board in a prominent location where you can see it daily, reinforcing your commitment to your financial objectives.

Guided Imagery: Practice guided imagery exercises where you mentally walk through the process of achieving your goals. Engage all your senses to make the visualisation experience as vivid as possible. This technique helps create a positive mindset and enhances your belief in the attainability of your goals. It can be included in your daily meditation practice.

Affirmations: Use positive affirmations related to your financial goals. Affirmations are short, positive statements that you repeat regularly. For example, "I am financially abundant, and money flows effortlessly into my life." These affirmations reinforce positive beliefs and attitudes towards your financial journey to one million, or the goal you choose for yourself.

Regular Reflection: Take time regularly to reflect on your goals and visualise your success. This can be a part of your daily or weekly routine. Reflecting on your progress and visualising the achievement of your goals helps maintain focus and motivation.

"The greatest danger for most of us, is not that our aim is too high, and we miss it, but that it is too low, and we reach it."

Michelangelo

EMBRACING A GROWTH MINDSET

A growth mindset is essential for continuous learning and improvement. Build on strategies to embrace challenges, persist in the face of setbacks, and cultivate resilience as you navigate the fast-moving finance sector.

Embracing a growth mindset is a transformative approach that goes beyond the realm of personal development—it is a key to unlocking continuous learning and improvement, particularly in the pursuit of financial success. This section delves into the concept of a growth mindset and provides strategies to leverage this mindset on your journey towards wealth creation.

Understanding a Growth Mindset

Openness to Learning: A growth mindset is characterised by an eagerness to learn and an understanding that abilities and intelligence can be developed over time. Individuals with a growth mindset see challenges as opportunities to grow rather than insurmountable obstacles.

Viewing Challenges as Opportunities: Instead of avoiding challenges, those with a growth mindset embrace them. Challenges are seen as a chance to enhance skills, acquire new knowledge, and ultimately improve one's financial capabilities. This mindset fosters a proactive approach to problem-solving.

Persistence in the Face of Setbacks: A growth mindset encourages resilience and persistence. Rather than being discouraged by setbacks, individuals with this mindset see them as part of the learning process. They view failures not as indicators of their limitations but as stepping stones toward improvement.

Embracing Effort as the Path to Mastery: Effort is considered a pathway to mastery in a growth mindset. Instead of relying solely on inherent abilities, individuals understand that consistent effort and dedication lead to skill development and financial success.

Strategies to Cultivate a Growth Mindset in Finance

Embrace Challenges in Financial Learning: Actively seek out challenges in your financial education. Whether it's understanding complex investment strategies, learning about market trends, or delving into personal finance principles, approaching these challenges with curiosity and a willingness to learn fosters a growth mindset.

Learn from Setbacks: Rather than dwelling on failures, analyse them for valuable lessons. Right down your emotions and thoughts in the trade tracker, that way, you can start to work towards managing emotions and reactions as you move forward. Consider setbacks as feedback and adjust your financial strategies accordingly. Every setback is an opportunity to refine your approach and move closer to your goals.

Encourage a Positive Relationship with Effort: Recognise and celebrate your effort in financial endeavours. Acknowledge that the time and energy you invest in learning and making informed financial decisions contribute significantly to your growth and success.

Seek Feedback and Guidance: Actively seek feedback from financial mentors, advisors, or peers. Embrace constructive criticism as an opportunity to improve and refine your financial strategies. Feedback provides valuable insights that contribute to continuous learning and growth.

Set Incremental Financial Goals: Break down your financial goals into smaller, manageable tasks. This not only makes your objectives more achievable but also allows for a continuous cycle of setting, achieving, and setting new goals. Each small success contributes to the development of a growth mindset.
They might look like paying off a credit card off, purchasing a holiday to an exotic island, buying a new car, house deposit, you get the picture, these will be as unique as you are.

Foster a Culture of Learning: Surround yourself with a community that values continuous learning. Engage in financial discussions, join trading groups, join X.com crypto community and participate in workshops or seminars. Being part of a learning-oriented community provides support and encouragement for cultivating a growth mindset.

Celebrate Progress, Not Just Achievements: This is not about receiving a participation medal but more about celebrating how far you've come. You've set your own milestones, so acknowledge and celebrate your progress along the way, not just the ultimate achievement of financial goals. Recognising the journey and the effort put into improvement reinforces the mindset that growth is a continuous, evolving process.

Embracing a growth mindset in the pursuit of financial success is a powerful paradigm shift. By viewing challenges as opportunities, persisting in the face of setbacks, and recognising the value of effort in the learning process, you position yourself for continuous improvement. This mindset not only enhances your financial capabilities but also contributes to resilience and adaptability in navigating your path to your goals and, ultimately, one million dollars.

A growth mindset sees challenges as opportunities for growth. "

Anonymous

"The ability to discipline yourself to delay gratification in the short term in order to enjoy greater rewards in the long term, in the indispensable prerequisite for success."

Brian Tracy

MASTING THE ART OF DELAYED GRATIFICATION

Delayed gratification is a hallmark of successful wealth builders. This segment explores the power of delaying short-term gratification for long-term gains. Learn techniques to overcome impulsive behaviours and make disciplined financial choices that will lead to greater wealth accumulation in the future.

Mastering the art of delayed gratification is a critical skill that sets successful wealth builders apart. It involves resisting the temptation of immediate rewards in favour of more substantial, long-term gains.

With the use of compounding, delayed gratification on financial success provides techniques to cultivate discipline in making prudent financial decisions. Short-term pain for long-term gain, so essentially, this means maybe forgoing that next purchase and watching your wealth grow to the million and buying the car, house, and everything all at once!

Understanding Delayed Gratification

Long-Term Perspective: Delayed gratification requires adopting a long-term perspective on financial decision-making. Instead of focusing solely on immediate desires or impulses, individuals prioritise actions that contribute to their broader financial goals and objectives.

Trade-offs and Sacrifices: Making the choice to delay gratification often involves making trade-offs and sacrifices. It requires individuals to forego immediate pleasures, purchases, or indulgences in exchange for more significant rewards in the future, such as financial security, investments, or wealth accumulation.

Resisting Impulsive Behaviour: Delayed gratification necessitates resisting impulsive behaviour and cultivating the ability to pause and reflect before making financial decisions. Don't buy a new dress, shoes, handbag, tools, or beer brewing kit. You get the picture. This mindfulness helps individuals avoid spontaneous, short-term choices that may undermine their long-term financial goals.

Techniques for Cultivating Delayed Gratification

Set Clear Financial Goals: Clearly defined financial goals serve as a roadmap for delayed gratification. When individuals have a precise understanding of what they want to achieve, it becomes easier to resist immediate temptations that may divert them from their long-term objectives.

Create a Budget: Developing and adhering to a budget is a practical tool for implementing delayed gratification. A budget helps individuals allocate resources strategically, distinguishing between essential expenses, savings, and discretionary spending. By sticking to a budget, individuals reinforce disciplined financial habits. This is essential when trading your way to one million, as you will be able to resist the temptation to dip into your trading balance.

Prioritise Needs Over Wants: Distinguishing between needs and wants is fundamental to delayed gratification. Prioritising needs ensures that essential financial obligations are met before considering discretionary spending. This approach reinforces a disciplined mindset, emphasising the importance of long-term financial stability.

Practice Mindfulness: Mindfulness involves being present in the moment and making conscious choices. By practising mindfulness, individuals can become more aware of their impulses and emotions, allowing them to make deliberate decisions aligned with their long-term financial objectives.

Create a Waiting Period: Implementing a waiting period before making significant financial decisions can be a powerful technique. This allows individuals to step back, evaluate their choices, and consider the long-term consequences. It reduces the likelihood of impulsive actions that may undermine financial goals.

Reward Milestones: Acknowledging and rewarding milestones along the way reinforces the benefits of delayed gratification. Celebrating achievements, even the smaller ones, provides positive reinforcement and motivation to continue making disciplined financial choices. ***Automate Savings and Investments***: Automating savings and investments ensures that a portion of income is allocated towards long-term financial goals before discretionary spending occurs. This proactive approach minimises the temptation to spend impulsively and fosters consistent wealth-building habits.

Mastering delayed gratification is not just about curbing immediate impulses; it is a fundamental strategy for building wealth over time. By consistently making disciplined financial choices, you can accumulate savings, make strategic investments, and position yourself for long-term financial success. The ability to delay gratification is a hallmark of financial maturity, contributing to resilience, stability, and the achievement of wealth-building goals. You can do it! I know you can.

"Through discipline comes freedom."

Aristotle

"Self-discipline is often disguised as short-term pain, which often leads to long term gains.

The mistake many of us make is the need and want for short-term gains.

(Immediate Gratification)

which often leads to long term pain."

Charles F. Glassman

IMPORTANCE OF YOUR SURROUNDINGS

Surrounding Yourself with Success

We have all heard the saying don't be the smartest person in the room, the environment we immerse ourselves in profoundly impacts our mindset and success. This section emphasises the importance of surrounding yourself with individuals who support your financial goals and inspire your growth. Discover how to cultivate a network of success and leverage the power of collaboration and mentorship.

Surrounding yourself with success is a strategic and influential approach to achieving your financial goals. The people and environment you immerse yourself in play a crucial role in shaping your mindset, influencing your behaviours, and ultimately determining your level of success. It's true that you are shaped by the 5 closest people to you, you pick up their habits, good and bad and mannerisms. We explore the significance of cultivating a supportive network and leveraging collaboration and mentorship for financial growth.

Mindset Influence

The people you surround yourself with significantly impact your mindset. Positive, success-oriented individuals can inspire and motivate you, while a negative or unsupportive environment may hinder your progress. By choosing a positive and success-driven atmosphere, you create a conducive environment for achieving your financial aspirations.

Behavioural Impact: Surrounding yourself with success influences your behaviours and actions. Being part of a community that values financial responsibility, goal-setting, and continuous improvement fosters habits that align with your own financial objectives. It creates a collective energy that propels everyone towards success.

Inspiration and Role Models: Engaging with successful individuals provides inspiration and role models. Observing and learning from those who have achieved financial success can offer valuable insights, strategies, and perspectives. This inspiration can fuel your own determination and commitment to reaching your financial goals.

Cultivating a Network of Success

Identify and Engage with Like-Minded Individuals: Actively seek out individuals who share similar financial goals and values. Attend networking events, join online communities, and participate in forums where discussions revolve around wealth creation, financial literacy, and success. Engaging with like-minded individuals provides a sense of camaraderie and shared purpose.

Build a Diverse Network: Diversity within your network is valuable. Surrounding yourself with individuals from various backgrounds, industries, and experiences exposes you to a range of perspectives and insights. A diverse network can offer creative solutions, challenge your thinking, and broaden your understanding of financial opportunities.

Participate in Professional Organisations: Joining professional organisations related to your field or industry is an excellent way to connect with successful individuals. Attend conferences, seminars, and workshops where you can network with accomplished professionals, entrepreneurs, and experts in the financial domain.

Seek Mentorship: Mentorship is a powerful tool for personal and financial growth. Establishing mentor-mentee relationships allows you to benefit from the experiences and wisdom of those who have walked a similar path. A mentor can provide guidance, share insights, and offer valuable advice that accelerates your journey to financial success.

Contribute to Your Community: Actively contribute to the success of your community or network. Offer support, share your knowledge, and celebrate the achievements of others. By contributing positively to your surroundings, you reinforce a culture of collaboration and success that benefits everyone involved.

Leveraging the Power of Collaboration and Mentorship

Learn from Others' Experiences: Engage in conversations with successful individuals to learn from their experiences. Understand the challenges they faced, the strategies they employed, and the lessons they learned along the way. This firsthand knowledge can be invaluable in shaping your own financial journey.

Share Your Goals and Progress: Openly share your financial goals and progress with your network. Accountability is a powerful motivator, and sharing your journey with supportive individuals adds an extra layer of encouragement and guidance.

Actively Participate in Mentorship Programs: Seek out formal or informal mentorship programs within your industry or community. Many successful individuals are willing to share their expertise and provide guidance to those aspiring to achieve similar success.

If you would like to join me, it is https://thousandtomillions.com/ Surrounding yourself with success is a strategic and intentional choice that significantly influences your financial journey. Cultivating a network of individuals who support your goals, inspire your growth, and provide valuable insights enhances your chances of success. Leveraging the power of collaboration and mentorship creates a dynamic environment where collective success becomes a shared reality.

"Surround yourself with only people who are going to lift you higher."

Oprah Winfrey

"The values of the world we inhabit and the people we surround ourselves with have a profound effect on who we are."

Malcolm Gladwell

SETTING FINANCIAL GOALS TO 1 MILLION

Let's Go!

We're ready to drive into the excitement of turning $1,000 into a cool million! Buckle up because we're about to chart a course that takes you from financial aspirations to the sweet victory of a seven-figure milestone. We've got through the repetitive stuff (almost), and we'll be setting financial goals – your personal roadmap to financial freedom.

Setting the Destination: $1,000,000 in a year!

So, where are we headed? The ultimate goal is a million buckaroonies or dollars! 7 figures! But don't let the big number intimidate you. We're breaking it down into bite-sized, achievable chunks. This chapter is all about making your dreams tangible and creating clear goals that you can reach step by step.

Making Goals That Work: SMART Goals

First things first, let's recap SMART goals. What's SMART? Specific, Measurable, Achievable, Relevant, and Time-bound. It's like giving your goals a superpower. Instead of saying, "I want to be rich," say, "I'll trade to $5,000 in the next two to three months for a killer vacation." See the difference? Be specific, know when you want it, and make it something you can really do.

Crafting the Plan

Now that we know where we're headed, let's plot our course. Think of your financial situation as a map. What's your income, your expenses, and your debts? Let's get a lay of the land. This is your starting point.

Short Stops and Long Journeys: Short-Term vs. Long-Term Goals

Next, we need to decide on short-term and long-term goals. Short-term goals are like pit stops on the way to your million. Emergency funds and paying off credit cards – those are the short stops. Then, you've got the long journey goals, the big one being a million dollars. But don't worry, we're breaking that journey into manageable stretches.

Money Allocation: Where Does It Go?

Now that you've worked out if you are allocating one thousand dollars, or maybe you have room to add a bit more to start, now is the time to decide how much money you can put toward your trading.

REMEMBER - this is NOT from your budget; it is the money set aside that you can afford to live without. If the unforeseen happens in trading and you do something stupid and lose it all, while it may hurt a little, it won't impact your everyday living.

Create a budget – it's like a treasure map showing where your money is going. Make sure you have some savings and can put a bit aside – that's your compass pointing toward the million.

THE MUST HAVES IN LIFE!

Building Your Financial Safety Net: Emergency Fund

Ever had a flat tyre on the road? It's a pain. Your pet has gotten ill, and the vet gives you a four-figure bill? Something unforeseen happens, and you need to spend a few months away from your usual job? That's why we're creating an emergency fund – your financial safety net. It's a must for a smooth journey. Aim for three to six months' worth of living expenses tucked away. No one knows what is around the corner, so be prepared.

Trading: The Engine of Your Financial Vehicle

Now, let's talk about trading. It's like the engine that propels your financial vehicle. No need to be a Wall Street expert – we're talking about compound trading choices, as we have discussed throughout this book. So, head back through to SECTION 1 and start to put the theory into action.

GPS for Your Finances is Regular Review and Adjustment

Your roadmap needs a GPS. Regularly check in on your goals, track your progress, and adjust as needed. Life changes, and so does your journey. Flexibility is key.

Transforming Dreams into Reality with Commitment and Discipline

Here's the deal – turning dreams into reality takes commitment and discipline. Stick to your goals, develop habits that support them, and stay on the path even when it gets tough. You've got this!

Celebrate the Wins - Cheers to Your Success!

I cannot say this enough! Every milestone is a victory. Whether it's saving a certain amount or paying off a debt, celebrate it! Small wins build up to the big win – hitting that million-dollar mark.

Ready for the Adventure?

This could be the adventure of your lifetime, which may just change your life. Your goals are the compass, your roadmap is the guide, and that million dollars is the treasure at the end. It's time to turn your financial dreams into reality. Let's hit the road!

"You have to set goals that are almost out of reach. If you set a goal that is attainable without much work or thought, you are stuck with something below your true talent and potential."

Steve Garvey

MASTERING POSITION SIZING

Understanding and managing risk is paramount to making money. This chapter builds upon the essential concepts of risk, providing you with the tools and knowledge to navigate the intricate balance between mitigating potential losses and seizing lucrative opportunities.

By developing a comprehensive understanding of risk, you will be equipped to make informed decisions and safeguard your path to $1,000,000.

In the quest to become a millionaire in a year, understanding and mastering risk is the linchpin of success. Central to these strategies is the concept of the risk/reward ratio—a powerful tool in the arsenal of successful investors.

Risk is an inherent part of trading, investing and wealth building. Without risk, there can be no reward. There are different types of risks, including market risk and liquidity risk, that exist in trading. Understanding these risks is the first step in managing them effectively. This chapter emphasises the importance of acknowledging the unpredictable nature of the market and learning how to assess and mitigate various risks.

Risk Tolerance and Risk Appetite

Understanding your risk tolerance and risk appetite is crucial in formulating your trading strategy. This section builds on techniques to help you evaluate your risk tolerance and align it with your desired goals, ensuring that your investment decisions are in harmony with your risk profile.

Position Sizing Strategies

EXAMPLE 1 - 3%

In a One-Cancels-the-Other (OCO) order, you set both a take-profit order and a stop-loss order simultaneously. Let's calculate the risk/reward ratio for a trade with a $1000 investment, a 3% return target, and a 3% stop-loss level.

1. Calculate the Target Profit and Stop-Loss Levels:

- **Target Profit:**

  $\text{Target Profit} = \text{Investment} \times \text{Return Percentage}$

  \text{Target Profit} = $1000 \times 0.03 = $30

- **Stop-Loss:**

  $\text{Stop-Loss} = \text{Investment} \times \text{Stop-Loss Percentage}$

  \text{Stop-Loss} = $1000 \times 0.03 = $30

2. Calculate Risk/Reward Ratio:

- **Risk/Reward Ratio:**

  $\text{Risk/Reward Ratio} = \frac{\text{Target Profit}}{\text{Stop-Loss}}$

  \text{Risk/Reward Ratio} = \frac{$30}{$30} = 1:1

In this scenario, the risk/reward ratio is 1:1, meaning that the potential profit is equal to the potential loss. A risk/reward ratio of 1:1 implies that, on average, you aim to make as much as you are willing to risk on a trade.

It's worth noting that traders often strive for a risk/reward ratio greater than 1:1 to ensure that their potential profits outweigh potential losses. A ratio of 1:2 or higher is commonly sought to provide a buffer for losing trades.

In the context of this example, a 1:1 ratio suggests a relatively balanced trade where the potential reward matches the potential risk. Traders may adjust their strategy based on their risk tolerance and market conditions to achieve a more favourable risk/reward profile.

EXAMPLE 2 - 6%

Let's expand on the risk/reward calculations for a trade with a $1000 investment, a 6% return target, and a 3% stop-loss level using the One-Cancels-the-Other (OCO) order.

1. Calculate the Target Profit and Stop-Loss Levels:

- **Target Profit:**

  $$\text{Target Profit} = \text{Investment} \times \text{Return Percentage}$$

  \text{Target Profit} = \$1000 \times 0.06 = \$60

- **Stop-Loss:**

  $$\text{Stop-Loss} = \text{Investment} \times \text{Stop-Loss Percentage}$$

  \text{Stop-Loss} = \$1000 \times 0.03 = \$30

2. Calculate Risk/Reward Ratio:

- **Risk/Reward Ratio:**

  $$\text{Risk/Reward Ratio} = \frac{\text{Target Profit}}{\text{Stop-Loss}}$$

  \text{Risk/Reward Ratio} = \frac{\$60}{\$30} = 2:1

In this scenario, the risk/reward ratio is 2:1. This means that for every dollar you are willing to risk (stop-loss), you aim to make two dollars in profit (target return). A 2:1 risk/reward ratio is generally considered favourable by many traders, as it provides a buffer where the potential reward is twice the potential risk.

A risk/reward ratio of 2:1 suggests that, on average, you are seeking trades where the potential profits are expected to be twice as large as the potential losses. This ratio is often used as a guideline to ensure that the overall strategy remains profitable even if not every trade is a winner.

EXAMPLE 3 - 10%

Another example on the risk/reward calculations for a trade with a $1000 investment, a 10% return target, and a 3% stop-loss level using the One-Cancels-the-Other (OCO) order.

1. Calculate the Target Profit and Stop-Loss Levels:

- **Target Profit:**

  $\text{Target Profit} = \text{Investment} \times \text{Return Percentage}$

  \text{Target Profit} = $1000 \times 0.10 = $100

- **Stop-Loss:**

  $\text{Stop-Loss} = \text{Investment} \times \text{Stop-Loss Percentage}$

  \text{Stop-Loss} = $1000 \times 0.03 = $30

2. Calculate Risk/Reward Ratio:

- **Risk/Reward Ratio:**

  $\text{Risk/Reward Ratio} = \frac{\text{Target Profit}}{\text{Stop-Loss}}$

  \text{Risk/Reward Ratio} = \frac{$100}{$30} = \frac{10}{3} \approx 3.33:1

In this scenario, the risk/reward ratio is approximately 3.33:1. This means that for every dollar you are willing to risk (stop-loss), you aim to make around $3.33 in profit (target return). A risk/reward ratio of 3.33:1 is considered quite favourable by many traders, as it indicates a potential for high returns relative to the risk taken.

Allowances for Errors

A higher risk/reward ratio often allows for a greater margin of error in trade execution. Even if not all trades are successful, the strategy can still be profitable as long as a sufficient number of trades achieve the targeted risk/reward ratio.

Remember, the risk/reward ratio is a crucial aspect of trade planning, and traders often tailor their strategies based on their risk tolerance and market conditions. Adjustments may be made to the ratio depending on the specific objectives and preferences of the trader.

Traders commonly adjust their risk/reward ratios based on their risk tolerance, market conditions, and the specific strategy they are employing. A higher risk/reward ratio often implies a more conservative approach, while a lower ratio may be associated with a more aggressive trading style.

Consider a more bullish market scenario where positive momentum and upward trends prevail. In such favourable conditions, a 10% profit target becomes not only feasible but potentially more attainable. The heightened optimism and increased trading activity characteristic of bullish markets can create opportunities for larger profit margins.

Conversely, in bear markets characterised by declining prices and negative sentiment, achieving substantial profits becomes more challenging. In such circumstances, a more conservative approach with a 3% profit target may be deemed prudent. This approach aligns with risk mitigation strategies, acknowledging the heightened volatility and increased uncertainty that often accompany bearish trends.

Choosing the appropriate profit target based on market conditions reflects a nuanced understanding of risk and reward. It allows traders to tailor their strategies to the prevailing market sentiment, optimising the potential for success. This adaptability is a hallmark of more experienced traders who recognise that market dynamics are always changing, and a flexible and well-informed approach is required to achieve consistent profitability.

Larger Profits = Less Trades

Achieving the milestone from one thousand to one million requires strategic planning and an understanding of trade outcomes. To illustrate, attaining this goal through 3% profit per trade would necessitate 234 successful trades while opting for a 6% profit target would reduce the required trades to 119. Now, introducing a 10% profit target transforms the landscape further, reducing the necessary successful trades to a mere 48.

This signifies that each 10% profit trade, when compounded, contributes significantly to the exponential growth of the initial investment. While perfection in trade execution remains an elusive ideal, understanding the evolving number of required trades provides a pragmatic perspective on the temporal commitment and diligence essential to achieving the coveted financial objective of one million dollars.

Seizing Lucrative Opportunities - Identifying Favourable Risk/Reward Ratios

Successful traders are adept at identifying opportunities with favourable risk/reward ratios. Look for setups where the potential reward significantly outweighs the risk. This might involve thorough technical analysis, market research, and staying informed about upcoming events that could impact prices.

A good place to continue learning is https://gettingstartedincrypto.com/

Risk Management Strategies - Standard Practices 2:1

The Risk/Reward Ratio Demystified

Understanding the Ratio

The risk/reward ratio is a fundamental principle that guides investment decisions. It quantifies the potential profit versus potential loss in a trade, helping investors make informed choices based on a calculated assessment of risk. The ratio is expressed as a formula:

$$\text{Risk/Reward Ratio} = \frac{\text{Potential Profit}}{\text{Potential Loss}}$$

Ideal Ratios

- **2:1 Ratio:** Many successful investors adhere to a 2:1 risk/reward ratio. This means that for every dollar at risk (potential loss), there's an opportunity to make two dollars in profit. This ratio provides a buffer, allowing for a higher percentage of winning trades to offset losses.

Stop-Loss Orders Revisited

Implementing tight and strategic stop-loss orders is a cornerstone of effective risk management. Especially in line with the ThousandtoMillions.com strategy. Set your stop-loss orders at a level where potential losses align with your predetermined risk tolerance. In most cases 3% to 5%. This disciplined approach prevents emotional decision-making during market fluctuations.

Seizing Opportunities in Risk

Mastering risk is not just about protecting wealth but unlocking opportunities for financial success. By adeptly managing risk, traders position themselves to capitalise on market shifts, emerging trends, and undervalued assets. This dynamic approach involves making informed decisions aligned with risk tolerance and financial goals.

Successful traders distinguish themselves by skilfully identifying opportunities with favourable risk/reward ratios. Look for setups where the potential reward significantly outweighs the risk. This might involve thorough technical analysis, market research, and staying informed about upcoming events that could impact prices.

Resilience and adaptability play crucial roles, allowing traders to learn from setbacks and thrive in an ever-changing market environment. Ultimately, the synergy between risk management and seizing opportunities defines a journey marked by growth and the achievement of financial success.

Mastering risk in the pursuit of millionaire status involves a meticulous blend of strategic risk management, deliberate loss mitigation, and shrewd identification of market opportunities. By incorporating the risk/reward ratio into your trading toolkit, you not only safeguard your capital but also position yourself to capitalise on opportunities that can propel you towards financial success. Remember, becoming a millionaire in a year is not just about making bold moves but making calculated, informed decisions that balance risk and reward.

"Embrace uncertainty and seize the risks before you, for it is in the daring pursuit of the unknown that we discover out true potential and unlock the doors to extraordinary possibilities."

Unknown

UNDERSTANDING LIQUIDITY

When attempting to buy or sell a trade in a market with insufficient liquidity, traders may encounter several challenges and potential issues. Liquidity refers to the ease with which an asset can be bought or sold in the market without causing a significant impact on its price. When a market lacks liquidity, it means there are fewer buyers and sellers actively participating, and the market may be more susceptible to extreme price movements. This often happens in new coins and tokens and bearish markets. Here are some consequences of trading in a market with low liquidity:

Slippage

- Definition: Slippage occurs when the actual execution price of a trade differs from the expected price.

- Impact: In illiquid markets, there may be a delay in executing trades, leading to slippage. Traders might end up buying or selling at a less favourable price than they anticipated.

Wide Bid-Ask Spreads

- Definition: The bid-ask spread is the difference between the highest price a buyer is willing to pay (bid) and the lowest price a seller is willing to accept (ask).

- Impact: In markets with low liquidity, bid-ask spreads tend to widen. This means that the cost of entering or exiting a trade becomes higher, as traders may need to accept less favourable prices.

Limited Market Depth

- Definition: Market depth refers to the quantity of buy and sell orders at different price levels.
- Impact: In illiquid markets, there may be limited market depth, making it challenging to execute large trades without significantly impacting the asset's price. Large orders may need to be broken down into smaller orders to avoid substantial price slippage.

Increased Price Volatility

- Definition: Volatility represents the degree of variation of a trading price series over time.
- Impact: Low liquidity often amplifies price volatility. With fewer participants, even a relatively small trade can cause noticeable price swings. This heightened volatility can lead to increased uncertainty and risk for traders.

Order Rejections or Partial Fills

- Definition: In illiquid markets, exchanges may struggle to match buy and sell orders efficiently.
- Impact: Traders may experience order rejections or partial fills, where only a portion of their order is executed. This can further contribute to frustration and hinder the desired trade outcomes.

Market Impact

- Definition: Market impact refers to the effect that a large order can have on the market price.
- Impact: In low-liquidity environments, executing a substantial trade can significantly impact the market price. As traders attempt to buy or sell larger positions, the scarcity of counterparties may cause prices to move against them.

Increased Risk of Market Manipulation

- Definition: Market manipulation involves artificially inflating or deflating the price of a security.
- Impact: In illiquid markets, the lack of participants may make it easier for manipulative activities to influence prices. Traders should be cautious about potential manipulation risks.

Trading in a market with insufficient liquidity introduces challenges such as slippage, wider bid-ask spreads, limited market depth, increased price volatility, order rejections, market impact, and a higher risk of market manipulation.

Traders need to be aware of these issues and always consider the liquidity of a market when making trading decisions. These decisions will form part of your comprehensive trading strategy, acting as the linchpin for successful navigation through the intricacies of all financial markets.

By understanding how market liquidity works, the choices you make become the foundation for managing risks effectively. Recognising that liquidity isn't just a minor detail but a crucial factor in how trades play out highlights the importance of a well-rounded strategy.

So, when you factor in the liquidity of a market in your decisions, you're essentially building a strong and flexible approach to trading. This careful consideration ensures that each decision is a deliberate move toward reducing risks, capitalising on opportunities, and reaching your financial goals on your path to one million dollars!

"If the plan doesn't work...

Change the plan, not the goal."

Unknown

DEVELOPING A SOLID TRADING PLAN

Trading is far from one-size-fits-all. As we gain experience, we learn which trading styles suit our preferences and lifestyles. This personalised approach acknowledges that success in trading is not about fitting into a rigid mould but adapting strategies to our risk tolerance, time commitments, and financial goals. Experienced traders often embrace a mix of styles or refine their chosen approach, recognising that the path to success evolves with changing market conditions.

Defining Your Trading Objectives

Before diving headfirst into trading, it is crucial to define your trading objectives. This section guides you to help find your 'style this is not just for fashion models; style is also for traders, and most traders don't trade alike. We will also explore styles to fit time restrictions. By understanding your desired outcomes, you can tailor your trading plan to align with your specific needs and aspirations.

Choosing a Trading Style

Different trading styles suit different individuals. This segment explores various trading styles, such as day trading, swing trading, and long-term investing. Discover the characteristics, advantages, and challenges of each style and identify the one that resonates with your personality, available time, and risk tolerance.

Technical Analysis and Charting

Mastering technical analysis and charting is pivotal for recognising trading opportunities and optimising entry and exit points. You don't need to know everything, but you do need to know and understand how markets work to be a proficient and profitable trader. Acquiring proficiency in these tools empowers traders to make well-informed decisions, significantly elevating the likelihood of success in the dynamic landscape of financial markets. We dive into a few different trading techniques below.

1. Elliott Wave Theory

Riding the Wave of Market Psychology

Overview:

Elliott Wave Theory, developed by Ralph Nelson Elliott in the 1930s, is a technical analysis approach that seeks to identify repetitive wave patterns in financial markets. This theory is rooted in the concept that market movements follow distinct and predictable patterns driven by crowd psychology. We cover this in depth in Section 3.

Key Principles:

- Wave Structure: Elliott Wave Theory categorises market movements into impulsive waves (trending) and corrective waves (countertrend).
- Fibonacci Ratios: The theory often incorporates Fibonacci ratios to identify potential reversal or extension levels within a wave structure.
- Psychological Phases: The theory suggests that the market moves in five waves during uptrends and three waves during downtrends, reflecting shifts in investor sentiment.

Execution:

- Traders use Elliott Wave analysis to anticipate trend changes, identify entry and exit points, and manage risk based on the expected wave structure.

2. Order Blocks

Unravelling Institutional Footprints

Overview:

Order Blocks is a trading concept that focuses on identifying key levels in the market where institutional traders place significant orders. These blocks are considered zones of strong support or resistance.

Key Principles:

- Institutional Influence: Order Blocks assume that significant market movements are often initiated by institutional traders, leaving behind discernible order imprints.
- Market Memory: The concept relies on the idea that the market "remembers" these order blocks, leading to future price reactions when the price revisits these levels.

Execution:

- Traders using Order Blocks seek to identify these levels on price charts and anticipate price reactions around them. This involves looking for signs of order absorption or initiation.

3. Day Trading

Navigating Intraday Price Swings

Overview:

Day trading involves opening and closing positions within the same trading day, capitalising on short-term price fluctuations. Day traders aim to profit from intraday trends and price volatility.

Key Principles:

- Technical Analysis: Day traders heavily rely on technical analysis, utilising chart patterns, indicators, and intraday price action to make quick and informed trading decisions.
- Leverage: Given the short-term nature of day trading, traders often use leverage to magnify small price movements.

Execution:

- Day traders enter and exit positions quickly, often employing tight stop-loss orders and predefined profit targets. They monitor intraday charts, volume, and news events to make rapid decisions.

4. Swing Trading

Capturing Medium-Term Trends

Overview:

Swing trading aims to capture price swings or "swings" within a trend. Unlike day trading, swing traders hold positions for a few days to weeks, capitalising on short-to-medium-term price movements.

Key Principles:

- Trend Identification: Swing traders focus on identifying trends using technical analysis. They enter positions at the start of a new swing within an existing trend.
- Risk-Reward Ratio: Emphasising risk management, swing traders look for favourable risk-reward ratios, often targeting larger price moves.

Execution:

- Swing traders analyse charts on a daily or weekly basis. They use technical indicators, trendlines, and chart patterns to identify potential entry and exit points.

5. Algorithmic Trading

Precision through Automated Strategies

Overview:

Algorithmic trading, also known as algo trading or black-box trading, involves the use of computer programs to execute trading strategies. These algorithms can analyse market conditions and execute trades at a speed and frequency impossible for human traders.

Key Principles:

- Quantitative Analysis: Algorithmic trading relies on quantitative analysis, utilising mathematical models and statistical techniques to identify trading opportunities.

- High-Frequency Trading (HFT): Some algorithmic strategies operate on a high-frequency basis, executing a large number of orders in fractions of a second.

Execution:

- Traders and institutions design algorithms based on specific criteria and parameters. These algorithms automatically execute trades, manage risk, and adapt to changing market conditions.

Each trading style offers a unique approach to the financial markets, catering to different risk tolerances, time horizons, and preferences.

Whether you're drawn to the psychological patterns of Elliott Wave Theory, the institutional imprints of Order Blocks, the rapid pace of day trading, the trend capturing of swing trading, or the precision of algorithmic trading, selecting the right style depends on your individual goals, risk appetite, and trading personality.

As you explore these styles, remember that successful trading often involves a combination of strategies and continuous adaptation to market dynamics, and knowing that the TREND is always your FRIEND!

"By failing to prepare…

You are preparing to fail "

Benjamin Franklin

"Our goals can only be reached through a vehicle of a plan, in which we must fervently believe, and upon which we must vigorously act. There is no other route to success."

Pablo Picasso

DEVELOPING TRADING RULES AND STRATEGIES

Consistency is key in trading. We run through the importance of developing trading rules and strategies that provide a systematic approach to decision-making. This will mean you know what to do and when, so you can keep the emotions at bay. Discover how to define entry and exit criteria, establish risk management rules, and adapt your strategies based on market conditions. Develop a set of rules that align with your trading objectives and facilitate disciplined execution.

Developing trading rules and strategies is a systematic process that involves careful analysis, testing, and refinement. Here's a general guide on how to develop trading rules, along with three examples:

1. Define Your Objectives:

- Clearly articulate your trading objectives, including financial goals, risk tolerance, and time commitment. Understanding what you aim to achieve guides the development of specific strategies.

2. Choose a Trading Style:

- Identify a trading style that aligns with your goals and personality. Whether it's day trading, swing trading, or long-term investing, your chosen style will shape the rules and strategies you employ.

3. Conduct Market Analysis:

- Analyse the market conditions, including trends, volatility, and key economic indicators. This analysis helps in identifying potential opportunities and risks that can inform your trading rules.

4. Set Risk Management Parameters:

- Establish clear risk management rules, including the maximum percentage of capital to risk per trade, stop-loss levels, and position sizing. Protecting your capital is a fundamental aspect of successful trading.

5. Utilise Technical and/or Fundamental Analysis:

- Choose between technical analysis, fundamental analysis, or a combination of both, depending on your preferred approach. Develop rules for entry and exit points based on your chosen analytical methods.

6. Back testing:

- Test your trading rules on historical data to assess their effectiveness. Back testing helps identify potential weaknesses and refine the rules for better performance in different market conditions.

7. Paper Trading:

- Practice your strategies in a simulated environment through paper trading. This allows you to see how your rules perform in real-time without risking actual capital.

8. Analyse and Refine:

- Regularly review the performance of your trading rules and strategies. Identify areas for improvement and adjust the rules accordingly. The ability to adapt is crucial in the ever-changing market landscape.

Three Examples of Trading Rules

Example 1: Moving Average Crossover (Trend-Following Strategy):

- Rule 1: Buy when the short-term moving average crosses above the long-term moving average.
- Rule 2: Sell when the short-term moving average crosses below the long-term moving average.
- Risk Management: Use a fixed percentage of capital for each trade and set a stop-loss based on volatility.

Example 2: Breakout Strategy (Volatility-Based):

- Rule 1: Buy when the price breaks above a predefined resistance level.
- Rule 2: Sell when the price breaks below a predefined support level.
- Risk Management: Determine position size based on the average true range (ATR) to account for market volatility.

Example 3: Earnings Momentum (Fundamental Analysis):

- Rule 1: Buy stocks of companies that consistently beat earnings expectations or Cryptocurrencies with constant building and partnerships, especially in bear markets.
- Rule 2: Sell stocks of companies that consistently miss earnings expectations. Similar for cryptocurrencies, where the teams miss deadlines on product launches.
- Risk Management: Limit exposure to a certain percentage of the portfolio for any single stock/crypto and use a trailing stop to protect profits.

Remember, trading rules should be specific, measurable, and adaptable. Regularly review and update them based on your evolving understanding of the market and your own trading performance.

Back testing and Performance Evaluation

Back testing allows you to assess the effectiveness of your trading strategies using historical data. We are about to delve into the process of back testing, evaluating performance, and making necessary adjustments based on the results.

Learn how to refine your trading plan, identify strengths and weaknesses, and continuously improve your trading performance.

Back testing in Trading

Back testing is a process in which a trading strategy or set of trading rules is applied to historical market data to assess how it would have performed in the past. Traders use back testing to evaluate the effectiveness of their strategies, identify potential strengths and weaknesses, and gain insights into the strategy's historical performance.

Key Steps in Back testing

- Define the Trading Strategy: Clearly articulate the rules and parameters of the trading strategy.

- Apply the Strategy to Historical Data: Execute the strategy on past market data, simulating trades as if they were made in real-time.

- Evaluate Performance: Analyse the results, including profitability, drawdowns, win-loss ratio, and other relevant metrics.

- Refine and Optimise: Identify areas for improvement and refine the strategy based on the insights gained during back testing.

Benefits of Back testing

- Performance Evaluation: Back testing provides a quantitative assessment of how well a trading strategy would have performed in historical market conditions.

- Risk Management: Traders can evaluate the risk-adjusted returns of the strategy, helping to refine risk management parameters.

- Strategy Optimisation: Back testing allows for the optimisation of parameters to enhance the strategy's performance.

- Confidence Building: Successful back testing instils confidence in traders, validating the effectiveness of their chosen strategies.

Performance Evaluation in Trading:

Performance evaluation in trading involves assessing the effectiveness of a trading strategy or the overall trading portfolio. It goes beyond back testing to consider real-time performance, considering factors such as execution slippage, transaction costs, and market conditions that may not be fully captured in historical data.

Key Aspects of Performance Evaluation:

- Real-Time Execution: Evaluate how the strategy performs in live market conditions, accounting for actual trade execution and potential slippage.

- Transaction Costs: Consider transaction costs, including commissions and spreads, which can impact the overall profitability of a trading strategy.

- Adaptability: Assess the strategy's adaptability to changing market conditions and its ability to remain effective over time.
- Continuous Monitoring: Regularly monitor and update performance metrics to reflect changes in the market or the trading environment.

Importance of Performance Evaluation:

- Reality Check: Performance evaluation provides a reality check, ensuring that the strategy performs as expected in live markets.
- Risk Management Refinement: It helps in refining risk management strategies by incorporating real-world transaction costs and slippage into the assessment.
- Continuous Improvement: Performance evaluation guides ongoing refinement and improvement of trading strategies based on real-time results.
- Decision-Making Confidence: Traders gain confidence in their strategies when they consistently perform well in live market conditions.

Both back testing and performance evaluation are essential components of a trader's toolkit. Back testing allows for the initial assessment of a strategy's historical performance, while performance evaluation ensures that the strategy remains effective in real-world conditions. Together, they contribute to informed decision-making and the continuous improvement of trading strategies.

FUNDAMENTAL ANALYSIS AND MARKET RESEARCH

Fundamental Analysis:

Fundamental analysis is a method of evaluating securities, such as stocks or bonds, by analysing the intrinsic value of an asset. It involves examining various economic, financial, and qualitative factors that can affect the value of an investment. The goal is to determine whether an asset is overvalued or undervalued in the market.

Key Aspects of Fundamental Analysis:

- Economic Indicators: Assessing economic indicators like GDP growth, unemployment rates, and inflation can provide insights into the overall health of an economy.

- Financial Statements: Analysing a company's financial statements, including the income statement, balance sheet, and cash flow statement, helps evaluate its financial health.

- Company Earnings: Understanding a company's earnings, revenue growth, and profit margins provides information about its financial performance.

- Management and Competitors: Evaluating the quality of management and understanding the competitive landscape are crucial factors in fundamental analysis.

Importance of Fundamental Analysis in Trading

- Long-Term Investment Decisions: Fundamental analysis is often used for long-term investment decisions, helping investors identify stocks with strong growth potential.

- Informed Investment Choices: It provides a comprehensive view of a company's financial health, enabling traders to make informed decisions based on a deeper understanding of the asset.

- Market Valuation: Fundamental analysis helps in assessing whether an asset is overvalued or undervalued, assisting traders in identifying potential market inefficiencies.

Market Research:

Market research involves gathering and analysing information about markets, including trends, competitors, and consumer behaviour. In the context of trading, market research helps traders understand the broader market environment and make more informed decisions.

Key Aspects of Market Research:

- Market Trends: Analysing trends in the financial markets helps traders identify potential opportunities and risks.

- Market Sentiment: Understanding market sentiment, whether it's bullish or bearish, can impact trading decisions.

- Global Events: Keeping abreast of global events, economic indicators, and geopolitical developments helps anticipate market movements.

- Industry Analysis: For stocks, understanding the industry and sector dynamics is crucial for making informed investment decisions.

Importance of Market Research in Trading:

- Risk Management: Market research aids in identifying potential risks and uncertainties, allowing traders to implement effective risk management strategies.

- Timing Entries and Exits: By understanding market trends and sentiment, traders can better time their entry and exit points for trades.

- Opportunity Identification: Market research helps traders identify new opportunities and stay ahead of market developments.

Both fundamental analysis and market research are crucial components of a comprehensive trading strategy. While fundamental analysis delves into the financial health of individual assets, market research provides a broader understanding of the market environment. Together, these tools empower traders to make well-informed decisions, manage risks effectively, and capitalise on market opportunities.

For short-term speculative traders, fundamental analysis is often deemed irrelevant. In this trading approach, the focus is primarily on immediate price movements, technical indicators, and chart patterns.

Decisions are driven by short-term market sentiment and momentum, with little consideration for the broader economic factors or long-term potential. The emphasis is on exploiting short-term market inefficiencies and capitalising on intraday or short-term trends.

While major economic events are still monitored, the primary tools for short-term traders are technical analysis indicators, allowing them to make rapid and informed decisions in the fast-paced trading environment.

"You don't learn to walk by following rules.

You learn by doing, and by falling over."

Sir Richard Branson

FUNDAMENTAL ANALYSIS IN CRYPTOCURRENCY

Fundamental analysis in cryptocurrencies involves evaluating the underlying factors that can impact the value and success of a digital asset. As cryptocurrency is often defined as a high-risk asset due to the young nature of the market and strong market volatility. Key considerations include:

- Blockchain Technology: Assessing the technology behind a cryptocurrency, especially the capabilities and security of its blockchain, is fundamental. The strength and innovation of the underlying technology can influence its long-term viability.

- Use Case and Utility: Understanding the practical use case and utility of a cryptocurrency is crucial. Cryptocurrencies with clear, real-world applications and utility tend to have more sustainable value.

- Development Team: Examining the experience and expertise of the development team is vital. A capable and reputable team can contribute to the ongoing development and improvement of the cryptocurrency.

- Regulatory Environment: The regulatory landscape significantly impacts cryptocurrencies. Changes in regulations can affect their legality, adoption, and overall market sentiment.

Market Research in Cryptocurrency

Market research in the cryptocurrency space involves monitoring trends, sentiments, and external factors that can influence market dynamics, including news. Key aspects include:

- Market Trends and Sentiment: Cryptocurrency markets are often influenced by trends and sentiment. Monitoring social media, forums, and news sources helps traders gauge market sentiment and identify potential trends.
- Adoption and Partnerships: Examining the adoption rate of a cryptocurrency and its partnerships with businesses or other projects can indicate its potential for growth and mainstream acceptance.

- Global Developments: Cryptocurrency markets are influenced by global events, technological advancements, and macroeconomic trends. Staying informed about these factors helps traders anticipate market movements.

- Network Upgrades and Forks: In the cryptocurrency space, network upgrades and forks can have significant implications. Traders need to be aware of planned upgrades and potential forks to make informed decisions.

The Importance of Fundamental Analysis and Market Research in Cryptocurrency Trading

- Volatility Management: Cryptocurrency markets are known for their volatility. Fundamental analysis and market research help traders manage and mitigate risks associated with market fluctuations.

- Long-Term Investment Decisions: For long-term cryptocurrency investors, understanding the fundamentals of a digital asset is crucial for making informed investment decisions.

- Identifying Opportunities: Cryptocurrency markets are dynamic, and opportunities arise as new projects emerge. Fundamental analysis and market research assist traders in identifying promising projects and timely investment opportunities.

- Navigating Regulatory Changes: Cryptocurrency markets are influenced by regulatory developments. Being aware of and adapting to regulatory changes is essential for cryptocurrency traders.

By incorporating fundamental analysis and market research into cryptocurrency trading strategies, you can provide a comprehensive approach.

Whether evaluating the technology behind a cryptocurrency or staying attuned to market sentiments, these tools enable traders to navigate the unique challenges and opportunities presented by the volatile cryptocurrency market.

"Learning never exhausts the mind."

Leonardo da Vinci

"Somewhere, something incredible is waiting to be known."

Carl Sagan

FUNDAMENTALS OF STOCK MARKET TRADING

The stock market has long been a vehicle for wealth creation. This chapter focuses on the fundamentals of stock market investing, equipping you with the knowledge and tools to build a strong foundation for successful wealth accumulation. By understanding the key principles of stock market investing, you will be able to navigate the markets with confidence and make informed investment decisions once you start getting closer to the magic million!

Understanding Stocks and Equity Ownership

Understanding stocks and equity ownership involves grasping several key aspects, including the nature of stocks, their valuation, and the rights and privileges associated with owning shares in a company. Here are some key points to consider:

- *Stock Basics*:
    - Definition: Stocks represent ownership in a company. When you own a stock, you own a piece of the company.
    - Types of Stocks: Common and preferred stocks are the two main types. Common stockholders have voting rights, while preferred stockholders typically do not vote but have priority in receiving dividends.
- *Valuation*:
    - Market Value: The price of a stock in the market, determined by supply and demand.
    - Earnings and Dividends: Investors often assess a company's earnings and dividend history to evaluate its financial health and growth potential.

- *Stock Exchanges*:
    - Listed and Unlisted Stocks: Listed stocks are traded on organised exchanges (e.g., NYSE, NASDAQ), while unlisted stocks may be traded over the counter (OTC).
    - Liquidity: Stocks traded on major exchanges tend to be more liquid, meaning they can be bought or sold more easily.
- *Ownership Rights:*
    - Voting Rights: Common stockholders usually have the right to vote on certain company decisions, such as the board of directors.
    - Dividends: Stockholders may receive a portion of the company's profits in the form of dividends.
    - Liquidation Rights: In the event of bankruptcy or liquidation, stockholders may have claims on the company's assets after bondholders and preferred stockholders.
- *Privileges of Ownership:*
    - Capital Gains: Stockholders can benefit from capital gains if the value of their stocks increases.
    - Limited Liability: In most cases, individual shareholders are not personally responsible for the company's debts.
- *Risks:*
    - Market Risks: Stock prices can be volatile due to market conditions, economic factors, or company-specific events.
    - Business Risks: The performance of a company and its stock is influenced by its industry, competition, and management decisions.

- *Investor Considerations:*
    - Diversification: Spreading investments across different stocks can help manage risk.

    - Research: Informed decision-making involves researching a company's financial health, industry trends, and management.

Regulatory Framework:

- SEC Regulations: In the United States, the Securities and Exchange Commission (SEC) regulates the securities industry to protect investors and maintain fair and efficient markets.

Regulatory bodies vary by region, and each has its own set of rules and organisations overseeing the financial markets. Here are examples from different regions:

United States:

- Regulatory Body: Securities and Exchange Commission (SEC)
- Example Markets: New York Stock Exchange (NYSE), NASDAQ

United Kingdom:

- Regulatory Body: Financial Conduct Authority (FCA)
- Example Markets: London Stock Exchange (LSE), Alternative Investment Market (AIM)

European Union:

- Regulatory Body: European Securities and Markets Authority (ESMA)
- Example Markets: Euronext, Frankfurt Stock Exchange

Japan:

- Regulatory Body: Financial Services Agency (FSA)
- Example Markets: Tokyo Stock Exchange (TSE)

Hong Kong:

- Regulatory Body: Securities and Futures Commission (SFC)
    - Example Markets: Hong Kong Stock Exchange (HKEX)

India:

- Regulatory Body: Securities and Exchange Board of India (SEBI)
- Example Markets: Bombay Stock Exchange (BSE), National Stock Exchange (NSE)

Australia:

- Regulatory Body: Australian Securities and Investments Commission (ASIC)
- Example Markets: Australian Securities Exchange (ASX)

Canada:

- Regulatory Body: Canadian Securities Administrators (CSA)
- Example Markets: Toronto Stock Exchange (TSX), TSX Venture Exchange (TSXV)

Brazil:

- Regulatory Body: Comissão de Valores Mobiliários (CVM)
- Example Markets: B3 (B3 Brasil Bolsa Balcão)

South Africa:

- Regulatory Body: Financial Sector Conduct Authority (FSCA)
- Example Markets: Johannesburg Stock Exchange (JSE)

It's important for investors to thoroughly understand the terms and conditions associated with owning a particular stock and to stay informed about the company's performance and the broader economic environment. This knowledge can empower investors to make informed decisions about buying, holding, or selling stocks.

The Role of Stock Exchanges and Marketplaces

Stock exchanges and marketplaces play a crucial role in the financial markets by providing a platform for buying and selling securities, including stocks. The primary functions of stock exchanges, such as the New York Stock Exchange (NYSE) and NASDAQ, and alternative marketplaces like electronic communication networks (ECNs), include facilitating the trading of stocks and ensuring a fair and efficient marketplace. Here are key aspects of their roles:

- *Facilitating Trading*:
    - Matching Buyers and Sellers: Stock exchanges bring together buyers and sellers, creating a centralised marketplace where securities can be traded. This helps establish fair and transparent prices based on supply and demand.

- *Providing Liquidity*:

    - Market Makers: Exchanges often have market makers or specialists who facilitate trading by quoting bid and ask prices. This helps ensure liquidity, allowing investors to buy or sell securities at relatively stable prices.

- *Price Discovery*:
    - Transparent Pricing: Exchanges provide a transparent mechanism for price discovery. The continuous buying and selling of stocks on the exchange contribute to establishing real-time market prices.

- *Market Surveillance*:
    - Regulatory Oversight: Exchanges have regulatory functions to monitor trading activities, prevent market manipulation, and enforce compliance with trading rules. This oversight is crucial for maintaining market integrity.

- *Order Execution*:
    - Centralised Order Book: Exchanges maintain a central order book, where buy and sell orders are matched. Trades are executed based on the best available prices at any given time.

- *Market Index Calculation*:
    - Benchmarking: Exchanges often calculate and maintain market indices (e.g., S&P 500, Dow Jones Industrial Average), providing benchmarks for overall market performance.

- *Listing and Delisting*:
    - Listing Requirements: Exchanges establish criteria for companies to be listed, ensuring a certain level of financial health and transparency.
    - Delisting: Companies failing to meet listing requirements may be delisted from the exchange.

- *Alternative Marketplaces (ECNs)*:
    - Electronic Trading Platforms: ECNs are alternative trading systems that operate electronically, matching buyers and sellers outside traditional exchanges.
    - Increased Efficiency: ECNs can offer faster and more cost-effective trading, often with lower transaction costs.
- *Order Types:*
    - Market Orders: Executed at the best available price.
    - Limit Orders: Executed at a specific price or better.
    - Stop Orders: Triggered when a stock reaches a specified price level.
- *After-Hours Trading*:
    - Extended Hours: Some exchanges and ECNs allow trading outside regular market hours, providing additional flexibility for investors.

Understanding the mechanics of placing orders, the role of market participants, and the rules and regulations governing stock exchanges is essential for investors looking to navigate the financial markets effectively. Whether trading on a traditional exchange or through alternative marketplaces, investors benefit from a well-functioning and regulated marketplace that promotes transparency and fairness.

Key Financial Metrics for Evaluating Stocks

Evaluating the financial health and performance of a company is critical before investing in its stock.

Key financial metrics play a crucial role in evaluating stocks and assessing the financial health and performance of a company. Investors use these metrics to make informed decisions about buying, holding, or selling stocks. Here are some key financial metrics and why they are important:

- *Earnings per Share (EPS)*:
  - Calculation: Net Income / Average Outstanding Shares
  - Importance: EPS indicates a company's profitability on a per-share basis. Investors often look for consistent or growing EPS over time.

- *Price-to-Earnings Ratio (P/E)*:
  - Calculation: Market Price per Share / Earnings per Share
  - Importance: P/E ratio reflects the market's valuation of a company relative to its earnings. A higher P/E may suggest higher growth expectations.

- *Dividend Yield*:
  - Calculation: Annual Dividends per Share / Market Price per Share
  - Importance: Dividend yield indicates the annual dividend income as a percentage of the stock's market price. It's relevant for income-oriented investors.

- *Return on Equity (ROE)*:
  - Calculation: Net Income / Shareholders' Equity
  - Importance: ROE measures a company's ability to generate profit from shareholders' equity. A higher ROE suggests efficient use of equity capital.

- *Debt-to-Equity Ratio*:
  - Calculation: Total Debt / Shareholders' Equity
  - Importance: Indicates the proportion of a company's funding that comes from debt. Lower ratios may suggest lower financial risk.

- *Current Ratio*:
  - Calculation: Current Assets / Current Liabilities
  - Importance: Current ratio assesses a company's short-term liquidity. A ratio above 1 indicates the company can cover its short-term liabilities.

- *Free Cash Flow (FCF):*
  - Calculation: Operating Cash Flow - Capital Expenditures
  - Importance: FCF measures the cash generated by a company after covering its capital expenditures. Positive FCF is essential for growth and dividend payments.

- *Price-to-Book Ratio (P/B)*:
  - Calculation: Market Price per Share / Book Value per Share
  - Importance: P/B ratio compares a stock's market value to its book value. A lower P/B ratio may suggest a potentially undervalued stock.

- *Gross Margin:*
  - Calculation: (Revenue - Cost of Goods Sold) / Revenue
  - Importance: Gross margin measures the profitability of a company's core operations. Higher gross margins indicate better profitability.

- *Revenue Growth:*
  - Calculation: (Current Year Revenue - Previous Year Revenue) / Previous Year Revenue
  - Importance: Investors often seek companies with consistent or accelerating revenue growth as it indicates business expansion.

- *Operating Margin:*
  - Calculation: Operating Income / Revenue
  - Importance: Operating margin reflects a company's operating efficiency. Higher margins suggest better cost control.

- *Beta:*
  - Calculation: Measures a stock's volatility relative to the overall market.

  - Importance: Beta helps assess a stock's risk compared to the broader market. A beta of 1 indicates market-level risk.

These financial metrics provide investors with insights into a company's profitability, financial stability, growth potential, and valuation. It's essential to consider these metrics collectively and in the context of industry benchmarks for a comprehensive analysis of a stock's investment potential.

Long-term Investing vs. Short-term Trading

Once we are reaching highs close to or past one million, we need assess the market differently and more time efficiently. Investors have different approaches, ranging from long-term investing to short-term trading which are two distinct approaches to engaging in the stock market, each with its own set of objectives, time horizons, and strategies.

Here are the key differences between long-term investing and short-term trading:

Long-Term Investing

- *Time Horizon*:
  - Long-term: Typically involves holding investments for an extended period, often measured in years or decades.
- *Objective*:
  - Long-term: Aims to build wealth gradually over time through the appreciation of assets, dividends, and compound interest.
- *Strategy*:
  - Buy and Hold: Investors often buy stocks with strong fundamentals and the intention of holding them through market fluctuations.
- *Research Focus*:

    - Fundamentals: Emphasis on analysing a company's fundamentals, such as earnings, dividends, and growth potential.
- *Risk Tolerance*:
    - Higher Tolerance: Long-term investors may tolerate short-term market volatility, expecting the market to trend upward over time.
- *Tax Implications:*
    - Tax Efficiency: Holding investments for more than one year may qualify for lower long-term capital gains tax rates.
- *Monitoring*:
    - Infrequent Monitoring: Long-term investors typically do not need to monitor their investments on a daily basis.
- *Psychological Aspect*:
    - Emotional Stability: Long-term investors are often advised to remain patient and not be swayed by short-term market fluctuations.

Short-Term Trading

- *Time Horizon*:
    - Short-term: Involves buying and selling securities over a relatively short time frame, ranging from seconds to months.
- *Objective:*
    - Short-term: Aims to capitalise on short-term price movements for quick profits.
- *Strategy:*
    - Active Trading: Traders actively buy and sell stocks based on technical analysis, market trends, or short-term news events.
- *Research Focus*:
    - Technical Analysis: Focus on analysing price charts, trends, and trading volumes rather than long-term fundamentals.
- *Risk Tolerance:*

    - Lower Tolerance: Short-term traders may be more sensitive to market volatility and aim to limit losses through quick decision-making.
- *Tax Implications:*
    - Higher Tax Rates: Short-term capital gains are typically taxed at higher rates than long-term gains.
- *Monitoring:*
    - Frequent Monitoring: Short-term traders need to closely monitor market movements, news, and their positions.
- *Psychological Aspect*:
    - Quick Decision-Making: Short-term trading often requires a more active and reactive approach, with quick decision-making in response to market changes.

Choosing between long-term investing and short-term trading depends on individual preferences, financial goals, risk tolerance, and especially time commitment. Long-term investing is often associated with a more passive, patient approach, while short-term trading involves a more active and potentially higher-risk strategy. Both approaches can be valid, but it's crucial to align with your investment approach with their financial goals and risk tolerance.

Overview of Stock Market Trading

By delving into the fundamentals of stock market trading, we can equip ourselves as investors with essential knowledge and tools to lay a solid foundation for successful wealth accumulation. As we approach or surpass significant milestones, such as the one-million mark, a nuanced and efficient market assessment becomes imperative.

Traders may become investors and vice versa. But both must employ diverse strategies, from the patient outlook of long-term investing to the dynamic tactics of short-term trading.

Understanding stocks and equity ownership involves delving into key aspects, including stock basics, valuation, ownership rights, privileges, risks, and regulatory frameworks. Thorough comprehension of these elements empowers investors to make informed decisions about buying, holding, or selling stocks, ensuring a strategic and informed approach to the market.

The role of stock exchanges and marketplaces is pivotal in facilitating the trading of stocks and maintaining a fair and efficient marketplace. Whether on traditional exchanges like the NYSE or NASDAQ or alternative platforms like ECNs, investors benefit from a well-regulated environment that promotes transparency and fairness.

Key financial metrics play a critical role in evaluating stocks, providing insights into a company's financial health, performance, and potential for growth. These metrics, including EPS, P/E ratio, dividend yield, and others, guide investors in making informed decisions aligned with their financial goals.

Lastly, the distinction between long-term investing and short-term trading lies in the time horizon, objectives, and strategies employed. Long-term investing emphasises patience, steady wealth accumulation, and fundamental analysis, while short-term trading involves active strategies, quick decision-making, and sensitivity to market volatility. The choice between these approaches depends on individual preferences, financial goals, risk tolerance, and time commitment.

"Everyone has the brainpower to make money in stocks. Not everyone has the stomach. If you are susceptible to selling everything in a panic, you ought to avoid stocks and mutual funds altogether."

Peter Lynch

"The first rule of investment is 'buy low and sell high,' but many people fear to buy low because of the fear of the stock dropping even lower.

Then you may ask: 'When is the time to buy low?' The answer is: When there is maximum pessimism."

Sir John Templeton

TRADING THE HIGH VOLATILITY CRYPTOCURRENCY MARKET

Cryptocurrency is often painted with a tarred brush, but I love the people, the projects, the belief in the new financial narrative. Despite the scepticism and occasional controversies surrounding the crypto space, there's a vibrant community that is passionate about reshaping the way we think about and engage with money.

This movement goes beyond just the digital currencies themselves; it encompasses a diverse range of projects and initiatives that aim to decentralise, democratise, and innovate within the financial sector. From decentralised finance (DeFi) platforms that provide new avenues for lending and borrowing to blockchain projects that address issues like supply chain transparency and identity verification, the crypto space is a hotbed of creativity and ambition.

The people involved in these projects are not just driven by profit; many are motivated by a desire to challenge the status quo and create a more inclusive and equitable financial system. It's a community that values transparency, autonomy, and the potential for positive social impact.

Sure, there have been bumps in the road, with regulatory challenges, market volatility, and the occasional bad actor grabbing headlines. But it's important to recognise that these challenges are part of the maturation process for any emerging technology. And, in many cases, the crypto community has shown resilience, adaptability, and a commitment to learning from mistakes.

Beyond the financial and technological aspects, what truly excites me is the belief in a new narrative for finance—one that transcends borders, empowers individuals, and challenges traditional power structures. It's a narrative that envisions a future where financial services are more accessible, transparent, and accountable.

In the midst of the noise and controversy, it's essential to remember that behind every cryptocurrency or blockchain project, there are real people with real visions for a better financial future. So, while the tarred brush may linger, it's worth taking a closer look at the canvas to appreciate the artistry, innovation, and optimism that define the cryptocurrency landscape.

Let's break down trading in the high volatility cryptocurrency market. While it can be both rewarding and challenging, it essential to enter the space with basic knowledge of what you are diving into. And trading crypto isn't vastly different to trading the stock market, in penny stocks and newer technology businesses we often see similar volatility.

And before you say anything, we are all in crypto for the Tech!

I'm going to touch on a few benefits and disadvantages:

Benefits

- *Profit Potential*:
    - High volatility often means larger price movements, providing more opportunities for traders to profit. Skilled traders can capitalise on price swings to make significant gains.
- *Liquidity*:
    - High volatility can also be associated with increased liquidity, making it easier to buy and sell assets without a significant impact on their prices.
- *Diverse Trading Opportunities*:
    - Cryptocurrency markets are open 24/7, providing traders with opportunities around the clock. Additionally, the vast number of cryptocurrencies allows for diversification.

- *Market Sentiment Opportunities*:
    - Cryptocurrency markets are heavily influenced by market sentiment and news. Traders can use these factors to their advantage by identifying trends and making informed decisions.
- *Innovative Technology*:
    - Cryptocurrencies are at the forefront of financial technology. Trading in this market allows participants to engage with innovative technologies and financial instruments.

Disadvantages

- *Risk of Loss*:
    - High volatility means higher potential profits, but it also comes with increased risk. Prices can swing dramatically in a short period, leading to significant losses if the market moves against a trader.
- *Market Manipulation*:
    - Cryptocurrency markets are less regulated compared to traditional financial markets. This lack of regulation can make them susceptible to market manipulation, pump-and-dump schemes, and other fraudulent activities.
- *Lack of Fundamental Analysis*:
    - Cryptocurrencies often lack the fundamental analysis that traditional assets have, making it challenging to evaluate their intrinsic value. This can lead to speculative trading and increased volatility. As a speculative asset class fundamentals can vary from coin to token and be non-existent in tokens like "Meme-coins."

- *Security Concerns*:
    - The cryptocurrency market is susceptible to hacking and security breaches. Exchanges and wallets can be targets for cybercriminals, potentially leading to the loss of funds for traders. You must obtain a thorough knowledge of the ever-changing security needed to keep your funds safe.
- *Emotional Stress*:
    - The high volatility and rapid price movements can create emotional stress for traders. Fear and greed can drive impulsive decisions, leading to losses. It requires discipline and a strong emotional mindset to navigate these markets successfully.
- *Regulatory Uncertainty:*
    - Cryptocurrency markets face ongoing regulatory uncertainties in many jurisdictions. Changes in regulations or government policies can have a significant impact on market dynamics and trader activities.
- *Market Sentiment Risks:*
    - While market sentiment can present opportunities, it can also lead to herd behaviour and irrational decision-making, contributing to market bubbles and crashes.

Trading a high volatility cryptocurrency market can be lucrative for those who understand the risks and have a well-thought-out strategy, similar to what we have been discussing in this book. However, it's crucial for traders to stay informed, manage their risks, and be prepared for anything to happen in the crypto market.

Trading the cryptocurrency market involves understanding various fundamentals, including market dynamics, investment possibilities, and the influence of factors like technology, regulation, and market sentiment. Here are key fundamentals to consider:

Market Dynamics:

- Supply and Demand: Understand the basics of supply and demand in the cryptocurrency market. Limited supply (as in the case of Bitcoin) can influence price dynamics.

- Market Capitalisation: Market cap reflects the total value of a cryptocurrency. It's an important metric to consider when assessing the relative size of different cryptocurrencies.

Investment Possibilities:

- Long-Term Investment (HODLing): Some investors choose to buy and hold cryptocurrencies with the expectation of long-term price appreciation.

- Day Trading: Involves making short-term trades to take advantage of intraday price movements.

- Swing Trading: Capitalises on price "swings" or short- to medium-term trends.

Centralised and Decentralised Exchanges:

- Centralised Exchanges (CEX):

    - Examples: Bybit, Binance, Coinbase, Kraken, OKX.

    - Pros: High liquidity, user-friendly interfaces, a wide range of trading pairs.

    - Cons: Centralised control, potential security risks.

- Decentralised Exchanges (DEX):

- Examples: Uniswap, SushiSwap, PancakeSwap, 1inch.
- Pros: Greater user control, reduced reliance on intermediaries, enhanced privacy.
- Cons: Lower liquidity compared to major centralised exchanges.

Market Influences:

- Regulation: Changes in regulatory environments can significantly impact the cryptocurrency market. Regulatory clarity or uncertainty can affect investor confidence.
- Technology and Innovation: Developments in blockchain technology, new projects, and upgrades to existing networks can influence the market.
- Market Sentiment: Social media, news, and public perception play a crucial role. Market sentiment can lead to rapid price movements.
- Macroeconomic Factors: Economic indicators, global events, and monetary policies can impact the overall market.

Risk Management:

- Diversification: Spread investments across different cryptocurrencies to reduce risk.
- Stop-Loss and Take-Profit Orders: Set predefined levels to automatically exit trades at acceptable profit or loss points.
- Position Sizing: Determine the amount of capital to allocate to each trade based on risk tolerance.

Technical Analysis:

- Use technical analysis tools like charts, indicators, and patterns to make informed trading decisions.

Security Measures:

- Cold Wallets: Use hardware wallets for long-term storage to reduce the risk of hacking.
- Two-Factor Authentication (2FA): Enhance security on exchanges and wallets.

Education and Research:

- Continuously educate yourself about blockchain technology, specific cryptocurrencies, and market trends.

Psychological Factors:

- Emotions like fear and greed can influence decision-making. Developing a disciplined and rational mindset is crucial.

Network Effects:

- Consider the network effects of a cryptocurrency — the more users and developers, the stronger the network.

Tokenomics:

- Understand the token economics of a cryptocurrency, including its use cases, utility, and distribution model.

Market Cycles:

- Recognise that cryptocurrency markets often go through cycles of bull and bear markets.

Successful cryptocurrency trading requires a combination of technical knowledge, risk management, and a thorough understanding of market dynamics. It's important to stay updated on industry news, be adaptable to changing market conditions, and continually refine your trading strategy.

Additionally, the high volatility of the cryptocurrency market brings both opportunities and risks. It's essential for traders to be aware of the potential pitfalls and challenges. Here's an expansion on the risks associated with trading in the high volatility cryptocurrency market:

Scams and Fraud:

- The lack of regulatory oversight in the cryptocurrency space has led to the proliferation of scams and fraudulent schemes. Traders should be cautious of Ponzi schemes, pump-and-dump groups, and fake ICOs (Initial Coin Offerings).

Token and Exchange Risks:

- Token Collapse: Some tokens may become worthless due to project failures, lack of development, or regulatory issues.

- Exchange Collapse: Exchanges can face technical issues, insolvency, or even exit scams, resulting in significant losses for users. For example, FTX and Mt Gox.

Rug Pulls:

- In decentralised finance (DeFi), investors may face the risk of "rug pulls," where developers or liquidity providers unexpectedly withdraw funds, causing the value of a token to collapse.

Lack of Investor Protections:

- Traditional financial markets often have investor protections, such as insurance on deposits. Cryptocurrency markets generally lack these safeguards, exposing investors to higher levels of risk.

Market Manipulation:

- Due to lower market capitalisation compared to traditional markets, cryptocurrencies are more susceptible to market manipulation. Whales (large holders) can influence prices through coordinated buying or selling. This is becoming less common as the market matures, but always something you must be aware of.

Liquidity Risks:

- While high volatility can lead to increased liquidity, certain low-cap coins may lack sufficient liquidity. This can result in slippage, where the executed trade deviates significantly from the expected price.

Overleveraging:

- Trading platforms offering high leverage can amplify both gains and losses. Overleveraging increases the risk of liquidation, especially in highly volatile markets.

Regulatory Risks:

- Changing regulatory environments and government interventions can impact the legality and functionality of certain cryptocurrencies, exchanges, or trading practices.

Human Error and Hacking:

- Users can make mistakes, such as sending funds to the wrong address. Additionally, the risk of hacking and security breaches is inherent in both centralised and decentralised platforms.

Unpredictable Black Swan Events:

- External events, such as technological vulnerabilities, unexpected market shocks, or global crises, can lead to unpredictable and extreme price movements.

Market Information Risks:

- Cryptocurrency markets can be influenced by misinformation, fake news, or unverified rumours. Traders must exercise caution and verify information before making decisions.

Unstable Regulations:

- The regulatory landscape for cryptocurrencies is evolving. Sudden changes in regulations or legal actions against projects can have a significant impact on the market.

Environmental Concerns:

- Increased attention to the environmental impact of certain cryptocurrencies, especially proof-of-work based ones, can result in negative market sentiment and regulatory scrutiny.

FOMO and FUD:

- Fear of Missing Out (FOMO) and Fear, Uncertainty, and Doubt (FUD) can drive irrational decision-making, contributing to market bubbles and crashes.

While trading any high volatility market (cryptocurrency or traditional stocks) can be profitable, it's crucial to approach it with a clear understanding of the associated risks. Due diligence, risk management strategies, and staying informed about market developments are essential for navigating the challenges of the cryptocurrency landscape.

THE ART OF PORTFOLIO MANAGEMENT

Building and Maintaining a Balanced Portfolio

Portfolio management is the art of balancing risk and return across a diversified investment portfolio. We explore the principles and strategies of effective portfolio management to maximise the growth of your investments once you are reaching higher figures. By understanding asset allocation, diversification, rebalancing, and performance evaluation, you can optimise your portfolio's risk-adjusted returns and achieve long-term financial success.

Asset allocation refers to the strategic distribution of investments across different asset classes, such as stocks, bonds, cryptocurrencies, and cash, within a portfolio. The goal of asset allocation is to create a diversified investment mix that aligns with your financial goals as an investor, risk tolerance, and time horizon. This approach aims to optimise returns while managing risk by reducing the impact of poor performance in any single asset class.

Here's why asset allocation is important in a self-managed portfolio, considering different asset classes:

- ***Risk Management:***

    - Diversification: By spreading investments across various asset classes, the impact of poor performance in one area can be mitigated by potential gains in others. This helps reduce overall portfolio volatility.

- ***Return Optimisation:***

    - Balancing Risk and Return: Different asset classes have varying levels of risk and return potential. Proper asset allocation allows investors to balance their desired level of risk with the potential for returns that align with their financial goals.

- ***Market Conditions***:
    - Adaptability: Asset allocation enables investors to adjust their portfolios based on changing market conditions. For example, in times of economic uncertainty, a more conservative allocation with a higher proportion of bonds or cash might be preferred.
- ***Differing Market Cycles***:
    - Cyclical Trends: Asset classes often perform differently in various stages of economic cycles. A well-structured asset allocation allows investors to capitalise on opportunities in different market environments.
- ***Income and Growth***:
    - Income Generation: Bonds and dividend-paying stocks can provide regular income, while growth-oriented assets like stocks and certain cryptocurrencies offer the potential for capital appreciation.
- ***Liquidity:***
    - Cash Allocation: Maintaining a portion of the portfolio in cash provides liquidity, allowing investors to seize opportunities in rapidly changing markets or meet short-term financial needs.
- ***Long-Term Goals:***
    - Time Horizon Consideration: Asset allocation considers an investor's time horizon. For longer-term goals, a higher allocation to growth assets may be suitable, while shorter-term goals might warrant a more conservative approach.

- ***Risk Tolerance:***
    - Individual Preferences: Asset allocation can be tailored to an investor's risk tolerance. For those with a lower tolerance for risk, a more conservative allocation may be appropriate, while those comfortable with higher risk might favour a more aggressive approach. I prefer higher risk as often it leads to higher reward and faster growth.
- ***Inflation Hedge:***
    - Real Assets: Certain asset classes, like real estate or certain commodities, can act as a hedge against inflation, preserving purchasing power over the long term.
- ***Market Dynamics:***
    - Correlation Management: Understanding the historical and potential future correlations between different asset classes is crucial. Some assets may move in the opposite direction during market fluctuations, providing a counterbalance.

In a self-managed portfolio, you as the investor take on the responsibility of making investment decisions.

The thoughtful allocation of assets becomes paramount, allowing for flexibility and adaptation to changing market conditions while aligning with the investor's unique financial objectives and risk tolerance.

Regularly reviewing and rebalancing the portfolio based on changing market conditions and personal circumstances is a key aspect of effective asset allocation.

Diversification: Spreading Risk for Stability

Diversifying your portfolio and spreading risk across different asset classes is essential for several reasons, contributing to the stability and resilience of your investment strategy. Here's why diversification is a key principle in portfolio management, considering various asset classes like stocks, bonds, cryptocurrencies, and cash:

- ***Risk Reduction:***
    - Market Volatility: Different asset classes react differently to market conditions. For instance, stocks may be volatile, but bonds and cash are generally more stable. Diversifying across assets helps reduce the impact of poor performance in one area, mitigating overall portfolio risk.
- ***Preservation of Capital:***
    - Market Downturns: During economic downturns, certain asset classes may experience losses while others remain relatively stable. Diversification aims to preserve capital by minimising the overall impact of market downturns on the portfolio.
- ***Steady Returns:***
    - Risk-Adjusted Returns: Diversification allows investors to achieve a more stable, risk-adjusted return over time. While some assets may experience fluctuations, the overall portfolio performance is less likely to be subject to extreme highs and lows. This type of portfolio also ensures you won't feel FOMO as something is usually moving.

- ***Cyclical Adaptation:***
    - Economic Cycles: Different asset classes tend to perform well in various economic cycles. Diversification enables you to adapt your portfolio to changing economic conditions, benefiting from opportunities in different market environments.
- ***Income Generation:***
    - Combining Income and Growth: Combining assets that generate income (e.g., bonds) with those that offer potential growth (e.g., stocks) provides a balanced approach. This can contribute to consistent returns and meet both short-term income needs and long-term growth objectives.
- ***Liquidity Management:***
    - Cash Position: Maintaining a portion of your portfolio in cash provides liquidity. This ensures you have readily available funds to take advantage of investment opportunities or cover unexpected expenses.
- ***Asset Correlation:***
    - Correlation Management: Assets within the same class often exhibit correlation, meaning they move in similar directions. Diversification involves selecting assets with lower correlations, reducing the portfolio's vulnerability to simultaneous declines.
- ***Inflation Hedge:***
    - Real Assets: Investing in real assets like real estate or commodities can act as a hedge against inflation. Diversification with these assets helps protect your portfolio's purchasing power over the long term.

- ***Risk Tolerance Alignment:***
    - Personalised Approach: Diversification allows you to tailor your portfolio to your risk tolerance. A well-diversified portfolio can be customised to align with your comfort level for risk, ensuring a balance between potential returns and acceptable volatility.
- ***Behavioural Finance Considerations:***
    - Emotional Stability: Diversification can contribute to emotional stability during market turbulence. A well-diversified portfolio may experience less severe fluctuations, reducing the emotional stress associated with investing.
- ***Regulatory and Macro-Economic Factors:***
    - Global Events: Diversification across different geographic regions and industries helps mitigate risks associated with regulatory changes, geopolitical events, and economic fluctuations that may impact specific sectors.

Diversifying your portfolio across various asset classes is a fundamental strategy to manage risk, enhance stability, and optimise returns. It's a sensible approach to building a resilient investment portfolio that can weather different market conditions, align with your financial goals, and risk tolerance.

Diversification not only safeguards your investments against the unpredictable nature of financial markets but also acts as a powerful antidote to the fear of missing out (FOMO). By spreading your investments across different opportunities, you reduce the urge to chase short-term trends or succumb to emotional decision-making, fostering a disciplined and rational investment approach. This disciplined strategy, grounded in the principles of diversification, contributes to long-term financial success and a more secure financial future. This is essentially what we are aiming for.

Rebalancing: Maintaining Portfolio Alignment

Rebalancing is the process of periodically adjusting your portfolio's asset allocation to maintain your desired risk and return profile. This section discusses the importance of rebalancing and the triggers for rebalancing, such as changes in asset class performance or deviations from target allocations.

We also look at techniques for rebalancing your portfolio effectively, including threshold-based and calendar-based approaches. Understand the potential benefits of disciplined rebalancing in optimising long-term returns once we reached our million-dollar goal.

Rebalancing your portfolio is a critical aspect of maintaining a diversified investment strategy across various asset classes, including stocks, bonds, cryptocurrencies, and cash. Regularly reviewing and adjusting the allocation of assets helps ensure that your portfolio stays aligned with your financial goals, risk tolerance, and the ever-changing market conditions. Here's a guide on how to rebalance and maintain your portfolio:

- ***Establish a Target Asset Allocation:***
    - Begin by defining your target allocation for each asset class based on your financial goals, risk tolerance, and investment time horizon. This allocation serves as a roadmap for your portfolio.
- ***Set Rebalancing Thresholds:***
    - Determine acceptable ranges or thresholds for each asset class. For example, if your target allocation for stocks is 60%, you may set a threshold of 5%, meaning you would rebalance if the stock allocation deviated by more than 5 percentage points from the target.

- ***Regularly Monitor Your Portfolio:***
    - Schedule periodic reviews of your portfolio, such as quarterly or annually. Assess the current allocation of each asset class and compare it to your target allocation.
- ***Identify Deviations:***
    - Identify any significant deviations from your target allocation. If a particular asset class has drifted beyond the predetermined threshold, it may be time to rebalance.
- ***Rebalance Method:***
    - Decide on a method for rebalancing. There are two primary approaches:
    - Calendar-Based: Rebalance at regular intervals, such as annually or semi-annually.
    - Threshold-Based: Rebalance when the actual allocation deviates beyond a predetermined threshold.
- ***Sell High, Buy Low:***
    - When rebalancing involves selling assets that have performed well (and may be overallocated) and buying assets that are under allocated, you are essentially adhering to the principle of "selling high and buying low."
- ***Tax Considerations:***
    - Be mindful of tax implications when rebalancing, especially in taxable accounts. Consider selling assets that may result in minimal capital gains or, if possible, utilise tax-loss harvesting strategies.

- ***Review and Adjust the Plan:***
    - Periodically review your investment plan, considering any changes in your financial situation, goals, or market conditions. Adjust your target allocation if necessary to reflect evolving circumstances.
- ***Automate the Process:***
    - Consider using automated tools or investment platforms that offer automatic rebalancing features. These tools can help streamline the process and ensure timely adjustments.
- ***Document Decisions:***
    - Keep a record of your rebalancing decisions, including the reasons behind each adjustment. This documentation can provide insights into your investment strategy and serve as a reference for future adjustments.
- ***Stay Informed:***
    - Stay informed about market trends, economic conditions, and developments in each asset class. This knowledge can guide your rebalancing decisions and help you make informed adjustments.
- ***Seek Professional Advice*:**
    - If you find rebalancing challenging or have a complex financial situation, consider seeking advice from a financial advisor. A professional can provide personalised guidance based on your unique circumstances.

Rebalancing is an essential process that ensures your portfolio remains in line with your investment objectives. It's a proactive strategy that helps you adapt to changing market conditions and maintain a disciplined approach to investing. Regularly reviewing and adjusting your portfolio can contribute to long-term financial success.

"The best time to plant a tree was 20 years ago. The second-best time is now."

Chinese Proverb.

Three "Hypothetical" Examples of Portfolios

Three hypothetical examples of portfolios form Low to higher risk, that may need rebalancing due to different triggers:

Example 1: Threshold Deviation

- Initial Target Allocation:
    - Stocks: 60%
    - Bonds: 30%
    - Crypto: 5%
    - Cash: 5%
- Current Allocation:
    - Stocks: 65%
    - Bonds: 25%
    - Crypto: 7%
    - Cash: 3%
- Trigger for Rebalancing:
    - The actual allocation of stocks has exceeded the threshold of 5% above the target allocation. Rebalancing is triggered to bring the portfolio back to the desired balance.

Example 2: Time-Based Rebalancing

- Initial Target Allocation:
    - Stocks: 50%
    - Bonds: 40%
    - Crypto: 5%
    - Cash: 5%
- Current Allocation:
    - Stocks: 48%
    - Bonds: 42%
    - Crypto: 6%
    - Cash: 4%
- Trigger for Rebalancing:
    - The investor follows a semi-annual rebalancing schedule, and it's time for the routine review. The portfolio is adjusted based on any deviations from the target allocation.

Example 3: High-Risk Profile with Increased Crypto Allocation

- Initial Target Allocation:
    - Stocks: 40%
    - Bonds: 30%
    - Crypto: 20%
    - Cash: 10%
- Current Allocation:
    - Stocks: 35%
    - Bonds: 25%
    - Crypto: 50%
    - Cash: 5%
- Trigger for Rebalancing:
    - The cryptocurrency market has outperformed other asset classes, leading to an overallocation in crypto. Given the high-risk profile and the deviation from the target allocation, the investor decides to rebalance to maintain the desired risk exposure and bring the portfolio back to the original target allocation.

These examples illustrate various scenarios where rebalancing might be necessary. Investors can use a combination of threshold-based triggers, periodic reviews, and adjustments based on market conditions to ensure their portfolios stay in line with their financial goals and risk tolerance. The specific triggers for rebalancing will depend on the individual investor's strategy and preferences.

"Your time is limited, so don't waste it living someone else's life."

Steve Jobs

SUSTAINING MOMENTUM TO ONE MILLION

We all know the saying "it's not going to be easy, but it will be worth it"... And to sustain momentum when trading from one thousand dollars to the life-changing amount of one million, will not be without challenges and obstacles. In this chapter, we explore the importance of building resilience and overcoming setbacks to retain momentum.

From handling losses to adapting to changing market conditions and maintaining discipline, I will equip you with the tools and strategies to navigate through adversity and stay focused on your ultimate goal. By building resilience and learning from challenges, you can overcome setbacks and continue moving forward.

Losses are Normal

Yes, that is correct, losses are normal and are an intrinsic and inescapable facet of trading. Wouldn't it be nice if you could win every trade and become an instant millionaire? But rather than viewing losses through a lens of defeat, it is imperative to perceive losses as invaluable learning opportunities.

The unpredictable nature of financial markets ensures that setbacks will occur, regardless of one's expertise or strategy. Acknowledging this inherent reality is the first step towards cultivating a resilient and adaptive mindset. Every loss is a potential source of insight, offering the chance to scrutinise decisions, reassess risk management strategies, and refine trading approaches. Embracing losses not only fosters a healthier psychological outlook but also contributes to the continuous evolution and improvement of one's trading skills. The ability to learn from losses becomes an indispensable tool for traders seeking long-term success.

Let's consider an example of a trader implementing a 5% stop loss on a $1,000 Bitcoin trade. If the trader sets a 5% stop loss, it means that if the price of Bitcoin falls by 5% from the entry point, the trade will automatically be exited to limit potential losses.

If the trader enters the market with a $1,000 investment and the price of Bitcoin subsequently drops by 5%, the stop loss would trigger, and the trade would be closed. In this case, the loss incurred would be 5% of $1,000, which is $50. Thus, the trader would exit the trade with $950 remaining from the initial $1,000 investment.

On thc other hand, if a trader does not implement a stop loss and the price of Bitcoin experiences a significant decline, the potential loss becomes unlimited. For instance, if the value of the $1,000 trade drops by 10%, 20%, or more without a stop loss in place, the trader could face a substantial loss without any automatic mechanism to limit the damage. This underscores the importance of risk management strategies, such as stop losses, to safeguard capital and manage potential downsides while trading.

Adapting to Changing Market Conditions

Navigating changed conditions in any trading market is an intrinsic part of the learning journey. Markets are subject to fluctuations influenced by economic shifts, geopolitical events, or technological advancements.

If we think back to the chapter on impermanence, we know nothing stays the same and traders especially must possess a keen awareness of changing conditions to adjust their strategies effectively. Whether it be sudden market volatility, regulatory developments, or macroeconomic shifts, adaptability is crucial.

Successful traders embrace changed conditions as opportunities to reassess risk, fine-tune their approaches, and capitalise on emerging trends. In the face of evolving market dynamics, those who can swiftly recalibrate their trading strategies are better positioned to mitigate risks and capitalise on new opportunities, embodying the resilience necessary for sustained success.

Overcoming Psychological and Emotional Challenges

An integral aspect of personal growth and resilience is overcoming psychological and emotional challenges. In various facets of life, be it in relationships, career pursuits, or personal endeavours, we often encounter psychological and emotional hurdles that can impede progress. Confronting and surmounting these challenges requires a combination of self-awareness, emotional intelligence, and coping strategies.

Developing a resilient mindset involves acknowledging and understanding your own emotions, whether it be fear, self-doubt, or anxiety, and actively working towards managing and transforming them. Seeking support from other traders, or professional mentors can provide valuable perspectives and assistance in navigating emotional obstacles. Embracing challenges as opportunities for growth rather than insurmountable barriers is a powerful mindset shift that fosters resilience.

Ultimately, the journey of overcoming psychological and emotional challenges is a transformative process that builds inner strength, adaptability, and a greater capacity for facing life's uncertainties with courage and determination.

Staying Disciplined and Focused

Staying disciplined and focused is essential for sustaining momentum while trading. These attributes form the foundations of a successful trading plan, acting as the guiding principles that navigate the unpredictable waves of the financial markets.

Discipline involves adhering to predetermined strategies, risk management protocols, and maintaining emotional composure even in the face of market volatility. It's the unwavering commitment to a set course of action that prevents impulsive decision-making and helps you weather inevitable fluctuations.

Concurrently, focus directs attention to critical market indicators, timely information, and the overarching goals of a trading strategy. In the midst of rapidly changing conditions, maintaining focus ensures that traders can swiftly adapt to emerging trends and capitalise on opportunities. Together, discipline and focus serve to fortify a trader's resilience, enhancing the likelihood of making informed decisions and achieving long-term success.

Learning from Mistakes and Continuous Improvement

Engaging in continuous improvement is synonymous with learning from mistakes, and a pivotal tool in this process is the trading journal. Documenting emotions, thoughts, and reactions to market conditions provides a tangible record of your trading journey, offering invaluable insights into decision-making processes.

A trading journal becomes a personalised record of experiences, enabling traders to conduct post-trade analyses that go beyond the mere financial outcomes. By scrutinising entries, traders can identify patterns of behaviour, emotional triggers, and cognitive biases that may be hindering progress.

This introspective approach facilitates a deeper understanding of individual strengths and weaknesses, fostering a more disciplined and resilient mindset. The ability to recognise and address recurring mistakes will empower you to implement corrective actions, refining strategies, and enhancing overall performance.

In essence, a well-maintained trading journal becomes a compass for continuous improvement, guiding you toward a more informed and adaptive approach to placing your trades.

Seeking Support and Mentorship

Seeking support from experienced traders and mentors is a strategic move that can significantly accelerate growth on your trading journey. Aligning with a mentor or group that shares your trading style and goals is crucial for personalised growth and deeper understanding.

To find the right mentor, explore online forums, social media groups, or attend trading events where experienced professionals share insights. Platforms like **Gettingstartedincrypto.com** offer an excellent avenue for connecting with like-minded traders and mentors who can provide invaluable perspectives.

Networking within these communities not only expands your knowledge base but also exposes you to diverse strategies and approaches. Leverage the wisdom and experience of those who have successfully navigated the challenges of the financial markets, as learning from their wins and losses can be a shortcut to achieving your own financial goals. The collective knowledge shared within supportive communities, and I place an emphasis on supportive, can be a powerful catalyst for refining your skills and attaining your financial goals.

Celebrating Milestones and Staying Motivated

Last but not least, celebrating milestones along the way is a way of maintaining motivation to one million dollars.

Celebrating milestones is not only a gratifying endeavour but also a crucial element in maintaining momentum. You choose the milestones, whether they involve reaching a specific profit target, successfully implementing a new trading strategy, or overcoming a challenging market phase, serve as markers of progress.

Taking the time to acknowledge and celebrate these achievements, no matter how small, provides a psychological boost and reinforces a positive mindset. This celebration becomes a fuel for motivation, propelling you forward with renewed determination. Whether it's treating yourself to a small reward, reflecting on lessons learned, or sharing successes within a trading community, these moments of recognition play a pivotal role in sustaining the enthusiasm needed to navigate the complexities of the financial markets.

"I think I can. I think I can. I think I can.

I know I can."

Watty Piper, The Little Engine That Could.

THE NEXT LEVEL SCALING UP YOUR WEALTH

READ THIS CHAPTER WHEN YOU ARE CLOSE TO ACHIEVING 1 MILLION DOLLARS!

Congratulations! YOU ARE HERE!
I'm so proud you are reading this, now what?

You've successfully turned your initial thousand dollars into a substantial sum of (Insert Dr. Evil pinkie finger) ONE MILLION DOLLARS! In this final chapter for Section 2, we explore the exciting realm of scaling up your wealth and taking your financial journey to the next level. From asset allocation and diversification to legacy planning and philanthropy, we delve into strategies that can help you preserve and grow your wealth for the long term. By leveraging your newfound financial success, you can create a lasting impact and secure a prosperous future for yourself and generations to come.

Advanced Asset Allocation Strategies

Strategies are crucial for managing risk and optimising returns as you navigate past one million dollars attained through trading. These strategies go beyond the basic allocation of assets and delve into sophisticated approaches that consider market dynamics, economic conditions, and individual risk tolerance. Here are three real-world examples highlighting the importance of advanced asset allocation:

Market Conditions and Dynamic Asset Allocation:

In response to changing market conditions, advanced asset allocation involves adjusting your portfolio to capitalise on opportunities and mitigate risks. For instance, during economic downturns, reallocating funds to defensive assets like bonds or gold can provide a hedge against market volatility. Conversely, in bullish markets, a more aggressive allocation towards cryptocurrency and equities may maximise returns.

Factor-Based Investing for Enhanced Diversification:

Factor-based investing is an advanced strategy that involves allocating assets based on specific factors such as value, momentum, or high/low volatility. For example, a portfolio might be constructed with a tilt towards value stocks during periods of economic recovery, aiming to capture potential undervalued opportunities. Buying cryptocurrencies at approximately the 3rd year of the 4 year cycle would see these close to the bottom of their patterns.

Taking a DCA -Dollar Cost Averaging approach over six to 12 months prior to a Bitcoin Halving can yield significant advantages for investors. This strategy involves spreading the purchase of cryptocurrencies over regular intervals, typically 6 to 12 months before a Bitcoin Halving event.

The rationale behind this approach is rooted in historical market patterns, specifically the four-year cycle associated with Bitcoin Halving. By buying cryptocurrencies around the third year of this cycle, investors position themselves close to the bottom of the market patterns, potentially capitalising on lower prices.

Dollar Cost Averaging (DCA) further enhances this strategy by mitigating the impact of short-term market fluctuations. Instead of attempting to time the market perfectly, DCA involves investing a fixed amount at regular intervals, regardless of the asset's price. This systematic approach helps smooth out the impact of market volatility, providing investors with a cost-effective average entry point.

The 6 to 12 months leading up to a Bitcoin Halving, characterised by historical bullish trends, creates an opportune environment for DCA. This method not only allows investors to benefit from potential price appreciation during the halving event but also reduces the risk associated with making significant investments at a single point in time. In essence, combining the timing advantage of the four-year cycle with the disciplined approach of Dollar Cost Averaging can yield favourable outcomes in the cryptocurrency market.

Alternative Investments for Risk Mitigation

Including alternative investments, such as private equity or real estate, in your asset allocation can enhance diversification and reduce correlation with traditional asset classes. For instance, allocating a portion of the portfolio to real estate investment trusts (REITs) can provide exposure to the real estate market while offering potential for income and capital appreciation.

Moreover, diversifying your investment portfolio can extend beyond traditional financial instruments into tangible assets like real estate.

Investment rental properties, when strategically acquired and managed, can offer a unique avenue for wealth accumulation. The concept of negative gearing, commonly employed in real estate, involves borrowing funds to invest in a property with the expectation that the income generated from the property (rental income) will be less than the costs associated with owning and managing it (interest on the loan, maintenance, etc.). This creates a 'negative' cash flow, which, when leveraged against taxable income, may result in potential tax benefits for the investor.

Investment rental properties, coupled with negative gearing, can provide dual benefits. First, they offer the potential for long-term capital appreciation as property values increase over time. A hedge against inflation. Second, the tax advantages associated with negative gearing can contribute to optimising overall investment returns. However, it's crucial to approach real estate investment with careful consideration of market conditions, location, and individual financial goals.

Including such alternative investments in your overall asset allocation strategy adds another layer of diversification, reducing the correlation with more traditional assets like stocks and bonds, and higher risk assets like cryptocurrency. This multifaceted approach not only enhances the resilience of your portfolio against market fluctuations but also broadens the scope for potential returns, offering a well-rounded and robust investment strategy.

In summary, advanced asset allocation strategies empower you to navigate diverse market scenarios, strategically allocate resources, and maximise the potential for sustained wealth growth. These strategies reflect a nuanced understanding of financial markets and contribute to a well-rounded and adaptive investment approach as you manage and grow your one-million-dollar portfolio.

Legacy Planning and Wealth Preservation

Building substantial wealth necessitates thoughtful legacy planning. Exploring effective strategies to preserve and transfer your assets to future generations while minimising tax implications is a strategic imperative. A brief overview into the intricacies of estate planning, trusts, and other tools that ensure your financial legacy endures reveals the importance of meticulous preparation in this process.

Generational wealth is not just made; it is preserved through intentional actions and prudent decisions.

Legacy planning and wealth preservation become paramount after reaching your trading goals for several crucial reasons. First and foremost, having accumulated substantial wealth through trading signifies a significant achievement, and ensuring its longevity is a responsible and strategic consideration. Legacy planning involves structuring your assets in a way that allows for the smooth transition of wealth to future generations or charitable causes. This ensures that your hard-earned financial success can continue to benefit your family or contribute to meaningful causes even after you're no longer actively managing your wealth.

Wealth preservation is equally essential to safeguard your financial legacy from potential threats such as taxes, economic downturns, or unforeseen circumstances. Implementing effective wealth preservation strategies can mitigate tax liabilities, protect assets from market volatility, and provide a sustainable framework for the continued growth of your wealth.

Moreover, legacy planning involves creating a comprehensive estate plan, including wills, trusts, and other legal mechanisms, to clearly outline your wishes and ensure a smooth transfer of assets. This not only minimises potential conflicts among beneficiaries but also helps in efficiently managing the distribution of your estate. Remember that the legacy you leave behind is a testament to your foresight and commitment to securing the financial well-being of generations to come.

International Investing and Global Opportunities

International investing and global opportunities are crucial components of a well-rounded investment strategy for several reasons. Firstly, diversifying your investment portfolio across different geographical regions allows you to tap into a broader spectrum of economic conditions and market cycles. This diversification can help mitigate risks associated with localised economic downturns, political instability, or currency fluctuations that may impact a single market.

Furthermore, exposure to international markets provides investors with access to industries and sectors that might not be prevalent in their domestic market. This can lead to enhanced opportunities for growth and profit, as different regions may experience varying economic trends and technological advancements.

Here are a few examples illustrating the importance of international investing:

Emerging Market Growth

- Investing in emerging markets such as those in Southeast Asia, Latin America, or Africa can offer significant growth potential. These markets often experience rapid economic expansion, providing opportunities for investors to capitalise on the development of new industries and consumer markets.

Global Technology Trends

- Technological innovations often emerge from various corners of the globe. By investing globally, you can gain exposure to leading technology companies that may not be available in your home market. For example, investing in Asian tech giants like Alibaba (China) or Samsung (South Korea) can diversify your technology holdings. New technology advances like Driverless cars and Artificial Intelligence are transforming industries and creating investment opportunities that extend beyond geographical borders.

- By investing globally, you position yourself to capitalise on cutting-edge developments in sectors such as autonomous transportation and artificial intelligence. Companies at the forefront of these technological breakthroughs, whether they're based in Silicon Valley, European tech hubs, or emerging markets like Japan, provide investors with a chance to participate in the revolutionary changes shaping the future.

- As innovations continue to evolve on a global scale, maintaining a diversified portfolio with exposure to international tech leaders ensures that you stay at the forefront of transformative advancements, fostering resilience and potential growth in your investment strategy.

Currency Diversification

Holding assets in different currencies including cryptocurrencies, can act as a hedge against currency risk. For instance, if your domestic currency depreciates, investments in regions with appreciating currencies can help offset potential losses.

Global Healthcare Opportunity

- Healthcare innovations and advancements are not confined to a single region. Investing in pharmaceutical companies, biotech firms, or healthcare technology on a global scale allows you to participate in breakthroughs and advancements worldwide.

In essence, international investing provides a broader scope for portfolio diversification, risk mitigation, and exposure to a multitude of investment opportunities that can contribute to a well-balanced and resilient investment strategy.

However, it's crucial to conduct thorough research, stay informed about global economic conditions, and consider consulting with financial professionals when venturing into international markets.

Wealth Management and Financial Advisory Services

And this brings us to wealth management and financial advisory services. Selecting reputable professionals to provide personalised guidance and comprehensive financial planning is crucial for achieving long-term financial goals for several key reasons. These professionals, often financial advisors, or wealth managers, bring expertise and experience to the table, offering tailored strategies that align with individual financial objectives.

Why It's Important

Expertise and Knowledge - Reputable professionals possess in-depth knowledge of financial markets, investment instruments, tax regulations, and estate planning. This expertise allows them to navigate complex financial landscapes, staying abreast of market trends and providing clients with informed advice.

Personalised Guidance - Every individual's financial situation is unique. Reputable professionals take the time to understand clients' specific circumstances, goals, risk tolerance, and time horizons. This personalised approach ensures that financial strategies are customised to meet individual needs, maximising the likelihood of success.

Comprehensive Financial Planning - Reputable professionals go beyond singular investment advice. They engage in comprehensive financial planning that considers various aspects, including retirement planning, tax optimisation, risk management, and estate planning. This holistic approach creates a well-rounded strategy that addresses diverse financial needs.

Risk Management and Mitigation - Financial professionals assess and manage risks associated with investments, helping clients build portfolios that align with their risk tolerance. This proactive risk management is vital for protecting wealth and ensuring financial stability, especially during volatile market conditions.

Long-Term Goal Achievement -Successful financial planning is about more than short-term gains; it's about achieving long-term financial goals. Reputable professionals work with clients to set realistic objectives, create actionable plans, and adjust strategies over time as circumstances change.

Overview of Their Role

Financial professionals, whether financial advisors or wealth managers, play a multifaceted role:

Assessment and Analysis - They assess a client's current financial situation, including income, expenses, assets, and liabilities, to gain a comprehensive understanding of their financial landscape.

Goal Setting -Professionals work with clients to define short-term and long-term financial goals, considering factors like retirement, education funding, wealth preservation, and legacy planning.

Strategic Planning - Based on the assessment and goals, they develop a strategic financial plan that may include investment strategies, tax planning, risk management, and estate planning.

Implementation - Once the plan is agreed upon, professionals assist in implementing the recommended strategies, whether it involves selecting investments, optimising tax structures, or setting up estate planning instruments.

Monitoring and Adjusting - Regular monitoring of the financial plan ensures that it remains aligned with the client's evolving circumstances. Adjustments are made as needed to adapt to changing goals, market conditions, or life events.

In summary, selecting reputable financial professionals is essential for receiving expert guidance tailored to individual needs, creating comprehensive financial plans, and ultimately, working towards the achievement of long-term financial goals.

Continuing Education and Lifelong Learning

Continuing education and lifelong learning are essential components of personal and professional development, offering individuals the opportunity to expand their knowledge, skills, and perspectives throughout their lives. Staying intellectually curious and committed to learning allows you to remain relevant and adaptable in their careers and personal pursuits. Lifelong learning goes beyond traditional academic settings; it encompasses a proactive and self-directed approach to acquiring new information and refining existing skills.

Why not invest in yourself?

One of the primary benefits of continuing education is the enhancement of career prospects. In emerging fields where technology and industry trends evolve rapidly, staying abreast of the latest developments through ongoing learning ensures that professionals remain competitive and capable of contributing meaningfully to their workplaces. Lifelong learning can also lead to increased job satisfaction, as individuals engage with new ideas, methodologies, and challenges, fostering a sense of accomplishment and fulfilment in their roles.

Beyond professional growth, the advantages of continuous learning extend to personal enrichment. It cultivates a curious and open-minded mindset, encouraging individuals to explore diverse topics and perspectives. This intellectual stimulation not only broadens your understanding of the world but also enhances critical thinking and problem-solving skills. Lifelong learners often report improved overall well-being, as the pursuit of knowledge fosters a sense of purpose, resilience, and adaptability, contributing to a more satisfying and fulfilling life. Embracing continuing education as a lifelong habit is an investment in personal growth, intellectual vitality, and a more enriching and meaningful existence.

If you want to dive deeper into finance, you can explore resources, courses, and networks that can enhance your financial acumen and keep you informed about the latest trends and opportunities.

Enjoying the Fruits of Your Success

Finally, savour the fruits of your success with a sense of fulfilment and accomplishment. After navigating the intricacies of wealth accumulation and strategic financial planning, it's crucial to take moments to appreciate the milestones achieved. Indulge in the lifestyle you've diligently worked towards, allowing yourself the pleasures and luxuries that align with your aspirations.

Whether it's exploring exotic destinations, Tahiti darling? Or pursuing enriching hobbies, maybe that old car you've always wanted to restore or contributing to meaningful philanthropic causes, donating time and money to endangered Turtles? This phase is about relishing the rewards of your hard work.

Emphasising the importance of balance is key as you open a new chapter of your financial and life journey. Achieving equilibrium between indulgence and responsibility ensures the sustainability of your prosperity. By striking this balance, you not only preserve your wealth but also cultivate a sense of well-being and contentment.

Remember, wealth is not just about monetary value; it's about creating a life that aligns with your values and brings joy.
Congratulations on reaching this pinnacle in your financial journey, and may this chapter be marked by both the enjoyment of success and the cultivation of a harmonious and fulfilling life.

"Luck is preparation meeting opportunity."

Oprah Winfrey

SECTION 3

TECHNICAL ANALYSIS

TRADE LIKE LISA -BE LIKE LISA

SECTION 4 - CHAPTER BREAKDOWN

Technical Analysis: Be Like Lisa - Trade Like Lisa

- Supply and Demand Basics
- Importance in Trading Crypto and Stocks
- Why is Market Psychology Important?
- Understanding historical price action and why it repeats

Elliott Wave Theory and Historical Price Action

- Theory of Elliott Wave
    - Wave Patterns
    - Fibonacci Ratios
    - Psychological Phases
    - Fractals
- Elliott Wave Simplified
- Motive Wave Rules
- Wave Extensions
- Corrective Waves
- ZigZag
- Flat
- Triangle
- Combination
- Fibonacci Relationships
- Retracements
- Multiples
- Additional Resources

LISANACCI – FIBONACCI "Lisa Style"

- Fibonacci in Trading
- Understanding Fibonacci Levels
- Fibonacci Retracements in Technical Analysis
- Understanding Fibonacci Ratios
- Applying Fibonacci Ratios
- Applying Fibonacci Ratios in Trading
- Drawing Fibonacci Retracements
    - Fibonacci Retracement
    - Fibonacci Extensions
- LISANACCI Method
- Application of LISANACCI with Fibonacci
    1. Example 1
    2. Example 2
    3. Example 3

"I am the master of my fate; I am the captain of my soul."

William Ernest Henley

TECHNICAL ANALYSIS: BE LIKE LISA – TRADE LIKE LISA

I'm often asked to breakdown my "Tools of the Trade" so to speak, so people can trade like I do and achieve or try to achieve similar results, this is how my trading community GettingStartedinCrypto.com was formed, from the huge demand on social media to break it all down, and now the theories are contained in this book.

I'm a huge fan and proponent of TA and FA – technical analysis and fundamental analysis, often the fundamentals are already reflected in the chart before events happen. But with that said, it's important to note that while technical analysis can be a valuable tool, it's not foolproof, and no strategy guarantees success in the financial markets.

Traders often combine technical analysis with other forms of analysis, such as fundamental analysis and risk management, to make well-rounded and informed trading decisions. Knowledge is always power when it comes to trading and investing.

Principles of Technical Analysis

This section introduces the fundamental principles of technical analysis. We explore the concepts of supply and demand, market psychology, and the notion that historical price action repeats itself. Gain an understanding of the underlying assumptions and principles that form the basis of technical analysis.

What is Supply and Demand?

Supply and demand are fundamental economic concepts that play a crucial role in determining the prices of goods and assets, including cryptocurrencies and stocks. Here's an overview of these concepts and their importance in trading.

Supply and Demand Basics:

Supply:

- Definition: Supply refers to the quantity of a good or asset that producers are willing to offer for sale at different prices during a specific period.
- Law of Supply: Generally, as the price of a good or asset increases, the quantity supplied also increases, assuming all other factors remain constant. Conversely, as the price decreases, the quantity supplied tends to decrease.

Demand:

- Definition: Demand represents the quantity of a good or asset that consumers are willing to buy at different prices during a specific period.
- Law of Demand: Generally, as the price of a good or asset decreases, the quantity demanded increases, assuming all other factors remain constant. Conversely, as the price increases, the quantity demanded tends to decrease.

Importance in Trading Crypto and Stocks:

Price Determination:

- The intersection of supply and demand curves determines the equilibrium price of an asset. In financial markets, this equilibrium is reflected in the market price of a cryptocurrency or stock.

Trend Identification:

- Changes in supply and demand dynamics can help traders identify trends. For example, if demand outstrips supply, prices may rise, indicating a bullish trend. Conversely, if supply exceeds demand, prices may fall, indicating a bearish trend.

Support and Resistance Levels:

- Supply and demand zones often create support and resistance levels on price charts. These levels are areas where buying or selling interest has historically been strong. Traders use these zones to make decisions about entry, exit, and stop-loss points.

Volume Analysis:

- Volume, which represents the number of shares or units traded, is often used as an indicator of changes in supply and demand. An increase in volume during an uptrend may indicate strong buying interest, while increased volume during a downtrend may suggest strong selling pressure.

Market Sentiment:

- Supply and demand dynamics are closely tied to market sentiment. Understanding whether the market is driven by bullish or bearish sentiment can help traders anticipate potential price movements.

Impact on Liquidity:

- High liquidity, resulting from balanced supply and demand, can lead to smoother price movements and narrower bid-ask spreads. Low liquidity, caused by imbalances, can result in more volatile and unpredictable price swings.

Macro-Economic Factors:

- Changes in economic conditions, regulatory developments, or technological advancements can influence both supply and demand for cryptocurrencies and stocks. Traders need to stay informed about these factors to anticipate shifts in market dynamics.

Understanding supply and demand dynamics is essential for traders who aim to make informed decisions based on market conditions. Technical analysis tools, such as support and resistance lines, trendlines, and volume indicators, can be used to assess these dynamics on price charts and guide trading strategies.

Why is Market Psychology Important?

Market psychology refers to the collective emotions, attitudes, and perceptions of market participants that influence buying and selling decisions in financial markets. Understanding market psychology is crucial for traders because it helps them anticipate and react to the emotional swings and behavioural patterns of other market participants. Market psychology can be a significant driver of price movements in both cryptocurrency and stock markets. Here are some key aspects of market psychology and its importance in trading:

- *Fear and Greed*:
    - Market participants often oscillate between fear and greed. During periods of fear, such as market selloffs, investors may panic and sell assets at lower prices. Conversely, during periods of greed, such as strong bullish trends, investors may become overly optimistic and buy assets at higher prices. In cryptocurrency, the FEAR & GREED index is the perfect tool for monitoring these fluctuations.

- *Herd Mentality*:
    - Many traders tend to follow the crowd, especially during times of heightened volatility or uncertainty. This herd mentality can lead to exaggerated price movements as traders rush to buy or sell based on the actions of others.
- *Overreaction and Underreaction*:
    - Market participants often overreact or underreact to news, events, or price movements. Overreaction can lead to panic selling or buying, creating opportunities for contrarian traders. Underreaction may result in slower price adjustments to latest information.
- *Confirmation Bias*:
    - Traders may seek information that confirms their existing beliefs or biases, leading to selective attention and interpretation of news. This bias can influence trading decisions and contribute to the persistence of trends.

FOMO (Fear of Missing Out):

- FOMO occurs when traders feel the pressure to enter a trade or investment because they fear missing potential profits. This psychological phenomenon can drive rapid price increases as more participants join the buying frenzy.

- *Panic and Capitulation*:
    - Extreme market downturns can trigger panic selling, where investors rush to exit positions to limit losses. This can lead to a state of capitulation, where selling reaches a climax, often signalling a potential reversal. This is often the best time to buy.

- *Sentiment Indicators*:
    - Various sentiment indicators, such as the Fear and Greed Index, sentiment surveys, and social media sentiment analysis, are used to gauge the overall mood of the market. Traders use these indicators to assess whether sentiment is excessively bullish or bearish.
- *Contrarian Opportunities*:
    - Understanding market psychology allows contrarian traders to identify opportunities when the crowd's behaviour seems irrational. Contrarians may go against prevailing trends when they believe that market sentiment is too extreme.
- *Behavioural Finance*:
    - Behavioural finance explores how psychological factors impact financial decision-making. Traders who are aware of common behavioural biases, such as loss aversion and recency bias, can make more rational and disciplined decisions.

Market psychology plays a crucial role in the ebb and flow of financial markets. Traders who incorporate an understanding of market psychology into their analysis can better navigate the emotional highs and lows of the market and make more informed decisions. It's important to complement technical and fundamental analysis with an awareness of the psychological factors driving market movements.

Understanding historical price action and why it repeats.

The idea that historical price action repeats itself is grounded in the observation that market participants often exhibit similar patterns of behaviour in response to similar circumstances over time. While not an absolute rule, the concept is based on the belief that certain market patterns and trends tend to recur due to consistent human reactions to economic and financial conditions. There are several reasons why historical price action may repeat:

- *Human Behaviour*:
    - Markets are influenced by the collective actions of individuals, and human behaviour tends to repeat patterns. Emotions such as fear and greed can drive market participants to make similar decisions in comparable situations.
- *Market Participants' Memory*:
    - Traders and investors may remember past price patterns and reactions, influencing their current decisions. If a particular pattern led to a successful trade in the past, traders may be more inclined to use the same strategy when they see a similar setup. Pattern memory is often reflected in the same stocks and cryptos as traders have their favourites.
- *Market Psychology*:
    - Behavioural patterns, such as trend-following or trend-reversal behaviours, can become ingrained in the collective psyche of market participants. As a result, these patterns may repeat as traders respond to market events in a consistent manner.

- *Market Structure*:
    - Certain market structures, such as support and resistance levels, can act as psychological barriers. When an asset approaches a historical support or resistance level, traders may react in a similar way to how they did in the past.

"The biggest risk is not taking a risk.

In a world that's changing really quickly, the only strategy that is guaranteed to fail is not taking risks."

Mark Zuckerberg

ELLIOTT WAVE & HISTROIAL PRICE ACTION

Elliott Wave Theory is a technical analysis approach that suggests that financial markets move in repetitive patterns, reflecting the natural order of human psychology and crowd behaviour. The theory was developed by Ralph Nelson Elliott in the 1930s and is based on the idea that market movements follow a sequence of waves, both impulsive and corrective, which are related to Fibonacci ratios.

I've been working with this theory in my trading for quite some time and am a huge believer in the benefits of fully understanding how the trading theory works. When a thorough understanding is applied to technical analysis, it maximises accuracy and what I like to call "the edge."

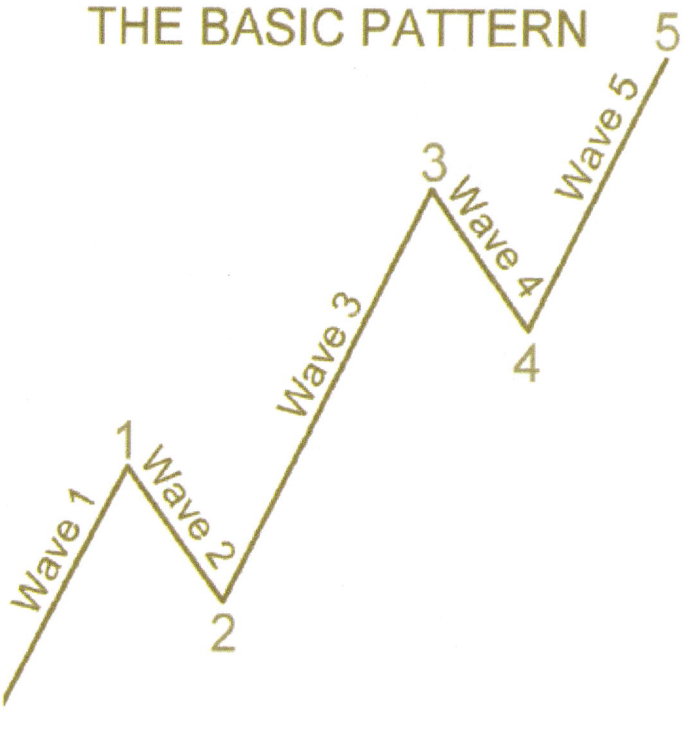

Image 5 wave pattern adapted from Elliott Wave Principle

Theory of Elliott Wave

Here's how Elliott Wave Theory incorporates the idea of historical price action repetition:

- ***Wave Patterns***:
    - Elliott Wave Theory identifies specific wave patterns, such as impulsive waves (trending) and corrective waves (countertrend). These patterns are said to represent the natural ebb and flow of market sentiment.
- ***Fibonacci Ratios***:
    - The theory suggests that the lengths of waves are often related to Fibonacci ratios. This implies that the market's self-similar structure is based on mathematical relationships, adding a layer of predictability.
- ***Psychological Phases***:
    - The theory divides market movements into different psychological phases, such as optimism and pessimism. These phases are thought to repeat in recognisable patterns, contributing to the repetitive nature of historical price action.
- ***Fractals***:
    - Elliott Wave Theory considers market movements as fractals, meaning that similar patterns can be observed at different time scales. This concept implies that the same wave patterns may repeat on smaller and larger time frames.

Elliott Wave Simplified

At its core, the 1930s Elliott Wave Theory offers a straightforward guide to understanding market movements. When tracking a trend, envision it unfolding in five waves (known as the motive wave), while corrections against the trend occur in three waves (the corrective wave). These directional waves are numbered 1 through 5, and the corrective waves are labelled a, b, and c. This wave pattern recognition is applicable to both long-term and short-term charts.

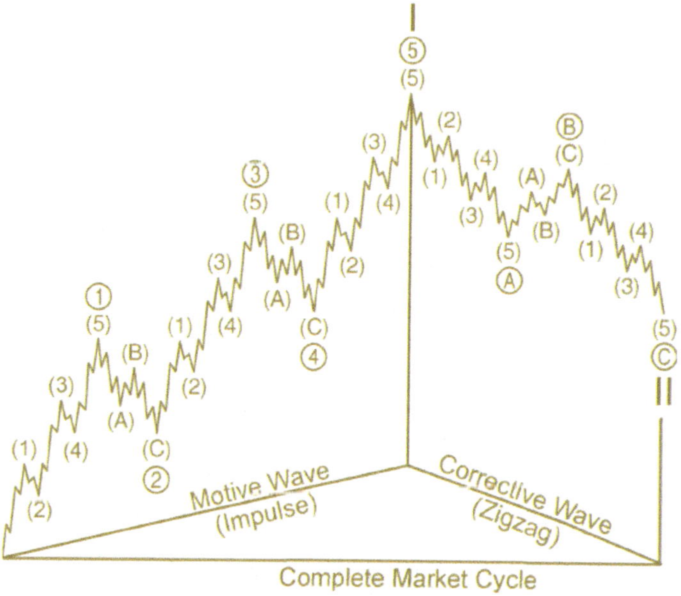

Consider the analogy of a financial jigsaw puzzle—within the broader market picture, smaller patterns interlock like puzzle pieces. In essence, Elliott Waves resemble assembling a puzzle, where extracting a smaller piece mirrors the larger whole. This concept, combined with the Fibonacci relationships existing between the waves, provides traders with a valuable framework for anticipating and predicting market movements. It's akin to piecing together a puzzle, allowing traders to uncover potential opportunities with compelling reward-to-risk ratios.

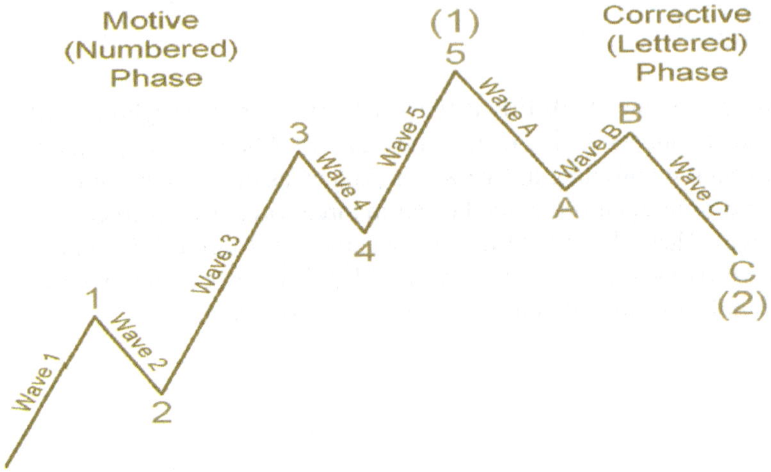

Motive Wave Rules

Elliott Wave Theory defines several rules for motive waves, which are the directional phases of market trends. These rules provide guidelines for identifying and validating wave patterns. Here are the key rules for motive waves:

- Wave 1 and Wave 4 Alternation Rule: If Wave 1 is a simple and quick move, Wave 4 is likely to be more complex and time-consuming, and vice versa. This alternation helps maintain balance and symmetry in the wave pattern.

- Wave 2 Correction Rule: Wave 2 should not retrace more than 100% of Wave 1. This rule emphasises that corrections in the second wave should not completely erase the gains made in the first wave.

- Wave 3 Rule: Wave 3 should never be the shortest wave among Waves 1, 3, and 5. Wave 3 is typically the most extended and powerful wave in a five-wave sequence.

- Wave 4 Rule: Wave 4 should not overlap with the price territory of Wave 1. (Wicks can happen in a leveraged market) This rule ensures that the corrective Wave 4 doesn't retrace too deeply into the region covered by the preceding Wave 1.
- Wave 5 Rule: Wave 5 should not exhibit significant overlaps with Wave 3. While Wave 5 often reaches a new high (in an uptrend), it should not extensively overlap with the price territory covered by Wave 3.
- Wave 5 and Wave 1 Equality Rule: In some cases, Wave 5 may be equal in length to Wave 1, contributing to the overall symmetry of the Elliott Wave pattern.

These rules serve as guidelines to validate the structure and integrity of motive waves within the Elliott Wave Theory framework. Analysts and traders use these rules to enhance the accuracy of their wave counts and predictions.

Rules play a crucial role in applying Elliott Wave Theory in real-time analysis.

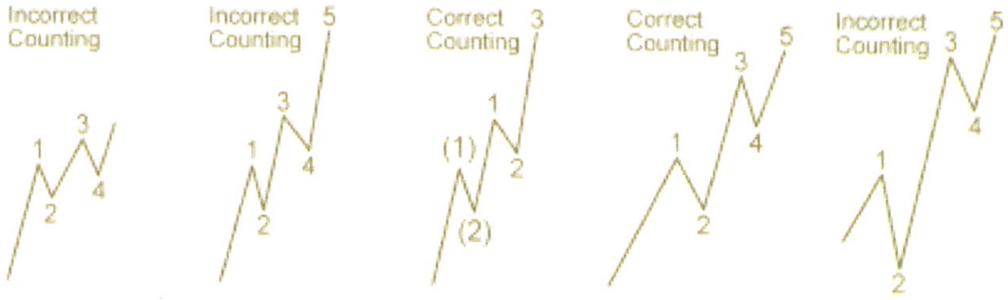

The image above shows:

The first wave count is incorrect because wave 4 extends into the price territory of wave 1.

The second wave count is flawed as wave 3 is the shortest motive wave.

The third wave count is accurate, correctly depicting the first three subdivisions of wave 3 - this shows Waves 1 and 2, then subwaves 1,2,3 of the 3rd motive wave.

The fourth wave count is correct because, although wave 3 isn't the longest motive wave, it also isn't the shortest.

However, the last wave count is inaccurate because wave 2 retraces more than 100 per cent of wave 1.

In an impulse wave, waves 1 and 5 are always motive waves (either impulse or diagonal), while wave 3 is always an impulse wave. Waves 2 and 4 are consistently corrective waves. This defines an impulse wave as a 5-3-5-3-5 structure.

Wave Extensions

Wave Extension refers to the phenomenon where one of the motive waves, typically wave 3 or wave 5, is elongated. An extended wave is an elongated impulse wave, and its motive subwaves at the next lower degree are as large as or larger than the non-extended motive wave(s) within the same impulse wave.

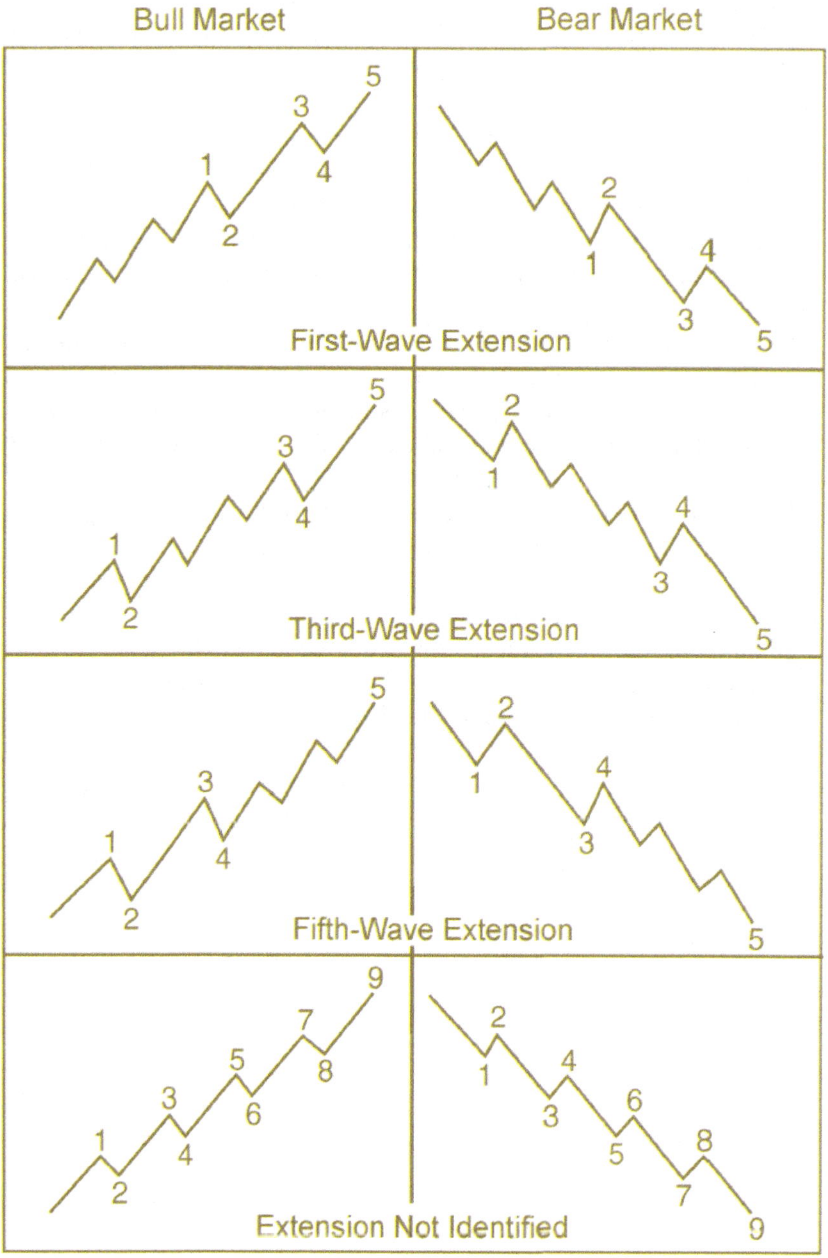

Bull Market
Bear Market
First-Wave Extension
Third-Wave Extension
Fifth-Wave Extension
Extension Not Identified

This diagram illustrates extensions for waves 1, 3, and 5. Sometimes, the initial subwaves of an impulse wave have similar lengths, making it challenging to pinpoint which motive wave is extended.

The bottom diagram exemplifies this uncertainty, where the extended wave could be 1, 3, or 5. In practical terms, it doesn't matter which one is extended as long as there are a total of nine waves. Notably, third-wave extensions are common in the cryptocurrency and stock markets, while fifth-wave extensions are often observed in commodity markets.

If wave 1 is extended, anticipate waves 3 and 5 to be roughly equal in length. If wave 3 is extended, expect wave 5 to be approximately equal to wave 1. When waves 1 and 3 are similar, anticipate wave 5 to be extended. Following the termination of a fifth-wave extension, expect a swift and sharp reversal back to the second subwave of the extension. It's rare for two motive waves to extend, but if it occurs, it's typically waves 3 and 5, referred to as a double extension.

In instances where an extension occurs within an extended wave, it's common for the extension at a lower degree to be in the same wave position as the extension it is part of. For instance, in a wave 3 extension, subwave 3 is often extended.

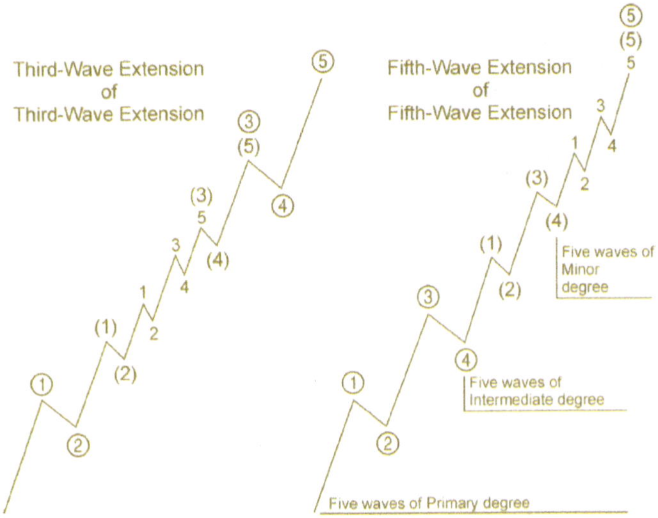

Truncation happens in an impulse wave when wave 5 doesn't extend beyond the end of wave 3. Despite this, a truncated fifth wave still follows the typical five-wave structure (see image below). This occurrence, indicative of exhaustion in the overall trend at a higher degree, usually occurs after an exceptionally robust third wave of the same degree. Following a truncated fifth wave, a rapid and sharp reversal is often observed.

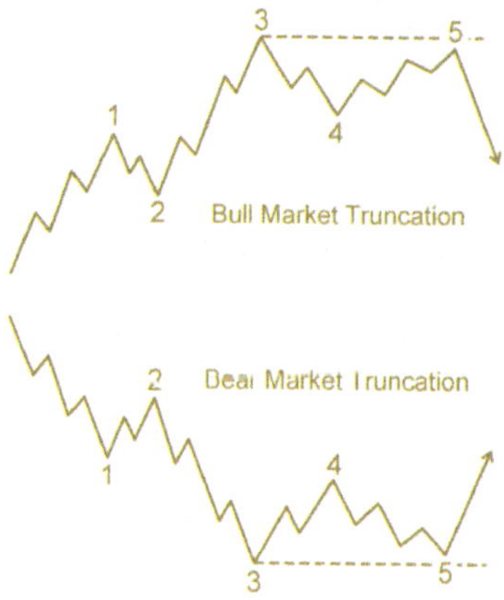

Diagonals, though classified as motive waves like impulses, deviate notably from impulses by adhering to the first two rules but disregarding the third rule. Unlike impulses, diagonals often see wave 4 entering the price territory of wave 1.

Diagonals generally take the form of contracting structures, occasionally expanding. In the contracting type, wave 3 is shorter than wave 1, wave 5 is shorter than wave 3, and wave 4 is shorter than wave 2. Conversely, in the expanding type, wave 3 is longer than wave 1, wave 5 is longer than wave 3, and wave 4 is longer than wave 2. Due to the rarity of expanding diagonals, our focus will be on the contracting variety.

Two main types of diagonals exist: leading diagonals and ending diagonals, with the latter being more common. Ending diagonals unfold as corrective waves, specifically zigzags, forming only as fifth waves of impulse waves or C waves of zigzags and flats.

In the image below, wave (5) exemplifies a contracting ending diagonal marked by converging trend lines, creating a wedge shape. These trend lines connect the termination points of waves 1 and 3 and 2 and 4. Wave 5 may conclude on, slightly above, or below the 1-3 trendline.

A move beyond this trendline is termed a throw-over, typically followed by a swift reversal back to the diagonal's starting point. This reversal usually takes one-third to one-half the time it took for the diagonal to form.

In leading diagonals, waves 1, 3, and 5 are either all impulse waves or all corrective waves in the form of zigzags, while waves 2 and 4 always take the shape of zigzags. Leading diagonals can form wave 1 of an impulse wave or the first wave of a zigzag, referred to as wave A, an exceptionally rare formation.

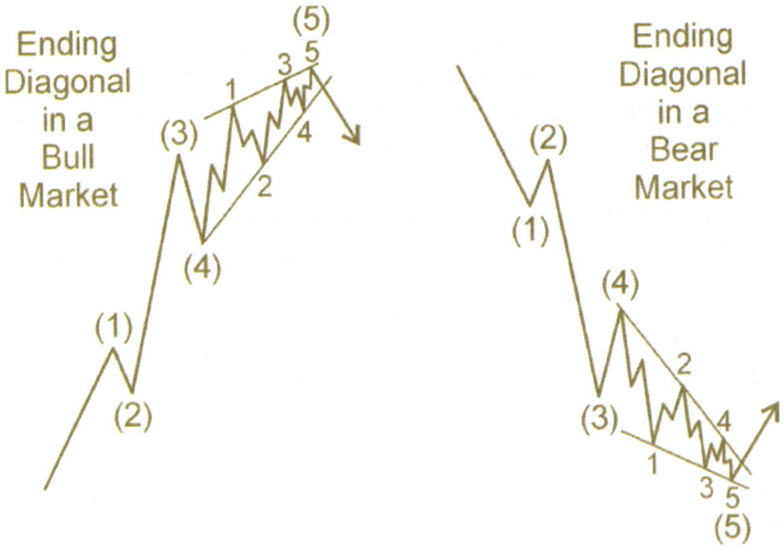

In the illustration below, wave (1) is portrayed as a contracting leading diagonal, sharing structural features with a contracting ending diagonal.

When a wave 1 leading diagonal concludes, anticipate wave 2 to retrace a substantial portion of wave 1. There is a saying that in this pattern, wave 2 will usually end close to where wave 1 began.

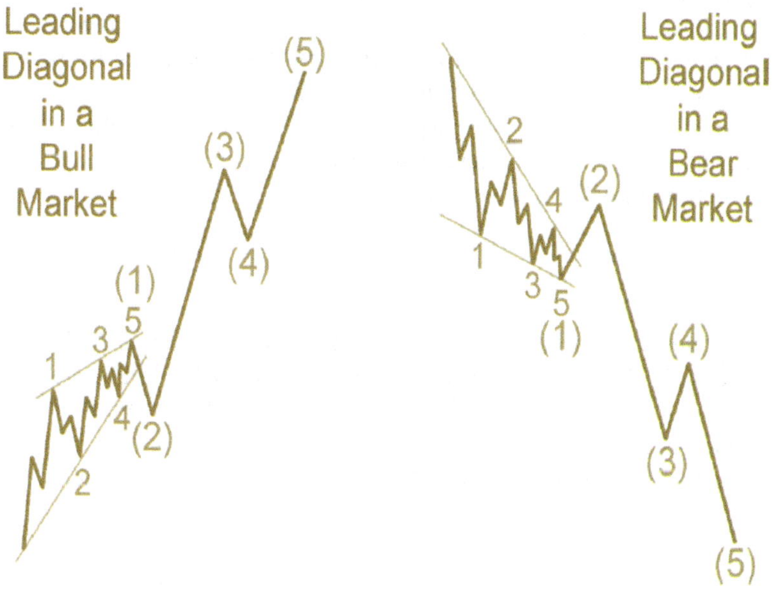

Corrective Waves

Corrective waves play a crucial role in market dynamics, adhering to the principle that "nothing moves in a straight line." These waves interrupt the natural flow of market trends and are categorised as either sharp or sideways.

A sharp corrective wave exhibits a steep angle and does not reach a new price extreme beyond the preceding wave it retraces. On the other hand, a sideways correction has boundaries closer to horizontal and typically records a new price extreme before completion. Despite their variations, all corrective waves involve some degree of retracement of the preceding wave of the same degree, posing a challenge for real-time identification and determining completion.
There are three fundamental types of corrective wave patterns: zigzag, flat, and triangle. When these patterns combine in a sideways correction, they form a "combination."

ZigZag

A zigzag is a sharp, three-wave corrective pattern labelled A-B-C. Wave A is always an impulse or a leading diagonal, while wave C is always an impulse or an ending diagonal. Wave B, situated in the middle, is consistently a corrective wave, taking the form of a zigzag, flat, triangle, or combination. This structure is referred to as a 5-3-5 pattern.

In a zigzag, wave B must not surpass the start of wave A, and wave C typically extends beyond the end of wave A. If wave C fails to surpass the end of wave A, it is termed a truncated wave C.

Zigzag corrections can manifest as one, two, or three zigzags, with three being the apparent limit. When there's more than one zigzag, an additional corrective wave connects them.

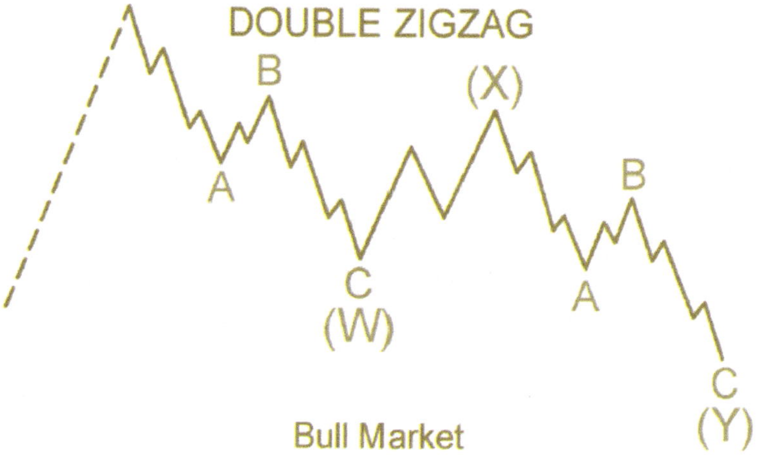

In a double zigzag, (above) the first zigzag is labelled W, the second as Y, and the connecting corrective wave as X. In a triple zigzag, the third zigzag is labelled Z, and wave X, which usually takes the form of a zigzag, moves in the opposite direction of wave W.

Flat

A flat is a sideways, three-wave corrective pattern labelled A-B-C. Waves A and B are consistently corrective waves, while wave C is always a motive wave. This structure is identified as a 3-3-5 pattern. In flats, waves A and B never take the form of triangles and seldom appear as flats. Notably, wave B typically retraces at least 90 percent of wave A.

There are three types of flats: regular, expanded, and running, with the expanded flat being the most common and running flats being a rare occurrence.

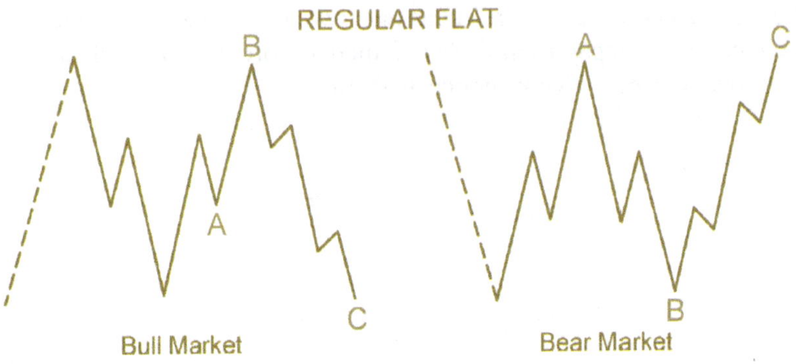

Above in a regular flat, wave B concludes at approximately the same level as the start of wave A, and wave C extends slightly beyond the endpoint of wave A.

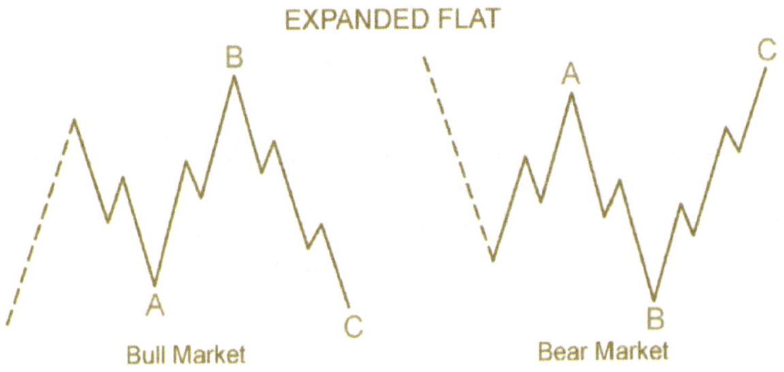

In an expanded flat, wave B finishes around the same level or just above where wave A begins, and wave C stretches a bit further past the conclusion of wave A.

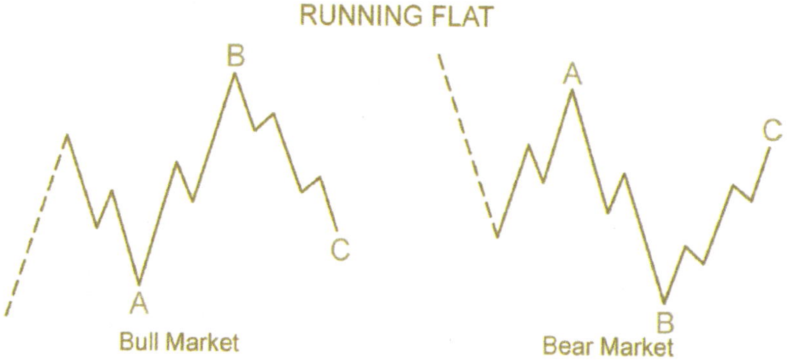

Above - In a running flat, wave B extends beyond the initiation point of wave A, and wave C doesn't quite reach the conclusion of wave A.

Triangle

A triangle is a sideways corrective wave characterised by subwaves labelled A-B-C-D-E. In most instances, all the subwaves within a triangle manifest as zigzags or multiple zigzag patterns.

This designates the triangle as a 3-3-3-3-3 structure. Occasionally, one of these subwaves adopts the form of another triangle, typically observed as wave E.

Among these subwaves, only one can be complex, meaning it stretches out over time, and this typically occurs with waves C, D, or E.

Variations of Elliott Wave Triangles

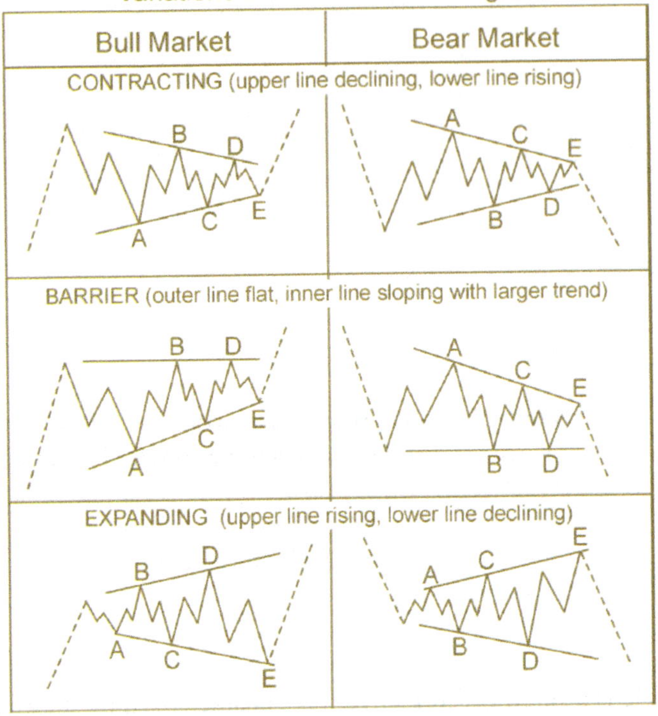

The image above illustrates the three types of triangles: contracting, barrier, and expanding.

In a triangle, we use two trendlines to understand its structure. The line connecting the termination points of waves A and C is called the A-C trendline, while the line connecting the termination points of waves B and D is referred to as the B-D trendline. Wave E may conclude at, just before, or beyond the A-C trendline.

For contracting and barrier triangles, the A-C and B-D trendlines come together. In barrier triangles, the B-D trendline is horizontal, and the A-C trendline aligns with the main trend at the next higher degree. In contrast, in expanding triangles, the A-C and B-D trendlines move apart.

In a contracting triangle, wave C stays within the limits of Wave A, wave D within Wave B, and Wave E within Wave C.

Wave B may or may not extend beyond the starting point of Wave A.

If wave B surpasses the start of wave A, it's termed a running contracting triangle, a common occurrence illustrated below.

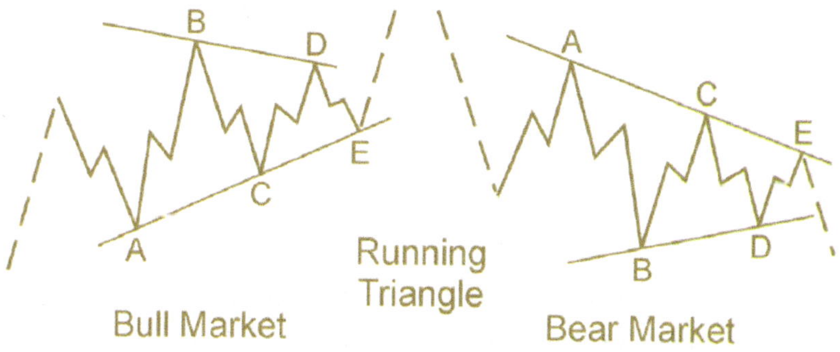

A barrier triangle shares characteristics with a contracting triangle, with one distinction: in a barrier triangle, the B-D trendline is horizontal, providing a unique structural element.

In a barrier triangle, wave D concludes roughly at the same level as wave B. Conversely, in an expanding triangle, each new subwave, after completing wave A, extends beyond the starting point of the preceding subwave.

It's important to note that a triangle consistently precedes the final motive wave in the direction of the main trend at the next higher degree.

This ultimate motive wave typically exhibits a swift and sharp move, known as the post-triangle breakout, as depicted below.

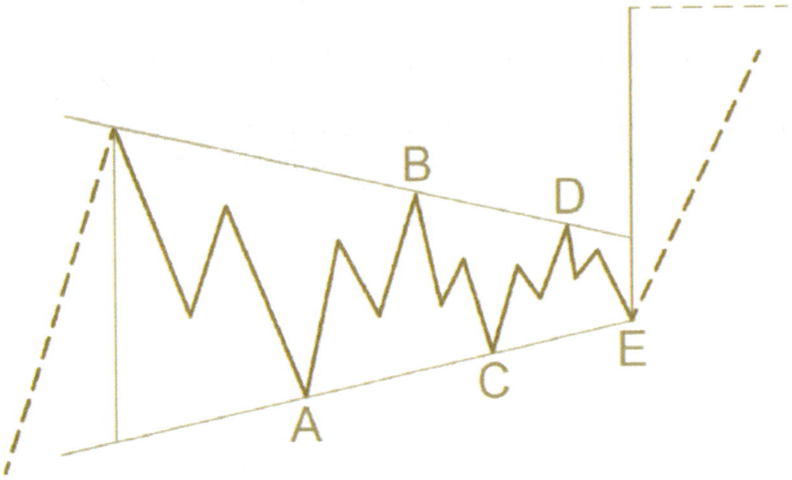

For a contracting or barrier triangle, we can estimate the minimum termination point of the thrust by extending the A-C and B-D trendlines back to the beginning of wave A.

Then, drawing a vertical line connecting these two trendlines helps define the "width" of the triangle. Applying this width to the end of wave E provides an estimate for the next move in the direction of the main trend at the next higher degree.

In the context of an impulse wave, the post-triangle thrust measurement serves to estimate the minimum length for wave 5. Should wave 5 surpass the initially estimated termination point, it indicates the likelihood of an extended and prolonged fifth wave.

Combination

A combination is a sideways corrective pattern comprising two or more corrective structures, with three corrective structures being the maximum limit. Each corrective structure is interconnected by an X wave, characterised by three key features: it can take any corrective pattern, consistently moves in the opposite direction of the previous corrective pattern, and is typically a zigzag. Notably, there never seems to be more than one triangle in a combination, and if one does appear, it tends to be the final corrective structure in the combination.

There are two types of combinations: double three and triple three.

In a double three combination, two corrective patterns labelled W and Y are linked by an X wave.

The image below illustrates one of many variations of a double three correction. On the other hand, a triple three combination comprises three corrective patterns labelled W, Y, and Z, each connected by X waves.

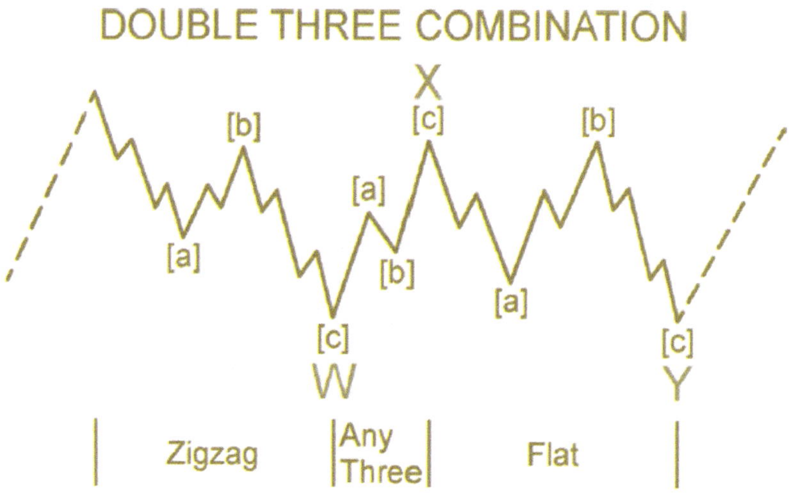

Triple threes are infrequent.

Within both double and triple threes, X waves typically manifest as zigzags and never as triangles.

TRIPLE THREE COMBINATION

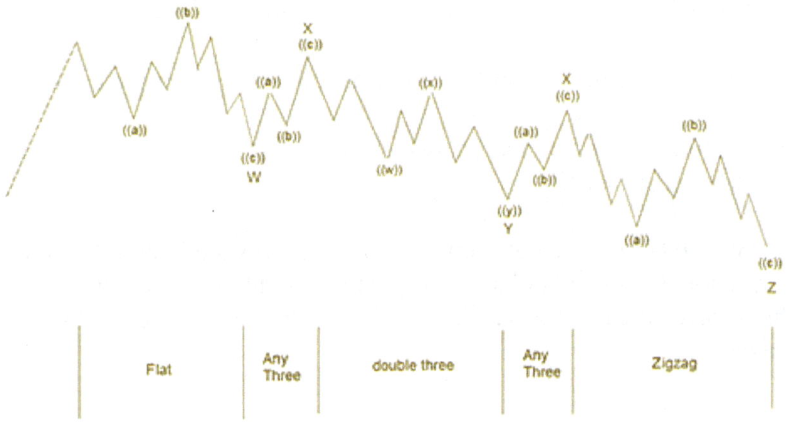

Fibonacci Relationships

Wave patterns frequently exhibit connections to Fibonacci ratios in both price and time aspects. The prominent Fibonacci ratio in wave formations is 0.618-0.65, renowned as the Golden Zone.

This key ratio is symbolised by the Greek letter phi (ϕ), pronounced as "fie." Its reciprocal is 1.618. An intriguing property of phi is that when added to one, it equals its inverse. Squaring phi or subtracting it from 1 yields another significant Fibonacci ratio, 0.382.

Fibonacci Ratios and Multiples

Ratio	Inverse	Φ^N
.618	1.618	$(1.618)^1$
.382	2.618	$(1.618)^2$
.236	4.236	$(1.618)^3$
.146	6.854	$(1.618)^4$
.090	11.089	$(1.618)^5$

In the image above, a variety of Fibonacci ratios is showcased. Each ratio can be expressed as phi—either 0.618 or its inverse 1.618—raised to a power.

Other notable Fibonacci numbers relevant to wave formation include 0.5 (1/2), 0.786 (the square root of 0.618), 1.0 (1/1), and 2.0 (2/1).

Within Elliott wave patterns, the key types of Fibonacci relationships include retracements, multiples, and dividers. While these relationships are commonly employed to gauge the length of specific waves concerning price, they also prove valuable for estimating the temporal length of waves.

Retracements

Impulse wave retracements: the second wave typically undergoes significant retracement, reaching approximately 0.618 times the length of wave one. Conversely, fourth waves tend to make shallower retracements, often hovering around 0.382 times the length of wave three (see image below).

In the context of a zigzag, how much wave B retraces wave A depends on the structure of wave B. For instance, as illustrated in below, if wave B takes the form of a zigzag, it should retrace between 0.5 to 0.786 of wave A. However, if wave B manifests as a triangle, it is expected to retrace approximately 0.382 to 0.50 of wave A.

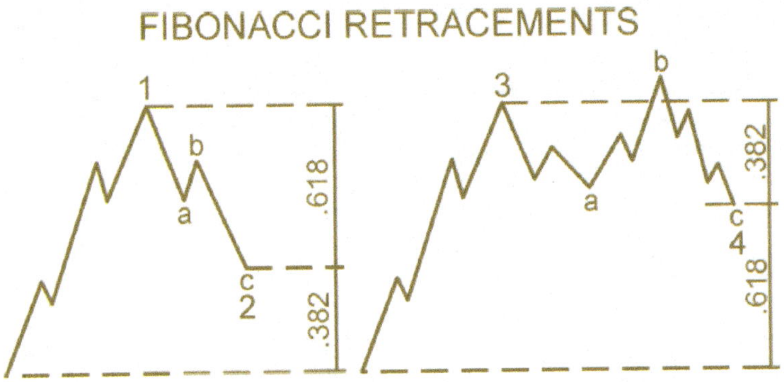

Multiples

In scenarios where wave 3 is extended, expect a connection between wave 5 and wave 1 through equality or roughly .618. When wave 5 is extended, anticipate wave 5, in terms of price, to travel about 1.618 times the net distance covered by waves 1 through 3. If this length is surpassed, watch for larger multiples, as illustrated next page.

FIBONACCI MULTIPLES IN IMPULSE WAVES

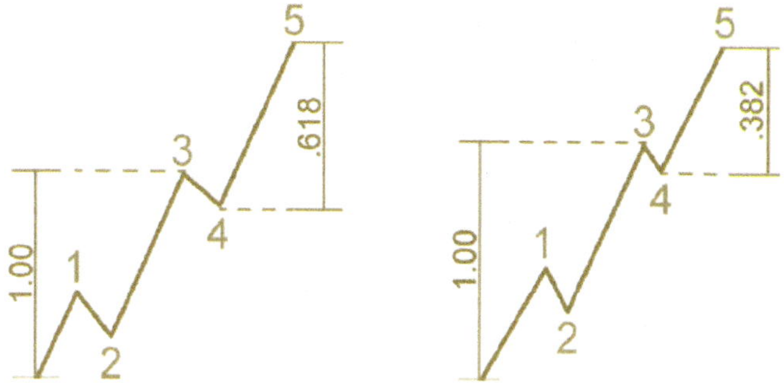

In instances of extended wave 1, the net distance travelled by waves 3 through 5 is likely to be roughly .618 times the length of wave 1 - see image below,

FIBONACCI MULTIPLES IN IMPULSE WAVES

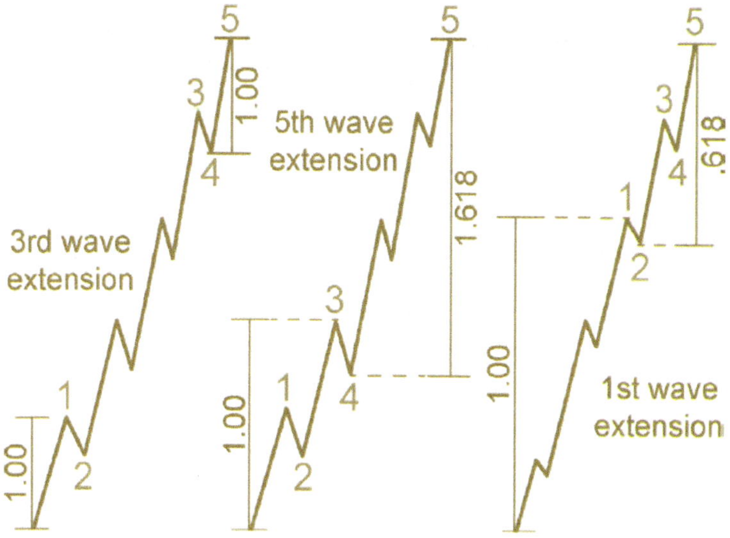

In single and multiple zigzag structures, equality is the most common Fibonacci relationship—like C equals A in the single zigzag, and Y equals W in the double zigzag - see image below.

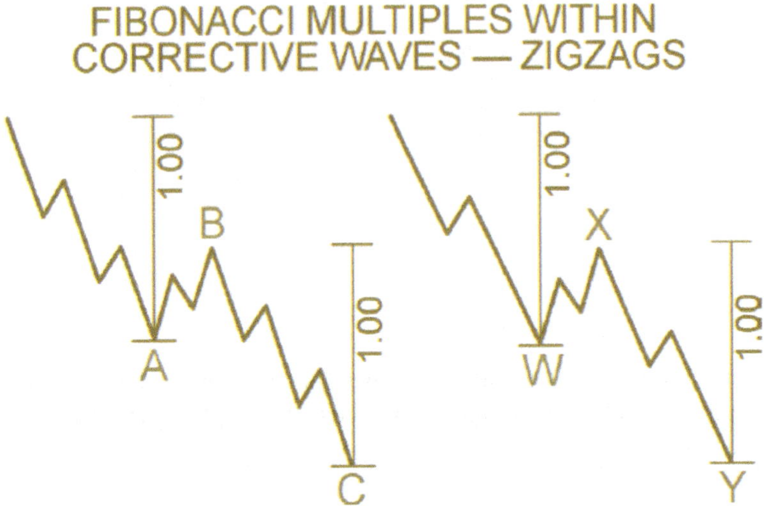

When equality isn't evident, explore other Fibonacci relationships, as depicted in the table below.

The relationships for multiple zigzags mirror those of a single zigzag.

Fibonacci Relationships
Single Zigzag
Wave C = Wave A
Wave C = .618 Wave A
Wave C = 1.618 Wave A
Wave C = .618 Wave A past Wave A
Double Zigzag
Wave Y = Wave W
Wave Y = .618 Wave W
Wave Y = 1.618 Wave W
Wave Y = .618 Wave W past Wave W
Triple Zigzag
Equality for W, Y, and Z
Ratio of .618, i.e., Wave Z = .618 Wave Y

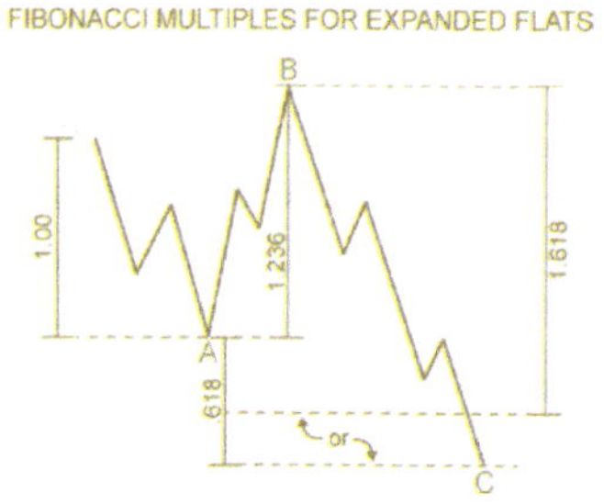

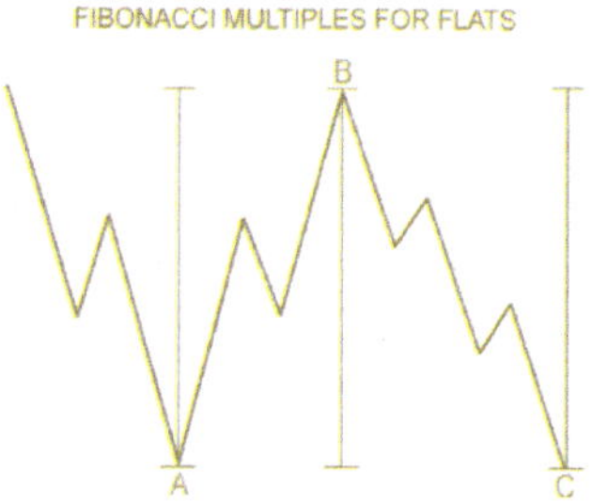

Let's make the concept of flat corrections clearer:

Regular Flat (Left)
In a regular flat correction, waves A, B, and C typically share an equal length.

Expanded Flat (Right)
For an expanded flat correction, envision wave C to either match the length of wave A multiplied by 1.618 or conclude at a price equivalent to 0.618 times the length of wave A beyond wave A.
Meanwhile, anticipate wave B to be 1.236 or 1.382 times the length of wave A.

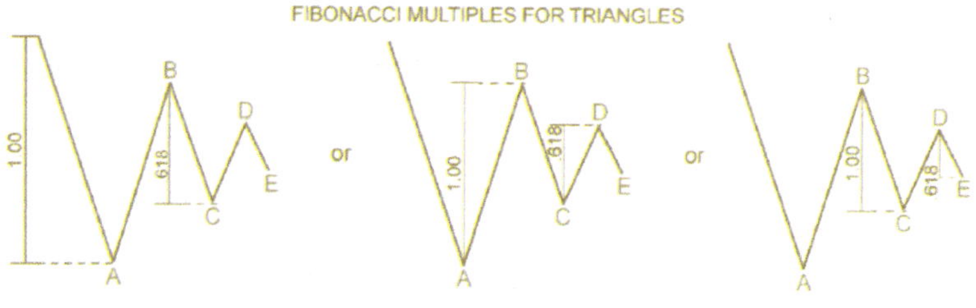

Let's simplify the concept of alternate waves in triangles:

Contracting Triangle:
In a contracting triangle, the alternate waves often exhibit a relationship to each other through the Fibonacci ratio of 0.618.

Expanding Triangle:
In contrast, for expanding triangles, this relationship is characterised by the Fibonacci ratio of 1.618.
Next, we simplify the idea of the Pink Zone and Fibonacci clusters:

Pink Zone:

The Pink Zone, resulting in a .382/.618 split, plays a significant role in wave patterns. Specific termination points within waves often lead to a division of the entire wave into the Pink Zone or a .50/.50 split. In an impulse wave, wave 4, usually at its origin or termination point, frequently divides the entire wave into the Pink Zone or two equal parts - see below.

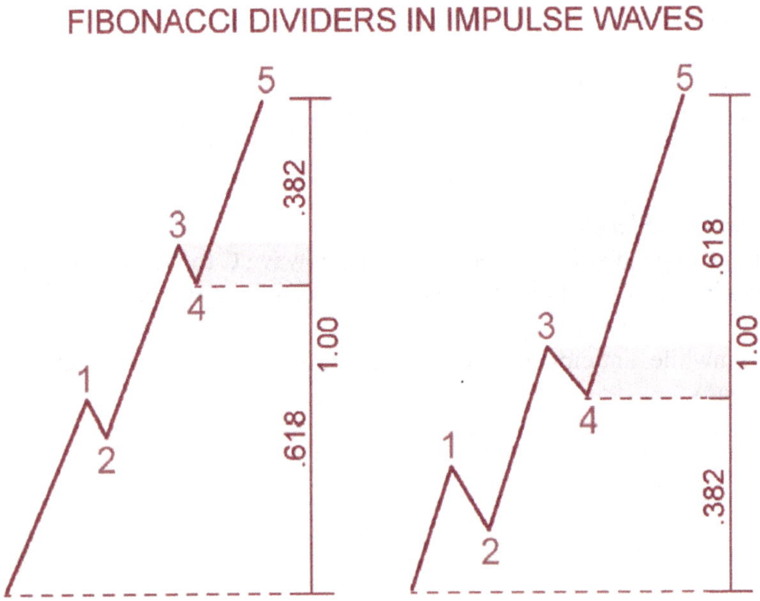

Clusters:

Instead of relying solely on a single Fibonacci relationship for predicting market movements, we find more potency in identifying Fibonacci clusters. A Fibonacci price cluster occurs when two or more Fibonacci price relationships align to approximately the same price level. Given that wave patterns unfold across various time frames simultaneously, there's often an opportunity to recognise a Fibonacci cluster.

Illustration of a Fibonacci price cluster.

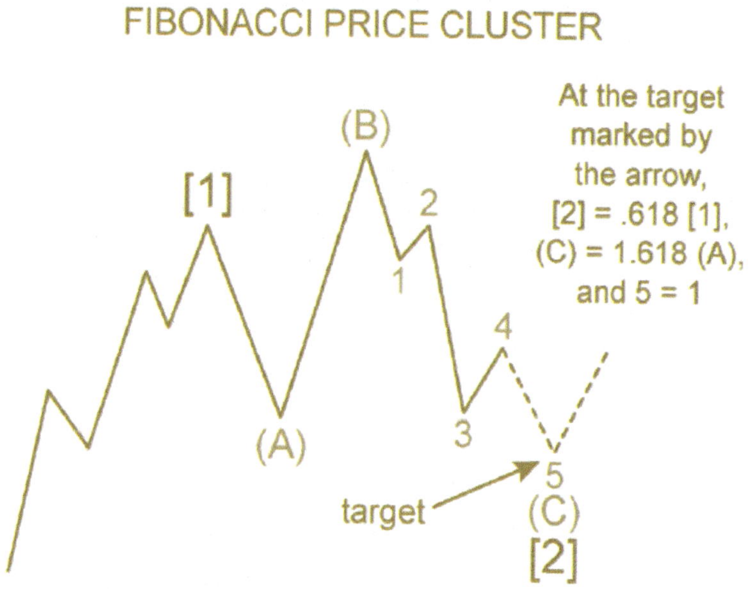

Let's simplify the information about Fibonacci relationships in the given image:

Fibonacci Relationships at a Common Price Level:

The image highlights three Fibonacci relationships converging around the same general price level:

1. Primary wave [2] retraces approximately 0.618 of Primary wave [1].
2. In the expanded flat, Intermediate wave (C) matches 1.618 times the length of Intermediate wave (A).
3. Within the Intermediate wave (C) impulse wave, Minor wave 5 is equivalent in length to Minor wave 1.

ADDITIONAL RESOURCES

If you want to learn more about Elliott Wave, I can suggest some general resources for learning about Elliott Wave Theory and technical analysis:

- Elliott Wave Principle by Frost and Prechter:
    - The book "Elliott Wave Principle" by Robert Prechter and A.J. Frost is a fundamental resource. While it's mentioned as available for free online, you may also find it in local libraries or online bookstores.

- Elliott Wave International:
    - The Elliott Wave International website (www.elliottwave.com) is a valuable resource. They offer educational materials and various resources on Elliott Wave Theory.

- Investopedia:
    - Investopedia (www.investopedia.com) provides a range of educational content on financial topics, including Elliott Wave Theory. Search for articles and tutorials to enhance your understanding.

- YouTube Tutorials:
    - There are many educational videos and tutorials on platforms like YouTube. Search for channels or specific videos that explain Elliott Wave Theory, its principles, and practical applications.

- Forums and Communities:
    - Engage with trading and investing communities to discuss Elliott Wave Theory.
    - Websites like www.gettingstartedincrypto.com often have discussions on technical analysis.

While many traders, including myself, find value in Elliott Wave Theory, it's essential to note that it is a complex and subjective tool.

Identifying and interpreting wave patterns requires skill and experience, and the theory is not universally accepted. Traders often use Elliott Wave analysis in conjunction with other technical analysis tools and indicators to make more comprehensive trading decisions. It's also important to recognise that market conditions can evolve, and historical patterns may not always repeat exactly.

I like to integrate Elliott Wave Theory with Moving Averages, support and resistance, RSI and MACD.

The next segment explores the tools I use in addition to Elliott Wave for successful trading.

"Don't focus on making money. Focus on protecting what you have."

Paul Tudor Jones

OSCILLATORS AND MOMENTUM INDICATORS

Oscillators and momentum indicators are crucial tools in technical analysis, particularly for trading cryptocurrencies and stocks. They provide insights into the speed and strength of price movements, helping traders identify overbought or oversold conditions and potential trend reversals.

Here's a breakdown of the Relative Strength Index (RSI), Stochastic Oscillator, Moving Average Convergence Divergence (MACD), Exponential Moving Averages (EMA) 9 and 21 and Volume Profile with Visual Range (VRVP) along with how to use them for trading purposes.

1. Relative Strength Index (RSI):

Purpose:

- RSI measures the magnitude of recent price changes to evaluate overbought or oversold conditions in an asset.

How to Use:

- Overbought Condition (Above 70): When RSI exceeds 70, it suggests the asset may be overbought, and a reversal or pullback could be imminent.
- Oversold Condition (Below 30): When RSI falls below 30, it indicates potential oversold conditions, suggesting a rebound or reversal may occur.

Trend Reversal:

- Look for divergences between RSI and price movements. For example, if the price makes new highs while the RSI does not, it could signal weakening momentum and an impending reversal.

2. Stochastic Oscillator:

Purpose:

- The Stochastic Oscillator measures the closing price relative to the high-low range over a specified period, indicating the strength of a trend.

How to Use:

- Overbought Condition (Above 80): Readings above 80 suggest the asset is overbought, and a potential reversal or pullback may be on the horizon.
- Oversold Condition (Below 20): Readings below 20 indicate potential oversold conditions, suggesting a rebound or trend reversal.

Trend Reversal:

- Look for divergence between the Stochastic Oscillator and price. A divergence can signal weakening momentum and a potential reversal.

3. Moving Average Convergence Divergence (MACD):

Purpose:

- MACD is a trend-following momentum indicator that shows the relationship between two moving averages of an asset's price.

How to Use:

- Crossover Signals: A bullish crossover (MACD line crossing above the signal line) can signal a potential uptrend, while a bearish crossover (MACD line crossing below the signal line) may indicate a potential downtrend.

Trend Reversal:

- Look for divergence between MACD and price. Divergences can signal potential trend reversals.

Signal Line Crossovers: A bullish crossover (MACD line crossing above the signal line) can signal a potential uptrend, while a bearish crossover (MACD line crossing below the signal line) may indicate a potential downtrend.

Histogram: The histogram, which represents the difference between the MACD line and the signal line, can also be used to identify potential trend changes. When the histogram approaches zero, it may suggest a possible trend reversal.

4. Exponential Moving Averages (EMA) 9 and 21:

Purpose:

- Exponential Moving Averages (EMAs) are trend-following indicators that give more weight to recent prices, providing a faster response to price changes compared to simple moving averages.

How to Use:

- EMA 9 and 21 Crossovers: A bullish crossover (EMA 9 crossing above EMA 21) suggests a potential uptrend, while a bearish crossover (EMA 9 crossing below EMA 21) may indicate a potential downtrend.

Trend Reversal:

- Pay attention to the relationship between the price and EMAs. If the price is making new highs or lows, but the EMAs are not confirming the trend, it may signal a potential reversal.

Support and Resistance: EMAs can function as dynamic support or resistance levels. In an uptrend, the EMA 21 may function as support, while in a downtrend, the EMA 21 may act as resistance.

General Tips for Using EMA 9 and 21:

- *Golden Cross and Death Cross*: A Golden Cross occurs when the shorter-term EMA (e.g., EMA 9) crosses above the longer-term EMA (e.g., EMA 21), indicating a potential bullish trend. Conversely, a Death Cross occurs when the shorter-term EMA crosses below the longer-term EMA, suggesting a potential bearish trend.

- *Consider the Trend Strength*: The angle and separation between the two EMAs can provide insights into the strength of the trend. Widening separation may indicate a strong trend, while narrowing could suggest weakening momentum.

- *Use in Conjunction with Other Indicators*: Combining EMAs with oscillators and other indicators can enhance the reliability of signals. Confirming signals across multiple indicators can strengthen the basis for a trade.

- *Adapt to Different Time Frames*: EMAs are versatile and can be applied to various time frames. Traders often use shorter-term EMAs for intraday trading and longer-term EMAs for trend identification in higher time frames.

As with any technical indicator, it's crucial to consider these EMAs in the context of the overall market conditions and in conjunction with other analytical tools.

While EMAs can provide valuable trend-following signals, no single indicator guarantees success and risk management remains a key component of my well-rounded trading strategy.

5. Volume Profile with Visual Range (VRVP):

Purpose:

- Volume Profile with Visual Range (VRVP) is a tool that analyses the distribution of trading volume at different price levels, providing insights into potential support and resistance zones.

How to Use:

- High Volume Nodes (HVN) and Low Volume Nodes (LVN): HVNs represent areas with significant trading activity, acting as potential support or resistance. LVNs, on the other hand, indicate areas with lower trading activity, suggesting potential breakout zones.

Trend Reversal:

- Look for shifts in the volume profile. If the market is consolidating around a specific price level with decreasing volume, it may indicate a potential reversal.

Point of Control (POC): POC is the price level with the highest traded volume. It often serves as a benchmark for market sentiment. If the price moves away from the POC, it may signal a shift in market dynamics.

General Tips for Using VRVP:

- *Value Area*: The value area represents the range where a significant portion of trading activity occurred. Traders often consider this area as a potential equilibrium zone and monitor price movements around it.

- *Volume at Price*: VRVP displays volume at different price levels, offering a visual representation of where traders are most active. High volume at specific levels can function as strong support or resistance.

- *Combine with Price Action*: Incorporate VRVP with traditional price action analysis. Confirming key levels identified by VRVP with other technical indicators or chart patterns can strengthen trading decisions.

- *Time Frame Consideration:* Adjust the time frame for VRVP analysis based on your trading strategy. Shorter time frames may be suitable for intraday trading, while longer time frames can provide insights into broader market dynamics.

As with any technical tool, it's essential to use VRVP in conjunction with other indicators and consider broader market conditions. VRVP provides a unique perspective on the market by focusing on volume distribution and incorporating it into a comprehensive trading strategy can enhance decision-making. I cannot emphasise enough that risk management remains crucial to mitigate potential downsides and protect capital in trading.

"We can't predict the future with certainty, and interestingly, we don't need to. What matters is your ability to use the information available at every moment to make the most appropriate decision."

Ray Dalio

General Tips for Using Indicators:

- *Confirmation with Other Indicators*: Use multiple indicators to confirm signals. If multiple indicators provide similar signals, it can increase confidence in a potential trade.

- *Consider the Overall Trend*: It's often more reliable to trade in the direction of the overall trend. Indicators are most powerful when they align with the broader market trend.

- *Combine with Price Action and Support/Resistance*: Incorporate these indicators with price action analysis and identify key support and resistance levels for more robust decision-making.

- *Avoid Relying on a Single Indicator*: No single indicator is foolproof. Use a combination of tools to build a comprehensive trading strategy.

Remember that while these indicators are valuable, they are not guarantees of future price movements. It's essential to consider other factors, including market conditions, news, and economic events, when making trading decisions. Additionally, practice and experience are crucial for refining your interpretation of these indicators in different market scenarios.

Technical analysis for trading crypto and stocks.

- *Price Patterns and Trends*: Technical analysis helps traders identify price patterns and trends in the market. By analysing historical price movements, traders can identify potential trend reversals, trend continuations, and key support and resistance levels. This information can be crucial for making informed trading decisions.

- *Entry and Exit Points:* Technical analysis provides tools and indicators that can help traders determine optimal entry and exit points. For example, moving averages, trendlines, and chart patterns can be used to identify potential buying or selling opportunities.

- *Market Sentiment:* Charts and technical indicators often reflect market sentiment. Traders use indicators like the Relative Strength Index (RSI) or Moving Average Convergence Divergence (MACD) to gauge whether an asset is overbought or oversold. This information can be valuable for predicting potential price reversals.

- *Risk Management:* Technical analysis can assist in setting stop-loss orders and defining risk-reward ratios. Traders can use technical indicators to assess the volatility of an asset and make decisions on the appropriate level for setting stop-loss orders to manage potential losses.

- *Historical Performance*: By analysing historical price data, traders can gain insights into how an asset has behaved in similar situations in the past. This historical performance can provide a basis for predicting future price movements.

- *Confirmation of Fundamental Analysis*: While fundamental analysis focuses on the underlying factors that may influence the value of an asset, technical analysis can be used to confirm or complement these findings. Traders often use both technical and fundamental analysis to make well-informed decisions.

- *Time Frame Analysis*: Technical analysis can be applied to various time frames, from short-term intraday trading to long-term investing. This flexibility allows traders to adapt their strategies based on their preferred time horizon.

- *Automation and Algorithmic Trading*: Technical analysis plays a crucial role in algorithmic and automated trading systems. Many trading algorithms are built on technical indicators and patterns, allowing for automated execution of trades based on predefined criteria.

While I express a strong endorsement of both technical analysis (TA) and fundamental analysis (FA) in trading and investing, it's important to underscore that these analytical approaches, when used without proper risk management, can expose traders to significant challenges.

Technical analysis and fundamental analysis provide valuable insights into market trends and underlying asset value, respectively. However, relying solely on these methods without incorporating risk management strategies can result in unforeseen losses. The unpredictable nature of financial markets, coupled with unexpected events, underscores the need for safeguarding investments through risk mitigation measures.

Traders should prioritise the implementation of effective risk management techniques, such as setting stop-loss orders, and one cancels the other (OCO) orders and sizing positions appropriately. By doing so, they can protect their capital, mitigate potential losses, and create a more sustainable and resilient trading strategy. The synergy of technical and fundamental analysis with robust risk management is essential for achieving long-term success.

"What is most important isn't knowing the future — it is knowing how to react appropriately to the information available at each point in time."

Ray Dalio

TIMING THE MARKET

Timing is often regarded as everything when trading. The ability to enter and exit the market at the right moments can make the difference between financial success and disappointment.

This chapter delves into the art and science of timing the market, exploring the strategies and considerations that can help you master entry and exit points with confidence. More importantly this will help you work out YOUR "trading Style."

The Illusion of Perfect Timing

Before we dive into the strategies for timing the market, it's essential to dispel a common myth: the belief in perfect timing. Many novice traders fall into the trap of waiting for the "perfect" moment to enter or exit an investment. They believe that by doing so, they can maximise profits and minimise losses. However, perfect timing is a mirage in the trading world, especially cryptocurrency. Markets are unpredictable, influenced by a multitude of factors, and subject to rapid shifts. Waiting for the perfect moment can often result in missed opportunities and frustration. That is why when we know pattern wise, we are nearing a bottom region, long term trades are best DCA'ed to get the best dollar cost averaged entry point for a long-term swing or HODL trade.

Understanding Market Cycles

To master market timing, one must first grasp the concept of market cycles. Markets move in cycles of expansion and contraction, and recognising these patterns can provide valuable insights. If you refer back to the Elliott Wave section, you will gain great knowledge of wave movement and momentum.

The four primary phases:

- Expansion: During this phase, economic conditions are improving, and investor confidence is high. Crypto and Stock prices rise, and it's generally a favourable time to invest and trade.

- Peak: At the peak of the market cycle, optimism is at its zenith, and asset prices reach their highest point. This is often when novice investors enter the market, only to see their investments decline shortly after.

- Contraction: In the contraction phase, economic conditions start deteriorating, and investor sentiment turns negative. Stock prices decline, and it's a challenging period for most investors.

- Trough: The trough represents the bottom of the market cycle, where pessimism is pervasive, and asset prices are at their lowest. Savvy investors often enter or add to their positions during this phase.

Strategies for Timing the Market

- Dollar-Cost Averaging (DCA): This strategy involves investing a fixed amount of money at regular intervals, regardless of market conditions. DCA reduces the impact of market volatility and allows you to buy more shares when prices are low and fewer when prices are high.

- Technical Analysis: Technical analysts use charts, patterns, and indicators to identify potential entry and exit points. They examine historical price and volume data to predict future price movements.

- Fundamental Analysis: Fundamental analysts assess a security's intrinsic value by examining factors such as earnings, financial health, and industry trends. They aim to buy when a security is undervalued and sell when it's overvalued.

- Sentiment Analysis: Market sentiment, driven by emotions like fear and greed, can significantly impact timing decisions. Contrarian investors often buy when sentiment is overly negative and sell when it's overly positive.
- Stop-Loss Orders: Setting predetermined stop-loss levels can protect your investments from significant losses. When a security's price reaches the stop-loss level, it triggers an automatic sell order.

Risk Management and Patience

Timing the market is an intricate skill that requires practice and discipline. It's essential to remember that no strategy guarantees success, and losses are an inherent part of investing. Risk management should always be a priority. Diversifying your portfolio, setting realistic goals, and having a long-term perspective can help you weather market fluctuations.

Patience is another key factor in mastering market timing. Emotional reactions to market movements can lead to impulsive decisions. By adhering to a well-thought-out strategy and resisting the urge to chase short-term gains, you'll be better equipped to make informed decisions about when to enter and exit the market.

"The universe knows the perfect timing for all those things you want and will find, through the crux."

Denis Waitley

Wall Street Cheat Sheet

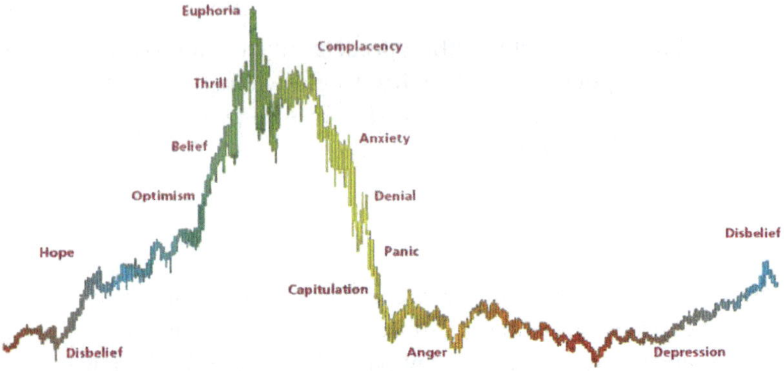

The Wall Street Cheat Sheet is a graphical representation of the typical psychological cycles that financial markets, including cryptocurrencies, go through. It was originally created for traditional stock markets but has been applied to various asset classes, including cryptocurrencies. The cheat sheet typically consists of different phases:

Bull Market: Accumulation Phase

- Description: This is the beginning of an upward trend. Prices are low, and there is pessimism among investors.
- Cryptocurrency Implication: This could be a period of low prices and negative sentiment in the crypto market. Smart investors might start accumulating assets.

Bull Market: Markup Phase

- Description: Prices start to rise, optimism increases. Positive news and developments may fuel the upward momentum.

- Cryptocurrency Implication: Prices of cryptocurrencies begin to rise, and traders may witness a series of positive developments in the space. FOMO (Fear of Missing Out) starts to kick in.

Bull Market: Distribution Phase

- Description: The market is at its peak, and euphoria is widespread. Investors may start taking profits, leading to a plateau or a slight decline.

- Cryptocurrency Implication: This phase could represent a peak in prices, with some early investors selling off their holdings to lock in profits.

Bear Market: Decline Phase

- Description: Prices start to decline, and optimism gives way to scepticism. Negative news may contribute to the downturn.

- Cryptocurrency Implication: This could be a period of decreasing prices and growing pessimism in the crypto market. Traders may become more risk averse.

Bear Market: Bottoming Phase

- Description: Prices reach a low point, and the market becomes oversold. Some long-term investors may start to see value at these levels.

- Cryptocurrency Implication: This phase might represent an opportunity for long-term investors to enter the market as prices hit rock bottom.

Bear Market: Rally Phase

- Description: Prices start to recover from the bottom, and some investors cautiously re-enter the market.

- Cryptocurrency Implication: This phase could indicate the beginning of a new bullish trend. However, it's essential to remain cautious, as it may be a temporary rally within an ongoing bear market.

While I personally love the idea behind the Wall Street Cheat Sheet and have even used this in my movie script COINRUNNERS to represent both emotions and the cycle it's important to note that the Wall Street Cheat Sheet is a tool for understanding market psychology, and it doesn't guarantee future market movements.

Cryptocurrency markets can be highly volatile and influenced by a variety of factors, including technological developments, regulatory changes, and market sentiment. Traders and investors should use a combination of technical analysis, fundamental analysis, and risk management strategies in addition to psychological frameworks like the Wall Street Cheat Sheet when making decisions in the cryptocurrency market.

"Being wrong is acceptable, but staying wrong is totally unacceptable."

Jack Schwager

NAVIGATING MARKET VOLATILITY

Strategies for Turbulent Times

Market volatility is an inherent part of trading and what I love in crypto, but it can present both opportunities and challenges. In this chapter, we explore strategies and techniques to navigate market volatility effectively, allowing you to protect your investments during turbulent times and capitalise on opportunities for growth. By understanding the causes of market volatility, managing emotions, implementing risk mitigation strategies, and seizing moments of uncertainty, you can navigate the markets with confidence and increase your chances of achieving financial success.

Understanding Market Volatility

This section provides a breakdown of market volatility, its causes, and its impact on investment/trading performance. Understand the different types of market volatility, including systematic and idiosyncratic risks. Learn how external factors, such as economic indicators, geopolitical events, and investor sentiment, can influence market volatility.

Market volatility is a measure of the degree of variation of trading prices over time. In the context of cryptocurrency trading, understanding, and managing market volatility is crucial for several reasons:

Opportunity for Profit:

- Positive Side: Volatility provides trading opportunities. In a volatile market, prices can change rapidly, creating opportunities for traders to profit from price swings.

- Negative Side: However, high volatility also comes with higher risk. Prices can move against traders just as quickly, leading to significant losses if not managed properly.

Liquidity:

- Positive Side: Volatility often attracts traders and liquidity to the market. Increased trading activity can lead to better liquidity, making it easier for traders to buy or sell assets without significantly impacting prices.

- Negative Side: During extreme volatility, liquidity can dry up, leading to wider bid-ask spreads and potential difficulties in executing trades at desired prices.

Risk Management:

- Positive Side: Understanding volatility is essential for effective risk management. Traders can adjust position sizes, set stop-loss orders, and employ other risk mitigation strategies based on the expected volatility.

- Negative Side: Ignoring or underestimating volatility can lead to unexpected losses, as price movements may be more extreme than anticipated.

Market Sentiment:

- Positive Side: Volatility often reflects shifts in market sentiment. Monitoring volatility can help traders gauge the overall mood of the market and make informed decisions.

- Negative Side: Excessive volatility can be driven by panic or fear, leading to irrational market behaviour. Traders need to be aware of these emotional aspects and avoid making impulsive decisions.

Market Volatility can be categorised into different types, including systematic volatility and idiosyncratic volatility. These terms are commonly used in finance to describe different sources of risk that can impact asset prices.

Systematic Volatility:

Definition: Systematic volatility, also known as market risk or undiversifiable risk, refers to the inherent risk associated with the overall market or a specific market segment.

Characteristics:

- It affects all securities in the market or a particular sector.
- Cannot be eliminated through diversification because it is a broad, market-wide phenomenon.
- Influenced by macroeconomic factors, geopolitical events, interest rates, and other systemic influences.
- Common measures of systematic volatility include beta, which indicates how closely an asset's price movements align with the market.

Idiosyncratic Volatility:

Definition: Idiosyncratic volatility, also known as specific risk or diversifiable risk, pertains to risks that are unique to a particular asset or a specific company.

Characteristics:

- It is company-specific and can be mitigated through diversification.
- Results from factors such as management decisions, company-specific news, and industry-specific events.
- Idiosyncratic volatility is often seen as company-specific price fluctuations that are not correlated with overall market movements.
- Investors can use diversification to reduce idiosyncratic risk by holding a diversified portfolio of assets.

Implied Volatility:

Definition: Implied volatility is a measure derived from option prices and reflects the market's expectations regarding future price volatility of a financial instrument.
Characteristics:

- It is forward-looking and represents the market's perception of potential future price swings.
- Implied volatility is particularly relevant in the options market, where it influences option premiums.
- Changes in implied volatility can provide insights into shifts in market sentiment and expectations.

Historical Volatility:

Definition: Historical volatility is a measure of past price movements of a financial instrument over a specific period.

Characteristics:

- It provides a retrospective view of how much an asset's price has fluctuated in the past.
- Historical volatility is often used to calculate standard deviation and other statistical measures to quantify the degree of past price variability.
- Traders and investors may use historical volatility to gauge potential future price movements.

Seasonal Volatility:

Definition: Seasonal volatility refers to patterns of increased or decreased volatility that occur at certain times of the year or during specific market seasons.

Characteristics:

- Some financial markets and assets may exhibit recurring patterns of volatility tied to seasons, months, or days of the week.
- Factors such as holidays, earnings seasons, or economic events can contribute to seasonal volatility.

Understanding these different types of volatility is crucial for investors and traders to manage risk effectively. Diversification can help mitigate idiosyncratic risk, while risk management strategies, such as the use of options and derivatives, can be employed to address systematic and implied volatility.

Additionally, staying informed about market conditions and economic indicators is essential for navigating various sources of volatility in financial markets.

Understanding Key Concepts

Volatility Measures:

- Historical Volatility (HV): Measures past price movements.

- Implied Volatility (IV): Reflects market expectations for future price movements (derived from options prices).

Volatility Index (VIX):

- Commonly known as the "fear index," it measures the market's expectation of future volatility. A rising VIX often indicates increased market uncertainty.

Average True Range (ATR):

- Measures market volatility by considering the true range of price movements.

News and Events:

- External factors, such as regulatory announcements, technological developments, or macroeconomic events, can significantly impact market volatility.

Technical Analysis:

- Chart patterns, such as triangles or channels, can be used to identify potential breakouts or breakdowns, indicating changes in volatility.

To navigate cryptocurrency market volatility successfully:

Stay Informed:

- Regularly monitor news and events that could impact the market.

Use Risk Management Strategies:

- Set stop-loss orders, diversify your portfolio, and avoid putting too much capital at risk in a single trade.

Adapt Trading Strategies:

- Adjust your trading strategies based on the level of volatility. Different strategies may be more suitable in ranging markets compared to trending markets.

Utilise Technical Analysis:

- Incorporate technical analysis tools to identify potential entry and exit points based on volatility patterns.

Be Disciplined:

- Stick to your trading plan, even in the face of high volatility. Emotional decision-making can lead to poor outcomes.

By understanding market volatility and implementing appropriate strategies, traders can navigate the challenges and capitalise on the opportunities presented.

Managing Emotional Responses to Volatility

Emotions play a significant role in investment decision-making, particularly during periods of market volatility. The heightened uncertainty and rapid price fluctuations characteristic of volatile markets can evoke emotions such as fear, greed, and anxiety.

To navigate these emotional challenges, it is crucial for traders and investors to implement strategies that help manage their emotional responses. One effective approach is to establish a well-defined trading plan before entering the market. This plan should include predetermined entry and exit points, risk tolerance levels, and profit-taking strategies. By adhering to a carefully crafted plan, investors can minimise impulsive decision-making driven by emotional reactions.

Additionally, setting realistic expectations and acknowledging that market volatility is an inherent part of trading can help individuals maintain a more rational and disciplined approach. Regularly reviewing and adjusting the trading plan in response to changing market conditions can also contribute to a sense of control, reducing the impact of emotional turbulence.

Furthermore, employing risk management techniques, such as setting stop-loss orders OCOs and diversifying portfolios, as discussed throughout this book, can provide a structured framework for handling risk and mitigating emotional stress. Finally, staying well-informed about market fundamentals, developments, and news can empower traders to make informed decisions, fostering a sense of confidence that can counteract emotional reactions in the face of volatility.

Long-Term Investing Amid Volatility

For your long-term strategies, once you reach the upper limits of your goals to one million,
it's crucial to maintain a long-term investing perspective and not succumb to market fluctuations.

This approach highlights the advantages of sustained investment over time, leveraging the potential for compounding returns. To succeed, focus on your investment goals, resist reacting to short-term market noise, and avoid impulsive decisions driven by temporary fluctuations.

Patience and consistency are key factors in achieving long-term financial success, emphasising the importance of staying committed to your investment strategy despite short-term market ups and downs.

Seizing Opportunities in Uncertainty

Uncertainty often accompanies market volatility, but it can also create opportunities for savvy investors. Exploring the mindset and strategies for seizing opportunities during uncertain trading market times involves a multi-faceted approach.

In cryptocurrency markets, identifying undervalued assets requires a deep understanding of the underlying technology, market trends, and potential for future adoption. Conduct thorough research, read TheMoonMag.com and consider the project's fundamentals, and evaluate its competitive positioning.

Assessing risk-reward ratios involves a meticulous analysis of potential gains versus potential losses. Establish clear entry, exit points, and use risk management tools, such as stop-loss orders, to protect investments. Having the courage to take calculated risks when others are fearful is a key component of successful trading.

Embrace a contrarian mindset, be wary of herd behaviour, and recognise that market fear can create buying opportunities. However, it's essential to maintain a disciplined approach and not succumb to impulsivity.

By combining a thorough understanding of the market, a calculated risk-taking mentality, and disciplined execution, traders can position themselves to capitalise on opportunities even in uncertain trading market times.

PSYCHOLOGY OF SUCCESSFUL TRADING

Mastering Your Mind

I love all things psychology; I love to understand how and why people do things, unravelling the intricacies of the human mind and gaining insights into the fascinating behaviours that shape our perceptions, decisions, and interactions with the world around us.

Why not, people watch the next time you sit down in a coffee shop, and you'll discover a captivating array of stories unfolding in the subtle gestures, expressions, and conversations of those around you, providing a window into the rich and diverse narratives that compose the human experience.

And next time you go to trade, open a TradingView chart on a low time frame and watch how the candles move, revealing intricate patterns reminiscent of Elliott waves shown in the earlier chapter. I guarantee you'll start to see patterns everywhere; the world is full of them, in people, nature, data, and beyond.

As you start seeing patterns more, the seemingly chaotic aspects of life begin to reveal underlying order and regularities.

In people, observe behavioural patterns and social dynamics; in nature, appreciate the symmetrical beauty of flora and the rhythmic cycles of ecosystems. Every year nature follows cycles and patterns turning Spring into Summer and Autumn into Winter.

Dive into data, and patterns emerge, guiding insights and predictions. It's a transformative perspective that invites you to uncover the intricacies woven into our very existence, providing a deeper understanding and appreciation for the patterns that shape the world around us.

Psychology is built into everything we do, influencing our thoughts, emotions, behaviours, and interactions daily. From the way we make decisions and form relationships to how we navigate challenges and perceive the world around us; the principles of psychology underpin the intricacies of human experience. Whether consciously or subconsciously, the study of psychology unveils the complexities of the human mind, shedding light on the motivations, biases, and cognitive processes that shape our every action and reaction.

The Role of Psychology in Trading

The role of psychology in trading is pivotal, influencing various aspects of a trader's decision-making process, risk management, and overall performance. Here's a quick recap of what I believe are key areas where psychology plays a significant role in trading:

Emotional Decision-Making:

- Fear and Greed: Emotions like fear and greed can significantly impact trading decisions. Fear of losses or the desire for quick profits can lead to impulsive actions that may not align with a well-thought-out strategy.

Risk Management:

- Risk Aversion: Traders' risk tolerance and aversion to losses are often influenced by psychological factors. Some traders may become overly conservative and miss opportunities, while others may take excessive risks driven by overconfidence.

Patience and Discipline:

- Impulse Control: Successful trading requires patience and discipline. Psychological factors such as impulsivity or a lack of self-control can lead to deviating from a trading plan, making decisions based on short-term emotions rather than a long-term strategy.

Cognitive Biases:

- Confirmation Bias: Traders may tend to seek information that confirms their existing beliefs and ignore data that contradicts their views. This confirmation bias can lead to flawed analyses and suboptimal decision-making.

Market Sentiment:

- Herd Behaviour: Traders often follow the crowd due to a fear of missing out or a desire to avoid losses. This herd behaviour can create market trends and bubbles, with traders making decisions based on the actions of others rather than independent analysis.

Adaptability:

- Ability to Learn: Psychological flexibility and the ability to learn from both successes and failures are crucial. Traders who can adapt to changing market conditions and continuously improve their strategies are more likely to succeed in the long run.

Stress Management:

- Handling Pressure: The high-pressure environment of trading can induce stress. Traders need effective stress management techniques to make rational decisions under pressure and avoid making emotionally driven mistakes.

Goal Setting:

- Motivation and Goals: Psychological factors influence a trader's motivation and goal setting. Clear goals and a strong sense of purpose can provide the psychological foundation for disciplined and focused trading.

By understanding and managing these psychological aspects, this is our why, how, when, and where are essential for traders aiming for long-term success. For me I believe traders must invest time in developing not just their technical skills but also their emotional intelligence and mental resilience and the reason the first third of this book completely focuses on that entirely.

Why, How, Where and When

The questions we covered in Section One "why, how, where, and when" serve as fundamental probes for understanding various aspects of human behaviour, cognition, and emotions.

Why:

- Purpose and Motivation: "Why" delves into the underlying motivations and purposes behind a behaviour or thought process. It explores the reasons individuals make certain choices or engage in specific actions.

How:

- Mechanisms and Processes: "How" focuses on the mechanisms and processes that contribute to a particular psychological phenomenon. It seeks to understand the steps or cognitive processes involved in the expression of behaviour or the formation of beliefs.

Where:

- Context and Environment: "Where" explores the environmental and contextual factors that influence behaviour. It considers the impact of physical settings, social environments, and cultural contexts on psychological processes.

When:

- Timing and Temporality: "When" investigates the timing and temporal aspects of psychological phenomena. It considers when certain behaviours or cognitive processes are more likely to occur and how they may change over time.

These questions are crucial in various branches of psychology, including clinical psychology, cognitive psychology, social psychology, and developmental psychology. For example:

- Clinical Psychology: "Why" might explore the reasons behind a specific mental health disorder, "How" could investigate the cognitive processes involved, "Where" might consider environmental triggers, and "When" could examine the timing of symptom onset.

- Cognitive Psychology: "Why" may investigate the purpose of certain cognitive processes, "How" could explore the mechanisms involved, "Where" might consider brain regions associated with these processes, and "When" could examine the timing of cognitive activities,

- Social Psychology: "Why" might focus on understanding social behaviours and motivations, "How" could explore the social mechanisms at play, "Where" might consider cultural influences, and "When" could examine the timing of social interactions.

These questions provide a systematic framework for to investigate, analyse, and understand everything we do.

"Today you are YOU!

That is truer than true there is NO ONE alive who is YOUER than YOU"?

Dr. Seuss

Emotional Intelligence and Self-Awareness

Emotional intelligence (EI) is the ability to recognise, understand, manage, and effectively use one's own emotions and navigate interpersonal relationships with empathy and sensitivity. In the context of trading, emotional intelligence is crucial for several reasons: Decision-Making:

- Managing Impulsivity: Emotional intelligence helps traders control impulsive decisions that may be driven by fear, greed, or anxiety. It allows for more rational and objective decision-making.

Risk Management:

- Self-Awareness: Traders with high emotional intelligence are more self-aware, allowing them to assess their risk tolerance accurately. This awareness contributes to better risk management and prevents taking unnecessary risks.

Adaptability:

- Flexibility in Changing Markets: Markets can be unpredictable. Emotional intelligence enables traders to adapt to changing market conditions, adjust strategies, and remain resilient in the face of setbacks.

Stress Management:

- Coping with Pressure: Trading is inherently stressful. Emotional intelligence equips traders with effective stress management techniques, ensuring they can make decisions under pressure without being unduly influenced by emotions.

Interpersonal Relationships:

- Understanding Others: Traders often interact with brokers, exchanges, colleagues, and other traders including those in trading communities - GettingStartedinCrypto.com, to create a sense of comradery and as a support network. . Emotional intelligence facilitates effective communication, conflict resolution, and the ability to understand the emotions and perspectives of others.

Patience and Discipline:

- Delayed Gratification: Successful trading requires patience and discipline. Emotional intelligence helps traders delay gratification, stick to their trading plans, and resist the urge to make impulsive moves for short-term gains.

Learning from Mistakes:

- Reflective Practice: Traders with high emotional intelligence are more likely to engage in reflective practices. They can objectively analyse both successful trades and losses, learning from mistakes and continuously improving their strategies.

Building and Maintaining Confidence:

- Positive Self-Regard: Emotional intelligence contributes to positive self-regard and confidence. Traders who are emotionally intelligent are more likely to bounce back from losses, maintaining a healthy mindset for future trading.

Intuition and Gut Feelings:

- Balancing Intuition: Emotional intelligence helps traders balance intuition with rational analysis. It allows them to trust their instincts when appropriate but also verify decisions with logical reasoning.

Goal Setting:

- Setting Realistic Goals: Emotional intelligence aids in setting realistic and achievable trading goals. Traders with high EI are more attuned to their strengths and weaknesses, allowing for more realistic goal setting.

Emotional intelligence is a crucial component of effective trading. It enhances decision-making, fosters adaptability, and contributes to successful risk management. Traders with high emotional intelligence are better equipped to navigate the complexities of financial markets and sustain long-term success. And hopefully after reading this book, I have helped paved your way to success.

Seeking Support and Continuous Learning

Traders can find valuable support and opportunities for continuous learning from a variety of online platforms and communities. Here are several options:

GettingStartedinCrypto.com:

- Websites dedicated to getting started in cryptocurrency, such as GettingStartedinCrypto.com, can provide educational content, tutorials, and community forums for crypto traders.

Reddit:

- Subreddits like r/Trading, r/StockMarket, and r/CryptoCurrency provide forums for traders to discuss strategies, share insights, and seek advice.

YouTube:

- YouTube channels like "Crypto Wendy O" "The Chart Guys," and "Crypto Daily" offer educational videos, market analysis, and trading strategies for traders at different skill levels.

Discord Communities:

- Discord servers like "Stock Market Alerts," and "TradingView" provide real-time discussions, alerts, and a community-driven environment for traders.

Investing and Trading Platforms:

- Platforms like Bybit, Bitget, Bitfinex, OKX, eToro, TradingView, and Interactive Brokers often have social features, forums, and educational resources for their users.

Twitter/ X.com:

- Follow reputable traders -Me - @LisaNEdwards , financial analysts, and trading platforms on the platforms to stay updated on market trends, news, and insights. Engaging in relevant hashtags like #Trading can lead to useful discussions.

Educational Websites and Blogs:

- Explore websites and blogs such as Investopedia, BabyPips (for forex), and CoinDesk or CoinMarketCap (for crypto) for in-depth educational content and market information.

Online Courses:

- Platforms like Udemy and Coursera offer various trading courses, ranging from beginner to advanced levels, covering topics such as technical analysis, algorithmic trading, and risk management.

Local Meetups and Conferences:

- Attend local trading meetups, "Crypto Mondays is Global or financial conferences to network with other traders, share experiences, and gain insights from industry experts. TheMoonMag.com often features there.

Books and Publications:

- Read trading books and financial publications to deepen your understanding. Authors like Jack Schwager, Nassim Taleb, and Edwin Lefèvre provide valuable insights into trading and markets.

Remember to approach information critically and verify the credibility of sources. Combining insights from various platforms can contribute to a well-rounded trading education. Always be cautious about the risks associated with trading.

"Believe you can, and you are halfway there!"

Theodore Roosevelt

"Self-control is strength.

Calmness is mastery. You have to get to a point where your mood doesn't shift based on the insignificant actions of someone else.

Don't allow others to control the direction of your life.

Don't allow your emotions to overpower your intelligence."

Morgan Freeman

LISANACCI – FIBONACCI "LISA STYLE"

After more than half my life trading, you develop easy ways to find setups and cheat codes for navigating the markets. LISANACCI works much like FIB Projection, but with a significant edge – it operates in tandem with algorithms, especially in cryptocurrency. Unlike traditional methods, LISANACCI leverages algorithmic levels, making it exceptionally accurate in predicting market movements. By incorporating how algorithms buy and sell into the process, I have been able to refine how LISANACCI works to coexist with these to enhance the precision of forecasting setups, providing more accurate trading setups.

To understand LISANACCI fully, you must first comprehend both Fibonacci Retracement and Extension and have a basic knowledge of Elliott Wave Principle, if you skipped that section, it's time to go back.

Fibonacci in Trading

Fibonacci retracement levels are a popular technical analysis tool used by traders to identify potential levels of support and resistance in financial markets. The Fibonacci sequence is a series of numbers where each number is the sum of the two preceding ones (e.g., 0, 1, 1, 2, 3, 5, 8, 13, 21, and so on).

The key Fibonacci levels used in trading are 23.6%, 38.2%, 50%, 61.8%, and 78.6%.

It's important to note that Fibonacci is usually used to identify changes in the trend, pullbacks, and potential reversal zones, providing traders with valuable insights into possible entry and exit points. By pinpointing levels of support and resistance, Fibonacci retracement assists in gauging the strength of a trend and anticipating where price movements may experience temporary setbacks or reversals.

This tool is most effective when integrated into a comprehensive trading strategy that incorporates other technical indicators as reflected in this section. It should include market analysis, and risk management principles to enhance decision-making accuracy and overall trading success.

Understanding Fibonacci Levels

Fibonacci retracement levels, derived from the famous Fibonacci sequence, are pivotal horizontal lines on a price chart indicating probable support and resistance zones. These levels correspond to specific percentages, representing how much of a previous price move has been retraced. The key Fibonacci retracement levels include 23.6%, 38.2%, 50%, 61.8%, and 78.6%, with 50%—though not an official Fibonacci ratio—also widely utilised.

The accuracy of this indicator lies in its applicability between any two significant price points, such as highs and lows. These levels are dynamically created based on the chosen price points. For instance, if the price rises by $10 and subsequently drops by $2.36, it retraces precisely 23.6%, a Fibonacci number. The prevalence of Fibonacci numbers in nature fuels the belief among traders that these ratios hold significance in financial markets.

Named after the Italian mathematician Leonardo Fibonacci, who introduced these numbers to Western Europe, Fibonacci retracement levels have their roots in ancient India, formulated between 450 and 200 BCE. Despite the historical association, Fibonacci did not originate the Fibonacci sequence but instead learned about it from Indian merchants.

Fibonacci Retracements in Technical Analysis

In technical analysis (TA), Fibonacci retracement levels pinpoint critical areas where the price may experience a reversal or stall in its price movement. Commonly used ratios include 23.6%, 38.2%, and 50%, among others. Traders leverage these levels to predict the potential future direction of a security's price movement, particularly between its high and low points.

Understanding Fibonacci Ratios

Fibonacci ratios stem from the Fibonacci sequence (0, 1, 1, 2, 3, 5, 8, 13, 21, 34, etc.), where each number is the sum of the two preceding ones. These ratios, including 23.6%, 38.2%, 50%, 61.8%, 78.6%, 100%, 161.8%, 261.8%, and 423.6%, are derived from mathematical relationships embedded in the sequence.

While 50% is not a pure Fibonacci ratio, it remains widely accepted as a support and resistance indicator. It is a psychological level that cannot be ignored.

Applying Fibonacci Retracement Levels in Trading

One of the most prevalent trading strategies involves using Fibonacci retracement levels to guide trade entries. For instance, a trader might observe the price experiencing a 38.2% decline after significant bullish momentum. Anticipating an upward trend, the trader enters the trade, considering the price arrival at a Fibonacci level as an opportune buying point.

Drawing Fibonacci Retracements

Fibonacci retracements are drawn as trend lines between two significant points, typically absolute lows, and highs, plotted on a price chart. Horizontal lines intersecting at Fibonacci levels are then placed, creating a visual representation of potential support and resistance levels.

Fibonacci retracements serve as valuable tools aiding traders in identifying support and resistance levels. Armed with this information, traders can strategically place orders, define stop-loss levels, and set price targets.

Fibonacci Retracement

Identifying a Trend: Before applying Fibonacci retracement, traders usually identify a trend. Fibonacci retracement is often used in trending markets to find potential levels where the price might retrace before continuing in the original direction.

Selecting Swing Points: Traders need to identify significant swing points in the price movement. A swing low to swing high is used in an uptrend, and a swing high to swing low is used in a downtrend.

Applying Fibonacci Levels: Once the swing points are identified, traders apply Fibonacci retracement levels to the chart. The tool is used to draw horizontal lines at the key Fibonacci levels (23.6%, 38.2%, 50%, 61.8%, and 78.6%) between the identified swing points.

Analysing Potential Reversal Zones: Traders use Fibonacci retracement levels to identify potential reversal zones. The idea is that after a significant price movement, the price may experience a retracement before continuing in the original direction. The retracement levels act as potential support or resistance levels.

Confirmation with Other Indicators: Traders often use Fibonacci retracement levels in conjunction with other technical indicators or chart patterns to increase the probability of accurate predictions. Common indicators include moving averages, trendlines, and candlestick patterns.

Trade Entry and Exit Points: Traders may use Fibonacci retracement levels to determine entry and exit points for trades. For example, they might enter a trade when the price approaches a Fibonacci support level in an uptrend or sell when it approaches a Fibonacci resistance level.

Fibonacci Extensions

Projection of Price Targets: Fibonacci extensions are used to project potential future price targets beyond the current trend. This is done by applying the Fibonacci extension tool to a significant price move, typically in the direction of the trend.

Identification of Extension Levels: The main extension levels used are 127.2%, 161.8%, 200%, and sometimes 261.8%. These levels represent potential areas where the price might reach after the trend resumes.

Trade Exit Points: Traders may use Fibonacci extensions to set profit targets. For example, in an uptrend, a trader might set a profit target at the 161.8% extension level.

Confirmation with Other Analysis: As with retracement, traders often use Fibonacci extensions alongside other technical analysis tools for confirmation.

Fibonacci retracement is primarily used to identify potential retracement levels within an existing trend, while Fibonacci extensions are used to project potential future price targets when a trend resumes. Both tools are part of the broader toolkit that traders use for technical analysis and decision-making.

It's important to note that while Fibonacci levels can be a useful tool, they are not foolproof, and trading decisions should not be based solely on them. Fibonacci retracement must be combined with other technical analysis methods like Elliott Wave and risk management strategies for more informed decision-making.

Additionally, market conditions can change, and no tool guarantees success in trading, so always use OCO, or some type of stop loss in line with money management practices discussed in this book.

LISANACCHI Method

The LISANACCI method by Lisa N Edwards is a specialised technique for predicting wave movements, particularly within the context of Elliott Wave theory and Fibonacci levels.

Here's a simplified breakdown:

- **Elliott Waves**: This is a theory that suggests financial markets move in distinct patterns or waves, and understanding these patterns can help predict future price movements.

- LISANACCI Method: This method, developed by Lisa N Edwards, is a way to predict the entire wave structure of a financial market using Elliott Wave principles.

- Fibonacci Levels: Fibonacci levels are mathematical ratios derived from the Fibonacci sequence (a series of numbers where each number is the sum of the two preceding ones). These ratios are often used in financial markets to identify potential levels of support and resistance.

In simple terms, the LISANACCI method is a systematic way of analysing market movements using a combination of Elliott Wave theory and Fibonacci ratios. By applying specific Fibonacci levels to each wave in the Elliott Wave sequence, traders can make more accurate predictions about the potential direction and magnitude of price movements in financial markets.

Application of LISANACCI with Fibonacci:

- **Wave 1:** Typically reaches 0.236 of its length.
- **Wave 2 (Correction):** Corrects to 0.382; in extended corrections, it might reach 0.5, and in Bearish Markets continue to the 0.786.
- **Wave 3:** Usually reaches 0.786, unless it's an extended wave, in which case it could reach 0.88-0.9, and in Bull markets 1.236.
- **Wave 4 (Correction):** Corrects within the golden zone of 0.618-0.65. In very bullish scenarios, it might reach 0.5; in bearish scenarios, it might reach 0.786.
- **Wave 5:** Generally, extends to a length of 1, although often stops at 0.9 unless it's an extended wave, in which case it could reach 1.618.

The overall correction will generally be similar to wave 3 ratio, if wave 3 goes to 0.786 the overall correction will reach this point. And the same for price the moves to 0.9 the overall correction will extend to 0.9 - for price that moves beyond this range we usually expect up to a 99% correction.

For retracements, we can look at what is known as pattern memory, as traders over time have observed recurring price patterns that tend to follow Fibonacci retracement levels. This phenomenon highlights the psychological aspect of trading, where market participants often exhibit similar behaviours in response to specific price movements.

Pattern memory involves recognising the historical tendencies of price retracements to halt or reverse at specific Fibonacci levels. Traders develop an intuitive sense of these patterns based on past market reactions, creating a collective memory within the trading community. This collective awareness influences decision-making, as traders anticipate potential reversals or continuation of trends at well-established Fibonacci retracement levels.

This pattern memory is not solely reliant on mathematical precision but is also shaped by the collective actions and reactions of market participants. As a result, traders may observe price behaviour around key Fibonacci levels and incorporate this observed pattern memory into their strategies.

However, it's crucial to acknowledge that while pattern memory can provide valuable insights, market conditions can evolve, and historical patterns may not always repeat. Therefore, careful traders combine pattern memory with ongoing analysis, adaptability, and risk management to make well-informed trading decisions in dynamic financial markets.

"Today you are YOU!

That is truer than true there is NO ONE alive who is YOUER than YOU"?

Dr. Seuss

EXAMPLE 1

If we look to the Bitcoin chart as an example

- WAVE 1 - 0.236
- WAVE 2 - 0.786
- WAVE 3 - 0.786
- WAVE 4 - 0.786
- WAVE 5 - POTENTIAL TARGETS
    - 0.9 Regular wave
    - 1:1 Standard wave
    - 1.618 Bullish wave

It's important to understand what part of the Elliott Wave cycle each wave falls into to have a greater understanding of the wave projections. . These are not actual targets, as BTC is in a Supercycle.

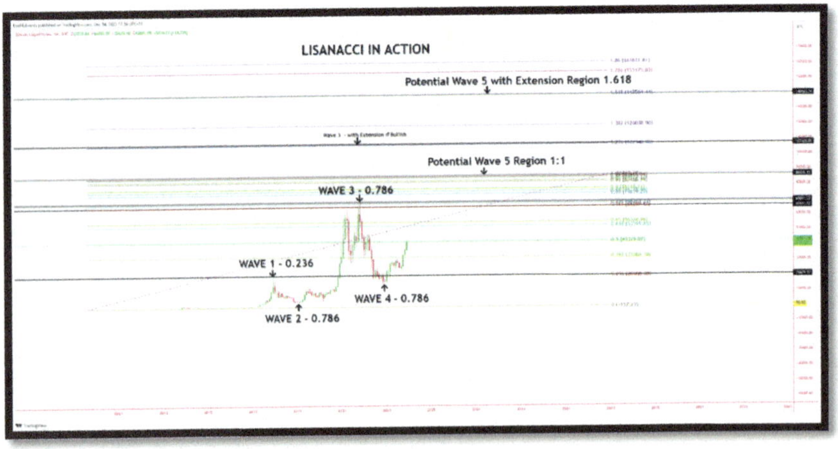

EXAMPLE 2

Step by Step with the Solana / Tether chart

- Wave 1 - 0.236

- Wave 2 - 0.65-0.618 Golden Zone

- Wave 3 -0.9 At this stage it is important to continue to move your STOP LOSS into profit.

- Wave 4 - 0.5 Standard retrace for Bullish Market
It's important to note the Fibonacci Retracement tool ONLY measures from the Wave high (0) to the wave 2 Low (1)

- Wave 5 - 1:1 in this case the market was extremely bullish pulling levels beyond the FIBs, we may have assumed 1.236 was possible and as the trade progressed past 1:1 we would have moved our STOP LOSS to lock profits.
-

- OVERALL RETRACE should be equal to WAVE 3 LISANACCI Level High or just beyond but not greater than 1:1

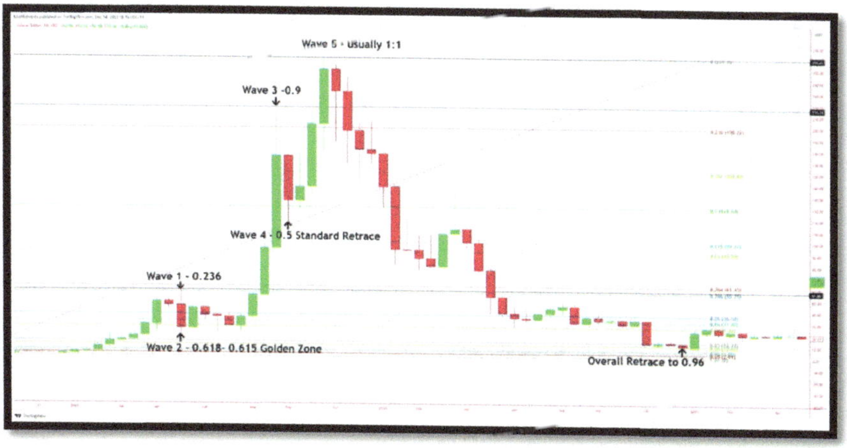

EXAMPLE 3

Applying to NASDAQ 100 INDEX

- Wave 1 - 0.236

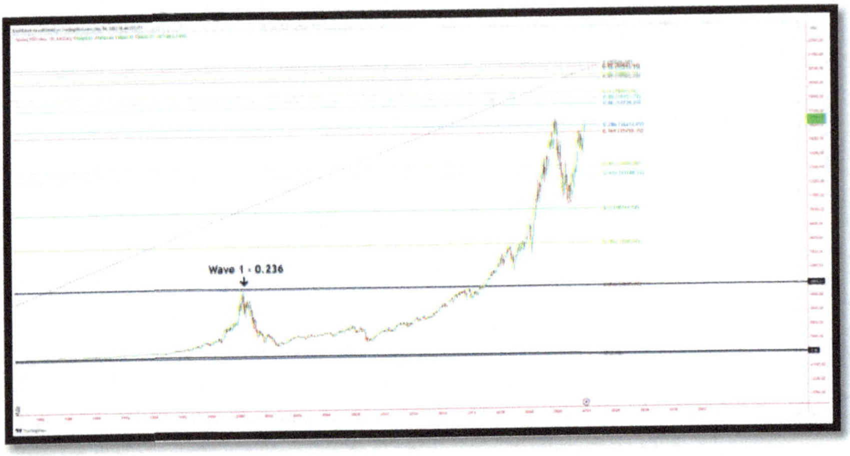

- Wave 2 - 0.786

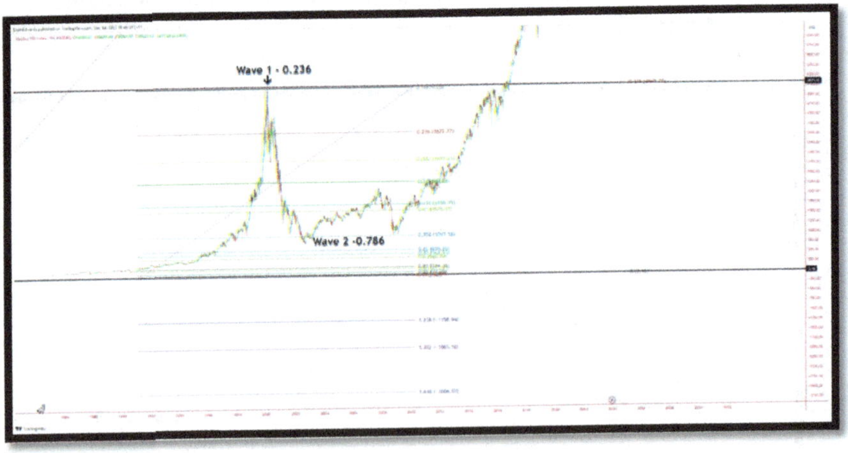

- Wave 3 - 0.786
  I often find if Wave 2 is 0.786 so will Wave 3

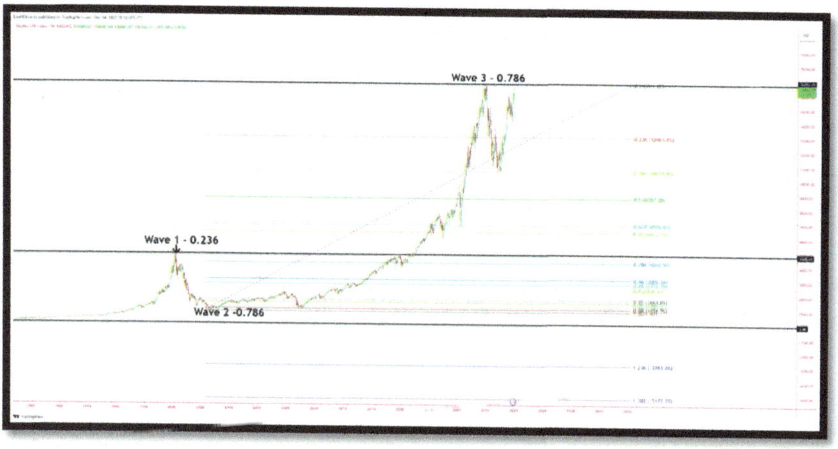

- Wave 4 - 0.382 which is a bullish retrace, but at this point it is important to refer to other indicators as to whether this wave is complete. If there is no breakout of the Wave 3 from this Wave 4 wave then it is likely the patten could decrease to form either a triangle or a wedge pattern, declining to lower FIB levels.

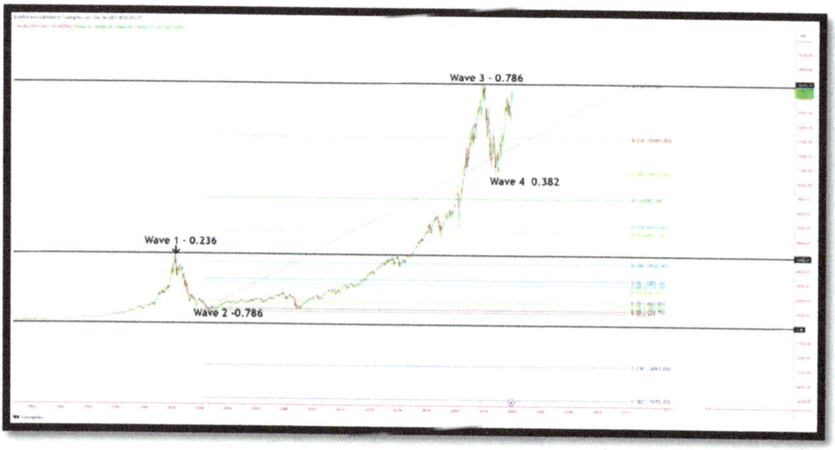

- Wave 5 Projections
  From a Standard Wave 1:1 to a Bullish 1.236 and Wave Extension 1.618

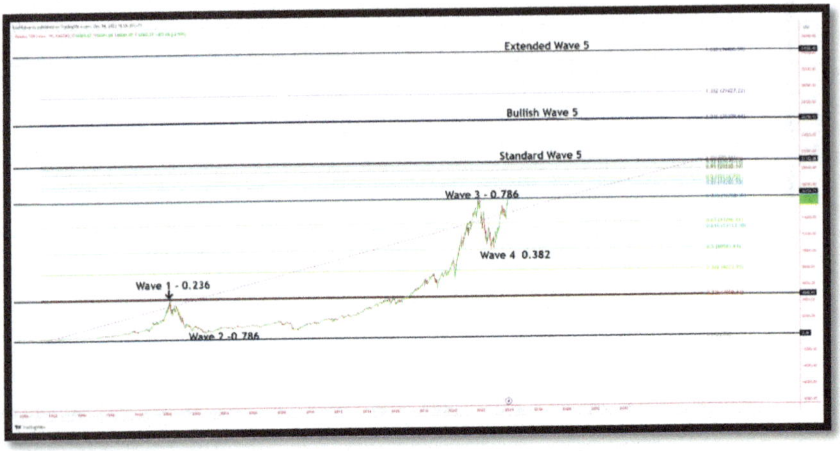

I have two basic rules about winning in trading as well in life...

1. If you don't bet, you can't win.
2. If you lose all your chips, you can't bet."

Larry Hite

SECTION 4

PRACTICAL CRYPTO LEARNING

10-week beginner trading course for crypto

IN THIS COURSE

- **Week 1: Introduction to Crypto Trading**
- **Week 2: Technical Analysis**
- **Week 3: Fundamental Analysis**
- **Week 4: Risk Management**
- **Week 5: Trading Strategies**
- **Week 6: Market Psychology**
- **Week 7: Trading Psychology**
- **Week 8: Cryptocurrency Investment**
- **Week 9: Technical Tools**
- **Week 10: Final Review and Assessment**

Week 1: Introduction to Crypto Trading

- What is cryptocurrency, and how does it work?
- Understanding blockchain technology
- Different types of cryptocurrencies
- Basic concepts of trading, such as buying, selling, and holding
- Setting up a crypto exchange account

Week 1: Introduction to Crypto Trading

Cryptocurrency is a digital or virtual currency that uses cryptography for security and operates independently of a central bank. It is based on blockchain technology, a decentralised ledger that records all transactions made on the network.

The first and most well-known cryptocurrency is Bitcoin, which was created in 2009 by an anonymous person or group using the pseudonym Satoshi Nakamoto. Since then, thousands of other cryptocurrencies, also known as altcoins, have been developed.

Cryptocurrencies are created through a process called mining, which involves solving complex mathematical equations using powerful computers. Once a block of transactions is verified and added to the blockchain, new cryptocurrency units are created as a reward for the miner.

Unlike traditional currencies, cryptocurrencies are not backed by a physical commodity or government. Instead, their value is determined by supply and demand on the market. The decentralised nature of the blockchain makes it more secure than traditional payment systems, as no central point of control can be hacked or manipulated.

Cryptocurrencies can be stored in digital wallets, and transactions can be made directly between users without needing a third party such as a bank. This allows for faster and cheaper transactions, especially for international payments.

Overall, cryptocurrency represents a new and exciting way of conducting financial transactions that challenge traditional banking systems and have the potential to disrupt many industries. However, it is important to understand the risks involved, such as the volatility of the market and the potential for fraud and scams.

Understanding Blockchain Technology

Blockchain technology is a decentralised digital ledger that records transactions securely and transparently. The blockchain is a distributed database maintained by a network of nodes or computers rather than a single central authority. Each node has a copy of the entire blockchain, and new transactions are verified and added to the ledger through a consensus mechanism.
One of the key features of blockchain technology is its transparency. Every transaction on the blockchain is visible to all participants, and once a block of transactions is added to the blockchain, it cannot be altered or deleted. This makes the blockchain immutable and resistant to tampering or fraud.

Another important aspect of blockchain technology is its security. Each block of transactions is linked to the previous block through a cryptographic hash function, creating a chain of blocks that is virtually impossible to modify without changing the entire chain. This makes the blockchain resistant to hacking and other forms of cyberattacks.

Blockchain technology is also fast and efficient. Transactions on the blockchain can be processed quickly and cheaply, making it an ideal solution for cross-border payments and other types of financial transactions. Additionally, the decentralised nature of the blockchain means there is no need for intermediaries such as banks or other financial institutions, reducing transaction costs and increasing efficiency.

Overall, blockchain technology has the potential to revolutionise many industries beyond just finance, including supply chain management, healthcare, and real estate. However, challenges and limitations to the technology, such as scalability and regulatory issues, which must be addressed before widespread adoption can occur.

Different types of cryptocurrencies

Thousands of different cryptocurrencies, also known as altcoins, are in circulation today. While Bitcoin is the most well-known and widely used cryptocurrency, many others offer unique features and benefits. Here are some types of cryptocurrencies – note these are represented in no particular order for no particular reason.

1. Bitcoin (BTC): the first cryptocurrency remains the most widely used and recognised. It is a decentralised digital currency that uses blockchain technology for secure and transparent transactions.
2. Ethereum (ETH): Ethereum is a decentralised platform that enables the creation of smart contracts and decentralised applications (dApps). It is also used as a cryptocurrency for transactions on the Ethereum network.
3. Ripple (XRP): Ripple is a real-time gross settlement system and currency exchange that uses blockchain technology. It is designed to enable fast and low-cost international payments.
4. Litecoin (LTC): Litecoin is a peer-to-peer cryptocurrency based on the Bitcoin protocol but with faster transaction times and lower fees.
5. Bitcoin Cash (BCH): Bitcoin Cash is a fork of the Bitcoin blockchain that was created in 2017. It is designed to offer faster transaction times and lower fees than Bitcoin.
6. Tether (USDT): Tether is a stablecoin pegged to the US dollar's value. It is designed to provide the stability of a fiat currency while still using blockchain technology for secure and transparent transactions.
7. Cardano (ADA): Cardano is a decentralised platform designed to offer more advanced features than Ethereum, such as proof-of-stake consensus and smart contract functionality.
8. Polkadot (DOT): Polkadot is a multi-chain platform that allows different blockchain networks to connect and interact with each other. It is designed to enable interoperability and scalability for blockchain applications.
9. Dogecoin (DOGE): Dogecoin is a decentralised cryptocurrency that was created as a joke but has gained a following due to its fun and lighthearted community. Also known as a meme coin. It is based on the Litecoin protocol but has faster transaction times and lower fees.

Overall, each type of cryptocurrency has its own unique features and benefits, and it's important to research and understand the differences before investing or trading.

Basic concepts of trading, such as buying, selling, and holding

Trading involves buying and selling assets, such as cryptocurrencies, with the goal of making a profit. Here are some basic concepts of trading:

1. BUYING: Buying involves purchasing an asset, such as a cryptocurrency, with the expectation that its value will increase over time. The price at which you buy an asset is known as the entry price.
2. SELLING: Selling involves selling an asset, such as a cryptocurrency, with the expectation that its value will decrease over time. The price at which you sell an asset is known as the exit price.
3. Holding: Holding involves keeping an asset, such as a cryptocurrency, for a period of time with the expectation that its value will increase over time. Holding can be a strategy for long-term investing or for waiting for the market to shift in your favour.
4. Market order: A market order is an order to buy or sell an asset at the current market price. Market orders are executed immediately, but the price at which the order is filled may differ from the current market price.
5. Limit order: A limit order is buying or selling an asset at a specific price. Limit orders are not executed immediately but are held until the market reaches the specified price.
6. Stop order: A stop order is an order to buy or sell an asset when it reaches a certain price level. Stop orders can be used to limit losses or to take profits at a specific price.
7. Margin trading: Margin trading allows traders to borrow funds to increase their buying power. Margin trading can be risky, as losses can exceed the initial investment.

Overall, it's important to have a solid understanding of these basic trading concepts before entering the cryptocurrency market. It's also important to conduct thorough research and analysis before making trades, as the market can be volatile and unpredictable.

Setting up a crypto exchange account

Setting up a cryptocurrency exchange account is necessary to begin trading cryptocurrencies. Here are some steps to follow when setting up a crypto exchange account:

1. Choose an exchange: Many cryptocurrency exchanges are available, so it's important to research and compare them before choosing one. Consider fees, security, supported cryptocurrencies, and user interface.
2. Create an account: Once you've chosen an exchange, create an account by providing your email address and a strong password. Some exchanges may require additional information, such as your full name and address, to comply with regulatory requirements.
3. Verify your identity: Most exchanges require users to complete a Know Your Customer (KYC) process to verify their identity. This may involve uploading a photo of your government-issued ID and a selfie.
4. Set up two-factor authentication (2FA): Two-factor authentication adds an extra layer of security to your account by requiring a second form of verification, such as a text message or app-based code, and your password.
5. Deposit funds: Once your account is set up and verified, you can deposit funds into your account using a bank transfer, credit card, or other payment method supported by the exchange. Some exchanges may also support cryptocurrency deposits.
6. Buy or sell cryptocurrencies: With funds in your account, you can buy or sell cryptocurrencies on the exchange. Follow the steps provided by the exchange to place orders and execute trades.

7. Withdraw funds: When you're ready to withdraw funds from your account, you can initiate a withdrawal to your bank account, or another payment method supported by the exchange. Some exchanges may also support cryptocurrency withdrawals.

It's important to remember that cryptocurrency exchanges can be vulnerable to hacking and other security threats. Be sure to follow best practices for securing your account, such as using a strong password and 2FA, and consider storing your cryptocurrencies in a secure offline wallet rather than leaving them on the exchange.

"The most important thing in making money is not letting your losses get out of hand.

When I became a winner, I said, 'I figured it out, but if I'm wrong, I'm getting the hell out, because I want to save my money and go on to the next trade."

Marty Schwartz

Week 2: Technical Analysis

- Introduction to technical analysis
- Understanding price charts and candlesticks
- Basic technical indicators such as Moving Averages, RSI, MACD, etc.
- How to use technical analysis to make trading decisions.

Week 2: Technical Analysis

Introduction to technical analysis

Technical analysis is a method of evaluating an asset's price movements and trends to make trading decisions. It involves analysing charts and using various tools and indicators to identify patterns and signals to help traders predict future price movements.

Here are some basic concepts and tools used in technical analysis:

1. Price charts: Price charts display an asset's price movements over a given period of time. Common types of charts include line charts, bar charts, and candlestick charts.

2. Support and resistance levels: Support and resistance levels are price levels where an asset has historically bounced back up or down. Traders use these levels to determine entry and exit points for trades.

3. Moving averages: Moving averages are lines that track an asset's average price over a specific period of time. Traders use moving averages to identify trends and potential support and resistance levels.

4. Relative Strength Index (RSI): The RSI is an indicator that measures an asset's strength and momentum by comparing the magnitude of its recent gains to its recent losses.

5. Fibonacci retracements: Fibonacci retracements are levels that indicate potential support and resistance levels based on a mathematical sequence.

6. Bollinger Bands: Bollinger Bands indicate potential price movements based on an asset's volatility. They are based on a moving average and standard deviation.

7. MACD: The Moving Average Convergence Divergence (MACD) is an indicator that measures an asset's momentum by comparing two moving averages.

Technical analysis is not foolproof, and it's important to use other tools and analysis methods in conjunction with technical analysis to make informed trading decisions. It's also important to remember that past price movements do not guarantee future price movements, and the cryptocurrency market can be volatile and unpredictable.

Understanding price charts and candlesticks

Price charts and candlesticks are important tools used in technical analysis to evaluate an asset's price movements and trends. Here's a closer look at how they work:

Price Charts:

Price charts display an asset's price movements over a given period of time. They can be displayed in various forms, such as line, bar, and candlestick charts. Each chart displays a different type of information, but candlestick charts are the most commonly used in technical analysis.

Candlestick Charts:

Candlestick charts represent an asset's price movements over a specific period of time, typically days or weeks. They are composed of individual candlesticks that show the opening, closing, and high, and low prices for that period.

Each candlestick comprises two parts: the body and the wick/shadow. The body represents the opening and closing prices, and the wick/shadow represents the high and low prices.

If the candlestick's body is filled or coloured, it indicates that the closing price was lower than the opening price, indicating a bearish trend. If the body is empty or white, it indicates that the closing price was higher than the opening price, indicating a bullish trend.

Candlestick charts also have patterns that can indicate potential trend reversals or continuations. Some common candlestick patterns include:

1. Doji: A Doji candlestick indicates indecision in the market and can signal a potential reversal.
2. Hammer: A Hammer candlestick has a small body and a long wick at the bottom, indicating a potential bullish reversal.
3. Shooting star: A Shooting Star candlestick has a small body and a long wick at the top, indicating a potential bearish reversal.
4. Engulfing: An Engulfing candlestick pattern occurs when a larger candlestick completely engulfs the previous smaller candlestick, indicating a potential trend reversal.

Understanding price charts and candlesticks are essential for technical analysis and can help traders make informed trading decisions. By analysing the patterns and trends displayed on these charts, traders can identify potential entry, exit points, and manage risk effectively.

Basic technical indicators such as Moving Averages, RSI, MACD, etc.

Basic technical indicators are tools used in technical analysis to help traders identify trends and potential price movements. Here are some of the most commonly used technical indicators:

1. Moving Averages: Moving averages are lines that track an asset's average price over a specific period of time. The most common types of moving averages are the Simple Moving Average (SMA) and the Exponential Moving Average (EMA). Traders use moving averages to identify trends and potential support and resistance levels.

2. Relative Strength Index (RSI): The RSI is an indicator that measures an asset's strength and momentum by comparing the magnitude of its recent gains to its recent losses. It ranges from 0 to 100, with readings above 70 indicating an asset is overbought and readings below 30 indicating an asset is oversold.

3. Moving Average Convergence Divergence (MACD): The MACD is an indicator that measures an asset's momentum by comparing two moving averages, typically a 12-period EMA and a 26-period EMA. It also includes a signal line, typically a 9-period EMA. Traders use the MACD to identify potential trend changes and momentum shifts.

4. Bollinger Bands: Bollinger Bands are lines that indicate potential price movements based on an asset's volatility. They are based on a moving average and standard deviation. The upper and lower bands represent potential resistance and support levels.

5. Fibonacci retracements: Fibonacci retracements are levels that indicate potential support and resistance levels based on a mathematical sequence. They are calculated by dividing an asset's price range by the Fibonacci ratios of 23.6%, 38.2%, 50%, 61.8%, and 100%.

6. Stochastic Oscillator: The Stochastic Oscillator is an indicator that measures an asset's momentum by comparing its closing price to its price range over a specific period of time. It ranges from 0 to 100, with readings above 80 indicating an asset is overbought and readings below 20 indicating an asset is oversold.

These are just a few examples of the many technical indicators available to traders. It's important to understand how each indicator works and how it can be used in conjunction with other indicators and analysis methods to make informed trading decisions.

How to use technical analysis to make trading decisions.

Technical analysis is a method used by traders to analyse an asset's price movements and trends based on historical data. It involves using various tools and indicators to identify potential entry, exit points, and manage risk.

Here are some steps to use technical analysis to make trading

decisions.

1. Identify the asset:-First, identify the asset you want to trade and gather historical price data, such as price charts and candlestick patterns.

2. Identify trends: Use moving averages and trend lines to identify the asset's overall trend. Is it trending upwards (bullish), downwards (bearish), or moving sideways (range-bound)?

3. Identify support and resistance levels: Use tools like Fibonacci retracements and Bollinger Bands to identify potential support and resistance levels. Support levels are areas where buyers may enter the market and drive prices up, while resistance levels are areas where sellers may enter the market and drive prices down.

4. Use indicators: Use technical indicators like the RSI, MACD, and Stochastic Oscillator to confirm trends, identify potential entry, and exit points. For example, if the RSI indicates that an asset is oversold and the MACD indicates a potential trend reversal, it may be a good time to enter a long position.

5. Set stop-loss orders: Set stop-loss orders to manage risk and limit potential losses. Stop-loss orders automatically close a trade if the asset's price reaches a certain level.

6. Monitor the market: Continuously monitor the market and adjust your trading strategy, as necessary. Use tools like price alerts and news feeds to stay up to date on market developments that may impact your trades.

It's important to note that technical analysis is not foolproof and cannot predict future price movements with certainty. However, by using technical analysis in conjunction with fundamental analysis and risk management strategies, traders can make informed trading decisions and improve their chances of success in the market.

"Don't worry about what the markets are going to do, worry about what you are going to do in response to the markets."

Michael Carr

Week 3: Fundamental Analysis

- Introduction to fundamental analysis
- Understanding news and events affecting the crypto market
- How to analyse market trends, market sentiment, and crypto projects
- How to use fundamental analysis to make trading decisions.

Week 3: Fundamental Analysis

- Introduction to fundamental analysis

Fundamental analysis is a method of evaluating an asset's intrinsic value by examining its underlying economic and financial factors. Unlike technical analysis, which focuses on price movements and trends, fundamental analysis takes a broader view of an asset's overall value.

Here are some key concepts and tools used in fundamental analysis:

1. Economic indicators: Economic indicators, such as GDP, inflation, and employment rates, can provide insight into the health of an economy and its potential impact on an asset's value. For example, a strong GDP growth rate may indicate a strong economy and increase demand for assets like stocks.

2. Company financial statements: Company financial statements, including income statements, balance sheets, and cash flow statements, can provide information on a company's financial health and potential for growth. For example, a company with strong revenue growth and low debt may be considered a good investment opportunity.

3. Industry trends: Analysing trends and developments in an asset's industry can provide insight into its potential growth and future demand. For example, a new technology or regulation may impact the demand for an asset like cryptocurrency.

4. Qualitative analysis: Qualitative analysis involves evaluating non-financial factors, such as a company's management team, brand reputation, and market positioning. These factors can impact investor sentiment and influence an asset's value.

5. Valuation methods: Several methods are used to value assets, including discounted cash flow analysis, price-to-earnings ratios, and price-to-book ratios. These methods compare an asset's current price to its underlying financial and economic factors to determine its potential value.

Fundamental analysis can be combined with technical analysis to make informed trading decisions. By examining an asset's underlying economic and financial factors, traders can better understand its potential value and make more informed investment decisions. However, it's important to remember that fundamental analysis is not foolproof and can be impacted by unexpected market developments and events.

Understanding news and events affecting the crypto market
News and events can significantly impact the cryptocurrency market, as they can influence investor sentiment and potentially impact an asset's value. Here are some key types of news and events that can affect the crypto market:

1. Regulatory developments: Regulatory developments, such as government actions to ban or regulate cryptocurrencies, can impact the demand for and value of cryptocurrencies. For example, news of a ban on cryptocurrency trading in a major market like China can lead to a sell-off and decreased demand for cryptocurrencies.

2. Technology advancements: Advances in blockchain technology and other related technologies can impact the demand for and value of cryptocurrencies. For example, news of a major upgrade to a cryptocurrency's underlying technology may lead to increased demand and a price increase.

3. Major company news: Major company news, such as partnerships, acquisitions, or product launches, can impact the demand for and value of cryptocurrencies. For example, news of a major retailer accepting cryptocurrency as payment can lead to increased demand and a price increase.

4. Market sentiment: General market sentiments, such as investor optimism or pessimism, can impact the demand for and value of cryptocurrencies. For example, positive market sentiment may lead to increased demand and a price increase.

5. Economic news: Economic news, such as inflation rates or interest rate changes, can impact the demand for and value of cryptocurrencies. For example, news of rising inflation rates may lead investors to seek out alternative assets like cryptocurrencies.

To stay up to date on news and events affecting the crypto market, traders can use news feeds, social media, and other sources of information. By staying informed and aware of potential market-moving events, traders can make more informed trading decisions and potentially profit from market movements. However, it's important to remember that unexpected events can always occur, and traders should always use proper risk management strategies to protect their investments.

- How to analyse market trends, market sentiment, and crypto projects

Analysing market trends, market sentiment, and crypto projects is a critical part of making informed trading decisions. Here are some key concepts and tools used in analysing these areas:

1. Market trends: Analysing market trends involves examining historical price data to identify patterns and potential future price movements. Traders can use technical analysis tools, such as moving averages and trend lines, to identify market trends and make informed trading decisions. Additionally, understanding market cycles and the factors that influence them can help traders anticipate potential price movements.

2. Market sentiment: Market sentiment refers to the overall attitude of investors and traders towards a particular asset or market. Traders can use sentiment analysis tools to track social media sentiment, news sentiment, and other data to gauge the

overall sentiment towards a particular asset. Understanding market sentiment can help traders anticipate potential price movements and make more informed trading decisions.

3. Crypto projects: Analysing crypto projects involves evaluating the potential of a particular cryptocurrency based on factors such as the team behind the project, the technology behind the project, and the potential use cases for the cryptocurrency. Traders can use tools like CoinGecko and CoinMarketCap to research different cryptocurrencies and evaluate their potential. Additionally, attending conferences and reading whitepapers can provide insight into the potential of different cryptocurrency projects.

By analysing market trends, market sentiment, and crypto projects, traders can gain a better understanding of the potential risks and rewards associated with different cryptocurrencies. This information can inform trading decisions and help traders make more informed investment choices. However, it's important to remember that analysis is not foolproof and unexpected events can always impact the market. Traders should always use proper risk management strategies and invest only what they can afford to lose.

How to use fundamental analysis to make trading decisions.

Fundamental analysis is a method of analysing the underlying value and potential of an asset based on its economic and financial factors. In the case of cryptocurrencies, fundamental analysis involves evaluating the project, technology, and market adoption of a particular cryptocurrency to determine its potential value. Here are some key steps to using fundamental analysis to make trading decisions:

1. Research the cryptocurrency: Start by researching the cryptocurrency and understanding its underlying technology, project roadmap, and use cases. Look for information about the development team, partnerships, and community engagement to gauge the potential value and adoption of the cryptocurrency.

2. Evaluate the market demand: Analyse the market demand for the cryptocurrency by looking at its trading volume, market capitalisation, and overall adoption. Look for any news or events that may have impacted the market demand for the cryptocurrency, such as new partnerships, regulatory developments, or technological advancements.

3. Look at the competition: Analyse the competition in the cryptocurrency market and compare the cryptocurrency in question to similar projects. Look for any advantages or disadvantages the cryptocurrency may have over its competitors, such as superior technology or better market adoption.

4. Evaluate the financials: Look at the financials of the cryptocurrency project, such as revenue, expenses, and profits. Evaluate any financial reports or public filings to understand the financial health of the project.

5. Plan: Use the information gathered from your research to decide on whether to invest in the cryptocurrency. If the fundamentals suggest that the cryptocurrency has strong potential for growth, it may be a good investment opportunity. Conversely, if the fundamentals suggest that the cryptocurrency is overvalued or has limited potential, it may be best to avoid the investment.

While fundamental analysis can provide valuable insights into the potential value of a cryptocurrency, it's important to remember that the cryptocurrency market is highly volatile and unpredictable. It's important to use proper risk management strategies and invest only what you can afford to lose. Additionally, it's important to stay up to date on news and events that may impact the cryptocurrency market and adjust your investment strategy accordingly.

Week 4: Risk Management

- Introduction to risk management
- Understanding the importance of risk management in trading
- Setting up a trading plan
- Identifying and managing risks
- Understanding leverage and margin trading

Week 4: Risk Management

- Introduction to risk management

Risk management is a critical aspect of trading any asset, including cryptocurrencies. It involves identifying and assessing potential risks associated with an investment and taking steps to minimise those risks. Here are some key concepts and strategies to consider when managing risk in cryptocurrency trading:

1. Risk assessment: The first step in risk management is identifying potential risks associated with your investment. Some common risks associated with cryptocurrency trading include market volatility, regulatory changes, and cybersecurity risks. By understanding and assessing these risks, you can make informed decisions about how to minimise them.

2. Diversification: One strategy for managing risk is to diversify your investment portfolio. This involves investing in various cryptocurrencies or other assets to minimise the impact of any one investment. By spreading your investments across different assets, you can reduce your overall risk and potentially increase your returns.

3. Stop-loss orders: A stop-loss order is an instruction to automatically sell a cryptocurrency at a certain price point. This strategy can be useful for limiting potential losses by automatically selling a cryptocurrency if its price drops below a certain level.

4. Position sizing: Position sizing involves determining the appropriate size of your investment based on the level of risk associated with the investment. By allocating a smaller portion of your portfolio to high-risk investments, you can limit potential losses if those investments don't perform as expected.

5. Risk-reward ratio: The risk-reward ratio is a calculation that compares the potential reward of an investment to the potential risk. By analysing the risk-reward ratio of an investment, you can make informed decisions about whether the potential reward justifies the potential risk.

Overall, risk management is a critical aspect of successful cryptocurrency trading. By understanding potential risks, diversifying your portfolio, using stop-loss orders, appropriately sizing your positions, and analysing risk-reward ratios, you can make informed decisions that help you minimise potential losses and maximise potential returns. It's important to remember that no investment strategy is foolproof, and unexpected events can always impact the market. As such, it's important to stay up to date on market news and adjust your investment strategy accordingly.

- Understanding the importance of risk management in trading

Risk management is a critical component of trading in any financial market, including cryptocurrency trading. Risks are always involved in trading, including market volatility, regulatory changes, and unexpected events that can impact the market. Effective risk management is essential for protecting your investments and minimising losses in the face of these risks.

Here are some reasons why risk management is important in trading:

1. Protects your capital: Effective risk management can help protect your trading capital by minimising losses. By managing your risk, you can reduce the likelihood of large losses that could wipe out your account.

2. Reduces emotional stress: Trading can be emotionally challenging, especially when the market is volatile. By having a risk management plan in place, you can reduce the emotional stress that comes with trading by knowing exactly when to exit a trade or cut your losses.

3. Increases long-term profitability: Successful traders understand the importance of long-term risk management. By taking small losses and avoiding big ones, you can maintain a consistent trading strategy and increase your overall profitability over time.

4. Provides a clear trading plan: Effective risk management requires a clear trading plan, which can help you stay focused on your goals and make informed decisions about when to enter and exit trades.

5. Reduces overall risk: Diversification and other risk management strategies can help reduce overall risk by spreading your investments across multiple assets and limiting your exposure to any one investment.

Overall, risk management is a critical component of successful trading in any financial market. By understanding the risks involved in trading, implementing effective risk management strategies, and staying disciplined and focused on your trading plan, you can increase your chances of success and minimise potential losses.

- Setting up a trading plan

A trading plan is a critical component of successful trading. It's a written document that outlines your trading goals, strategies, risk management rules, and other important details that can help you stay disciplined and focused when trading cryptocurrencies. Here are some key steps to consider when setting up a trading plan:

1. Define your trading goals: The first step in setting up a trading plan is to define your trading goals. What do you hope to achieve through trading? Are you looking to generate income, build wealth, or simply gain experience in the market? Defining your goals can help you stay focused on what's important and make informed decisions about how to achieve them.

2. Determine your risk tolerance: Risk tolerance refers to your willingness to take on risk when trading. It's important to understand your risk tolerance and set up risk management rules that align with it. For example, if you have a low-risk tolerance, you may want to limit your exposure to high-risk investments and use conservative risk management strategies.

3. Choose your trading strategy: There are many different trading strategies you can use when trading cryptocurrencies, including technical analysis, fundamental analysis, and trend following. Choose a strategy that aligns with your goals and risk tolerance.

4. Develop a risk management plan: A risk management plan is a critical component of any trading plan. It should outline the steps you'll take to manage risk, including how you'll determine your position size when you'll use stop-loss orders, and how you'll diversify your portfolio.

5. Set up a trading schedule: Setting up a trading schedule can help you stay disciplined and focused. Determine when you'll trade, how long you'll hold positions, and how you'll monitor market news and events.

6. Monitor your progress: Monitoring your progress is an important part of any trading plan. Keep track of your trades, analyse your performance, and adjust your plan as needed based on your results.

Overall, setting up a trading plan is a critical component of successful trading. By defining your goals, determining your risk tolerance, choosing a trading strategy, developing a risk management plan, setting up a trading schedule, and monitoring your progress, you can increase your chances of success and minimise potential losses when trading cryptocurrencies.

- Identifying and managing risks

Identifying and managing risks is an essential aspect of successful trading. Risk management involves identifying potential risks and developing strategies to minimise or mitigate them. Here are some key steps to consider when identifying and managing risks in cryptocurrency trading:

1. Identify potential risks: The first step in managing risk is to identify potential risks. These risks could include market volatility, unexpected news or events, liquidity issues, and technical issues with the trading platform.

2. Develop a risk management plan: Once you've identified potential risks, develop a risk management plan. This plan should outline the steps you'll take to minimise or mitigate each risk. For example, you may decide to use stop-loss orders to limit losses in case of market volatility or unexpected news.

3. Diversify your portfolio: Diversification is a key strategy for managing risk in trading. By spreading your investments across multiple cryptocurrencies or other assets, you can reduce your exposure to any one particular asset and potentially minimise losses.

4. Use proper position sizing: Position sizing refers to the amount of capital you allocate to each trade. Using proper position sizing can help you manage risk by limiting your exposure to any one trade. For example, you may decide to only allocate a small percentage of your portfolio to any one trade.

5. Use stop-loss orders: Stop-loss orders are a key risk management tool that can help you limit losses in case of market volatility or unexpected news. A stop-loss order is an order to sell an asset if it reaches a certain price. This can help you limit your losses if the market moves against you.

6. Stay informed: Staying informed about market news and events is an important part of managing risk. By keeping current on the latest developments in the cryptocurrency market, you can be better prepared to adjust your trading strategy in response to changing market conditions.

Overall, managing risk is a critical aspect of successful trading. By identifying potential risks, developing a risk management plan, diversifying your portfolio, using proper position sizing, using stop-loss orders, and staying informed, you can minimise potential losses and increase your chances of success when trading cryptocurrencies.

- Understanding leverage and margin trading

Leverage and margin trading are two concepts that can be confusing for beginner traders. Here is a closer look at what they mean and how they work in the context of cryptocurrency trading:

1. Leverage: Leverage refers to borrowing funds from a trading platform to increase your buying power. Essentially, leverage allows you to control a larger amount of assets than you would be able to if you only used your own capital. For example, if you have $1,000 in your trading account and your exchange offers 10:1 leverage, you can control up to $10,000 worth of cryptocurrency. This can potentially lead to larger profits but also magnify potential losses.

2. Margin trading: Margin trading refers to the practice of using borrowed funds (i.e., leverage) to open larger positions in the market. When you open a margin trade, you are required to put up a certain amount of collateral, which is used to cover any potential losses. For example, if you open a margin trade with $1,000 worth of cryptocurrency and the exchange requires a 50% margin, you will need to put up $500 as collateral. Margin trading can increase your potential profits but also magnify potential losses.

It is important to note that leverage and margin trading can be risky and are not recommended for beginner traders. If you decide to use leverage and margin trading, it is important to have a solid understanding of the risks involved and to use proper risk management strategies, such as setting stop-loss orders and using proper position sizing.

In summary, leverage and margin trading are tools that can increase your buying power and potentially lead to larger profits, but also come with increased risk. Before using these tools, it is important to have a solid understanding of how they work and to use proper risk management strategies to protect your capital.

"Being a successful trader also takes courage: the courage to try, the courage to fail, the courage to succeed, and the courage to keep on going when the going gets tough.

Perhaps the most important rule is to hold on to your winners and cut your losers."

Michael Marcus

Week 5: Trading Strategies

- Introduction to trading strategies
- Scalping, day trading, swing trading, and position trading
- Choosing the right strategy for your trading style and goals
- How to develop and back test your trading strategy.

Week 5: Trading Strategies

- Introduction to trading strategies

Trading strategies are a set of rules and guidelines that traders use to make trading decisions. A good trading strategy should consider a trader's personal goals, risk tolerance, and market conditions. Here are some common trading strategies that can be used in cryptocurrency trading:

1. Day trading: Day trading involves opening and closing trades within the same day, with the goal of profiting from short-term price movements. Day traders often use technical analysis to identify entry and exit points.

2. Swing trading: Swing trading involves holding positions for several days or weeks to profit from medium-term price movements. Swing traders often use a combination of technical and fundamental analysis to identify potential trades.

3. Position trading: Position trading involves holding positions for several months or even years to profit from long term price movements. Position traders often use fundamental analysis to identify strong crypto projects and hold their positions through market ups and downs.

4. Trend following: Trend following is a strategy that involves following the direction of the market trend. Traders using this strategy will typically wait for a trend to develop and then enter trades in the same direction as the trend.

5. Contrarian trading: Contrarian trading involves taking positions that are opposite to the prevailing market sentiment. Traders using this strategy will typically look for overbought or oversold market conditions and take positions in the opposite direction of the prevailing trend.

These are just a few examples of trading strategies that can be used in cryptocurrency trading. It is important to remember that there is no one-size-fits-all approach to trading, and that a successful trading strategy should be tailored to your own personal goals, risk tolerance, and market conditions. Additionally, it is important to continually test and refine your trading strategy over time to ensure that it remains effective in different market conditions.

- Scalping, day trading, swing trading, and position trading

Scalping, day trading, swing trading, and position trading are all common trading strategies used in various markets, including cryptocurrency. Here is an overview of each strategy:

1. Scalping: Scalping is a short-term trading strategy that involves making a large number of trades within a single day to capture small price movements. Traders who use this strategy will typically enter and exit positions quickly, often in a matter of seconds or minutes, and aim to make a small profit on each trade. Scalping requires a high level of discipline and focus, as traders must be able to quickly identify entry and exit points based on technical indicators or other market signals.

2. Day trading: Day trading involves opening and closing trades within the same day, with the goal of profiting from short-term price movements. Day traders often use technical analysis to identify entry and exit points and may make several trades per day. This strategy requires a high level of attention to market conditions and the ability to react quickly to changing prices.

3. Swing trading: Swing trading involves holding positions for several days or weeks to profit from medium-term price movements. Swing traders often use a combination of technical and fundamental analysis to identify potential trades and may make several trades per week. This strategy requires less attention to the market than day trading but still requires a significant amount of analysis and discipline.

4. Position trading: Position trading involves holding positions for several months or even years to profit from long-term price movements. Position traders often use fundamental analysis to identify strong crypto projects and hold their positions through market ups and downs. This strategy requires a long-term perspective and a high tolerance for risk.

Each of these trading strategies has its own advantages and disadvantages, and the best approach will depend on a trader's personal goals, risk tolerance, and market conditions. It is important to develop a trading strategy that aligns with your own strengths and preferences and to continually refine that strategy over time based on your experience and market conditions.

- Choosing the right strategy for your trading style and goals

Choosing the right trading strategy is an essential part of a successful trading journey. Here are some factors to consider when selecting the appropriate strategy for your trading style and goals:

1. Risk tolerance: Your risk tolerance is an essential factor in choosing the right trading strategy. Some strategies, such as scalping and day trading, are more high-risk, and high reward, while others, like position trading, are less risky but offer less potential for quick profits. Consider how much risk you are willing to take on and choose a strategy that aligns with your risk tolerance.

2. Time commitment: Different trading strategies require varying levels of time commitment. Scalping and day trading, for example, require a trader to be active in the market throughout the day, while position trading may only require checking in on the market a few times a week. Consider how much time you will dedicate to trading and choose a strategy that fits your schedule.

3. Market conditions: Market conditions can significantly impact the effectiveness of different trading strategies. For example, a volatile market may be better suited for day trading or scalping, while a stable market may be more conducive to position trading. Consider the current state of the market and choose a strategy that aligns with the current conditions.

4. Trading goals: Your trading goals will also play a significant role in selecting a trading strategy. Are you looking to make quick profits or generate steady returns over the long term? Are you looking to trade full-time or as a side income? Your goals will help you determine the appropriate strategy to pursue.

5. Trading experience: Finally, your level of experience as a trader will also impact your choice of strategy. Beginners may want to start with a more straightforward strategy like position trading, while experienced traders may be more comfortable with complex strategies like day trading or scalping.

In summary, choosing the right trading strategy requires careful consideration of your risk tolerance, time commitment, market conditions, trading goals, and experience level. By evaluating these factors, you can select a strategy that aligns with your unique needs and increases your chances of success in the cryptocurrency market.

- **How to develop and back test your trading strategy**

Developing and back testing your trading strategy is crucial to ensure it is effective and profitable. Here are some steps you can follow to develop and back test your trading strategy:

1. Define your strategy: Start by defining your strategy, including entry and exit criteria, stop-loss and take-profit levels, and risk management rules. Be as specific as possible to make testing and evaluating your strategy easier.

2. Choose a back testing platform: There are several back testing platforms available, such as TradingView, MetaTrader, and MultiCharts. Choose a platform that aligns with your trading style and provides the necessary features to test your strategy effectively.

3. Gather historical data: Collect historical price data for the cryptocurrency you want to trade. The data should include the open, high, low, and close prices, as well as trading volume and other relevant indicators.

4. Input your strategy into the back testing platform: Input your strategy into the back testing platform, including all the relevant rules and criteria you defined in step one.

5. Run the back test: Run the back test using the historical data you gathered in step three. The back testing platform will simulate your strategy over the historical data and provide you with performance metrics, such as the profit and loss, win-loss ratio, and maximum drawdown.

6. Analyse the results: Analyse the back testing results to determine the effectiveness of your strategy. Look for patterns in the data and identify any weaknesses or areas for improvement. Adjust your strategy and retest until you achieve the desired results.

7. Optimise your strategy: Once you have identified areas for improvement, optimise your strategy to enhance its performance. Adjust your entry and exit criteria, stop-loss and take-profit levels, and risk management rules to achieve better results.

8. Test your strategy in a demo account: After optimising your strategy, test it in a demo account using real-time market data. This will allow you to evaluate your strategy's performance in live market conditions and make any final adjustments before trading with real money.

Week 6: Market Psychology

- Introduction to market psychology
- Understanding emotions and biases in trading
- How to control emotions and avoid common trading mistakes
- The importance of discipline and patience in trading

Week 6: Market Psychology

- Introduction to market psychology

Market psychology studies how investors and traders make decisions in financial markets. It is based on the understanding that financial markets are not purely rational entities but rather are influenced by the emotions, biases, and beliefs of the people who participate in them.

There are several key concepts related to market psychology that are important for traders to understand:

1. Herding behaviour: This refers to the tendency of individuals to follow the crowd, even if it goes against their own beliefs or interests. This can lead to bubbles and crashes in financial markets as investors all move in the same direction without considering the underlying fundamentals.

2. Fear and greed: Fear and greed are two of the most powerful emotions driving financial markets. Fear can lead to panic selling and market crashes, while greed can lead to overvalued assets and bubbles.

3. Confirmation bias: This is the tendency to seek out information that confirms our existing beliefs while ignoring information that contradicts them. This can lead to traders becoming overly confident in their positions and ignoring warning signs of a market downturn in financial markets.

4. Anchoring bias: This refers to the tendency of individuals to rely too heavily on the first piece of information they receive when planning. In financial markets, this can lead to traders becoming fixated on a particular price or trend, even if the market has moved in a different direction.

5. Hindsight bias: This is the tendency to view past events as more predictable than they actually were. In financial markets, this can lead traders to believe that they could have predicted a market movement, even if it was not predictable at the time.

Understanding market psychology can help traders make better decisions by recognising the emotions and biases influencing their trading. By being aware of these concepts and learning to control their own emotions and biases, traders can make more informed and rational decisions in the cryptocurrency market.

- Understanding emotions and biases in trading

Emotions and biases play a significant role in trading decisions, as they can cloud judgment and lead to irrational decisions. Here are some of the common emotions and biases that traders need to be aware of:

1. Fear: Fear is a natural response to a potential loss or risk. In trading, fear can lead to selling assets prematurely or making decisions based on panic rather than analysis. This can result in missing out on profitable trades or taking unnecessary losses.

2. Greed: Greed is the desire to make profits quickly and excessively. In trading, greed can lead to taking excessive risks or not taking profits when they are available. This can result in significant losses and can cause traders to hold onto losing positions for too long.

3. Confirmation bias: This is the tendency to look for information that supports our pre-existing beliefs and ignore information that contradicts them. In trading, confirmation bias can lead to ignoring warning signals or market trends that go against our pre-existing beliefs, resulting in poor trading decisions.

4. Anchoring bias: Anchoring bias is the tendency to rely too heavily on the first piece of information that is available when making decisions. This can lead to traders becoming fixated on a particular price or trend, even if the market has moved in a different direction.

5. Overconfidence: Overconfidence is a bias that can lead traders to overestimate their ability to make profitable trades. This can result in taking unnecessary risks and making poor trading decisions.

By recognising these emotions and biases, traders can take steps to mitigate their impact on their decision-making. This includes using risk management strategies, creating a trading plan, and relying on technical and fundamental analysis to inform trading decisions rather than emotions and biases.

- How to control emotions and avoid common trading mistakes

Controlling emotions and avoiding common trading mistakes are essential for successful trading. Here are some tips to help you:

1. Have a trading plan: A well-defined trading plan outlining your entry and exit strategies can help you avoid impulsive decisions. To limit potential losses, your trading plan should also include risk management strategies, such as stop-loss orders.

2. Use technical and fundamental analysis: Relying on technical and fundamental analysis can help you make informed trading decisions based on market trends, news events, and other relevant data. This can help you avoid making decisions based on emotions or biases.

3. Practice good risk management: Implementing good risk management strategies, such as position sizing and diversification, can help you minimise potential losses and avoid making risky trades.

4. Stay disciplined: Sticking to your trading plan and avoiding impulsive decisions can help you stay disciplined and avoid common trading mistakes.

5. Manage your emotions: Recognise and manage your emotions, such as fear and greed, by taking breaks, practising meditation, or other stress-reducing techniques, and avoiding impulsive decisions when you are feeling emotional.

6. Learn from your mistakes: Review your trading decisions and learn from your mistakes. Analysing your mistakes can help you avoid repeating them in the future.

Remember, successful trading requires discipline, patience, and the ability to control your emotions. By following these tips, you can avoid common trading mistakes and make informed decisions based on analysis rather than emotions or biases.

- The importance of discipline and patience in trading

Discipline and patience are two critical traits that are essential for success in trading. Without them, developing a profitable trading strategy and sticking to it over the long term is difficult. Here are some reasons why discipline and patience are important in trading:

1. Helps you avoid impulsive decisions: Discipline and patience can help you avoid making impulsive trading decisions that are not based on sound analysis or market data. A well-thought-out trading strategy can help you identify profitable trading opportunities and avoid making decisions based on emotions or hunches.

2. Enables you to stick to your trading plan: this is only effective if you can stick to it consistently. Discipline and patience can help you follow your plan, even during volatile market conditions. This can help you avoid making rash decisions that could lead to significant losses.

3. Discipline and patience can help you manage risk effectively by allowing you to use risk management strategies such as stop-loss orders and position sizing. These strategies can help you limit potential losses and protect your trading capital.

4. Helps you to stay focused: Discipline and patience can help you stay focused on your trading goals and avoid distractions that could lead to poor decision-making. This can help you avoid common trading mistakes, such as overtrading or chasing losses.

5. Enables you to learn from your mistakes: Discipline and patience can help you take a more objective view of your trading decisions and learn from your mistakes. By analysing your trading results and identifying areas for improvement, you can refine your trading strategy and become a more successful trader.

In summary, discipline and patience are essential traits for successful trading. By developing a well-defined trading plan, sticking to it consistently, and managing risk effectively, you can improve your chances of market success. Remember, trading is a long-term endeavour; it takes discipline and patience to achieve lasting success.

"Make good decisions even with incomplete information. You will never have all the information you need. What matters is what you do with the information you have."

Michael Steinhardt

Week 7: Trading Psychology

- Introduction to trading psychology
- Understanding the psychology of winning and losing
- How to develop a winning mindset and positive attitude
- Dealing with stress and anxiety in trading

Week 7: Trading Psychology

- Introduction to trading psychology

Trading psychology refers to the mental and emotional factors that affect a trader's decision-making process. Managing emotions and staying disciplined is a crucial aspect of successful trading. Here are some key concepts that traders need to understand about trading psychology:

1. Emotions: Trading can be an emotional rollercoaster, and managing emotions is one of the most challenging aspects of trading. Fear, greed, and anxiety are common emotions that traders experience, and they can lead to irrational decision-making. To be a successful trader, developing emotional intelligence and learning how to manage these emotions effectively is essential.

2. Cognitive biases: Cognitive biases are mental shortcuts that people use to make decisions. In trading, cognitive biases can lead to irrational decision-making and can result in significant losses. Traders need to be aware of common biases such as confirmation bias, recency bias, and availability bias and learn how to avoid them.

3. Mental states: Mental states such as focus, concentration, and flow is essential for successful trading. Traders need to develop a mindset that allows them to stay focused on their goals, remain calm under pressure, and make rational decisions based on market data.

4. Self-discipline: Self-discipline is the foundation of successful trading. Traders must be disciplined to stick to their trading plan, follow their risk management strategy, and avoid making impulsive decisions. Developing self-discipline requires practice and persistence, but it's a critical factor in achieving long-term success in trading.
5. Mindfulness: Mindfulness is the practice of being present in the moment and aware of your thoughts and emotions.

Mindfulness can help you stay focused on your trading goals, manage emotions effectively, and make rational decisions. Traders can develop mindfulness through meditation, mindfulness exercises, and other practices.

In summary, trading psychology is an essential aspect of successful trading. Traders need to develop emotional intelligence, learn how to manage cognitive biases, develop a disciplined mindset, and practice mindfulness. By understanding these concepts and applying them to their trading, traders can improve their decision-making process and achieve long-term success in the markets.

- Understanding the psychology of winning and losing

Understanding the psychology of winning and losing is a critical aspect of trading psychology. How traders react to wins, and losses can significantly impact their decision-making process and overall trading performance. Here are some key concepts to understand about the psychology of winning and losing in trading:

1. Winning: Winning is an essential part of trading, and it can create a sense of euphoria and overconfidence in traders. However, excessive confidence can lead to complacency and a lack of discipline. Traders need to be aware of the potential risks of winning streaks and maintain their focus and discipline to avoid making mistakes.

2. Losing: Losing is a part of trading and can be emotionally challenging for traders. Losses can trigger negative emotions such as fear, anxiety, and frustration leading to irrational decision-making. Traders need to learn how to manage their emotions effectively and develop a mindset that allows them to learn from their losses and move on.

3. Loss aversion: Loss aversion is a psychological bias that causes people to feel the pain of losses more than the pleasure of gains. In trading, loss aversion can lead to traders holding onto losing positions for too long, hoping for a reversal.

Traders need to be aware of this bias and learn how to manage their risk effectively to avoid significant losses.

4. Risk management: Risk management is a critical aspect of trading, and it's essential to have a plan in place to manage potential losses. Traders need to set stop-loss orders and stick to their risk management strategy to avoid catastrophic losses.

5. Mindset: Developing a winning mindset is crucial for traders to achieve long-term success in the markets. Traders need to focus on the process of trading rather than the outcome, remain disciplined and patient, and stay positive and optimistic in the face of challenges.

In summary, understanding the psychology of winning and losing is crucial for traders to develop a winning mindset and achieve long-term success in the markets. Traders need to learn how to manage their emotions effectively, avoid cognitive biases, develop a disciplined mindset, and maintain their focus on the process of trading rather than the outcome. By applying these principles to their trading, traders can improve their decision-making process and achieve their trading goals.

- How to develop a winning mindset and positive attitude

Developing a winning mindset and positive attitude is an important aspect of trading psychology. Here are some tips on how to cultivate a winning mindset:

1. Focus on the process, not the outcome: It's easy to get caught up in the excitement of making money, but it's important to remember that trading is a process. Instead of focusing solely on profits, focus on following your trading plan and making disciplined, rational decisions.

2. Accept losses: Losing trades are a natural part of trading. Rather than dwelling on them or trying to avoid them at all costs, learn to accept losses as a normal part of the process. This will help you avoid emotional reactions and make better decisions in the long run.

3. Develop a positive attitude: Maintaining a positive attitude can help you stay motivated and focused during difficult times. This can involve setting realistic goals, surrounding yourself with supportive people, and practising gratitude.

4. Learn from mistakes: Everyone makes mistakes, but successful traders use these experiences as opportunities for growth and improvement. Analyse your trades and identify what went wrong, then adjust your trading plan to avoid making the same mistakes in the future.

5. Practice discipline: Discipline is crucial to successful trading. This means sticking to your trading plan, managing risk, and avoiding impulsive decisions based on emotions.

By cultivating a winning mindset and positive attitude, you can improve your overall trading performance and achieve your goals.

- Dealing with stress and anxiety in trading

Trading can be a high-stress activity, leading to anxiety and other emotional challenges. Here are some tips for dealing with stress and anxiety in trading:

1. Take care of your physical health: Physical health is important for managing stress and anxiety. Exercise regularly, get enough sleep, and eat a healthy diet.

2. Practice relaxation techniques: Meditation, deep breathing exercises, and yoga can all be helpful in reducing stress and anxiety.

3. Stay organised: Keep track of your trades and financial information in an organised manner to avoid feeling overwhelmed.

4. Set realistic goals: Setting unrealistic goals can increase stress and anxiety. Set achievable goals that are in line with your trading strategy.

5. Manage risk: Risk management is an important part of trading. By using stop-loss orders and other risk management techniques, you can minimise potential losses and reduce stress.

6. Take breaks: Trading can be a 24/7 activity, but taking breaks can be beneficial for reducing stress and anxiety. Step away from your computer and do something you enjoy.

7. Seek support: Don't be afraid to seek support from friends, family, or a mental health professional if you struggle with stress and anxiety.

Remember that stress and anxiety are normal experiences in trading, and everyone deals with them differently. By taking care of your physical and mental health, managing risk, and seeking support when needed, you can reduce the impact of stress and anxiety on your trading performance.

"Do more of what works and less of what doesn't."

Steve Clark

Week 8: Cryptocurrency Investment

- Introduction to cryptocurrency investment
- Understanding the difference between trading and investing
- How to choose the right investment strategy
- How to evaluate a crypto project and its potential
- Diversification and portfolio management

Week 8: Cryptocurrency Investment

- Introduction to cryptocurrency investment

Cryptocurrency investment is the act of buying and holding digital assets with the expectation of earning a return on the investment over time. Here are some key concepts to understand when it comes to cryptocurrency investment:

1. Cryptocurrency fundamentals: Before investing in any cryptocurrency, it's important to research and understand the fundamental factors that affect its value, such as the technology behind the cryptocurrency, its use case, and the team behind the project.

2. Market trends: Cryptocurrency markets are notoriously volatile, so understanding market trends and indicators can be crucial to making informed investment decisions. This includes analysing price charts, market sentiment, and news and events that may impact the cryptocurrency market.

3. Risk management: As with any investment, risk management is important in cryptocurrency investment. This includes diversifying your portfolio, setting stop-loss orders, and being aware of the risks associated with holding digital assets.

4. Long-term investment strategy: Cryptocurrency investment is typically a long-term strategy instead of short-term trading. This means investors need to have a long-term outlook and be patient with their investments.

5. Regulatory and legal considerations: The regulatory landscape around cryptocurrencies is still evolving, so it's important to be aware of the legal and regulatory risks associated with cryptocurrency investment.

6. Security: Cryptocurrency investment involves holding digital assets, which can be vulnerable to hacking and theft. Investors should take steps to secure their digital assets, such as using a secure wallet and following best security practices.

Overall, cryptocurrency investment can be a lucrative opportunity for those who are willing to put in the time and effort to research and understand the market. However, it's important to approach cryptocurrency investment with a long-term outlook and to be aware of the risks and regulatory considerations involved.

- Understanding the difference between trading and investing

Trading and investing are two different approaches to the financial markets, including the cryptocurrency market. Understanding the difference between the two can help you determine which approach is right for your financial goals.

Investing involves buying and holding an asset for an extended period of time with the expectation that it will increase in value over time. Investors typically base their investment decisions on the asset's underlying value, such as its fundamentals, future growth potential, and overall market trends. In the case of cryptocurrencies, investing may involve buying and holding a digital asset for a period of months or even years, with the expectation that it will increase in value as more people adopt it and the technology becomes more widely used.

Trading, on the other hand, involves buying and selling an asset in a relatively short period of time, usually with the goal of making a profit from the fluctuations in the asset's price.

Traders may use various strategies, such as technical analysis or news-based trading, to try to predict short-term movements in the market. In the case of cryptocurrencies, trading may involve buying and selling digital assets over the course of hours or days, with the goal of taking advantage of short-term price movements.

One of the key differences between trading and investing is the level of risk involved. Trading is generally considered to be a higher-risk strategy, as it requires a more active approach and involves making predictions about short-term market movements. On the other hand, investing is generally considered a lower-risk strategy, as it involves a longer-term approach and is based on the asset's underlying value.

Another difference between trading and investing is the level of time commitment required. Trading requires a more active approach, as traders must closely monitor the market and be ready to make quick decisions based on changing conditions. On the other hand, investing is generally a more passive approach, as investors may only need to monitor their portfolio periodically to ensure that it is still aligned with their long-term goals.

Ultimately, the choice between trading and investing comes down to your financial goals, risk tolerance, and the level of time and effort you are willing to commit to the market. Both strategies have the potential to be profitable, but they require different approaches and carry different levels of risk.

- How to choose the right investment strategy

When it comes to cryptocurrency investment, there are several strategies you can consider. Here are some of the most popular ones:

1. Buy and hold: This strategy involves buying a cryptocurrency and holding onto it for the long term, with the belief that its value will increase over time. This is also known as "HODLing" in the crypto community.

2. Dollar-cost averaging: This strategy involves buying a fixed amount of a cryptocurrency at regular intervals, regardless of its price. This helps mitigate the impact of market volatility on your investment.

3. Value investing: This strategy involves identifying undervalued cryptocurrencies with strong fundamentals and investing in them long-term.
4. Growth investing: This strategy involves investing in cryptocurrencies with high growth potential, even if they are currently overvalued.

5. Income investing: This strategy involves investing in cryptocurrencies that pay dividends or offer other forms of passive income.

6. Index investing: This strategy involves investing in a diversified portfolio of cryptocurrencies, either through a cryptocurrency index fund or by building your own portfolio.

When choosing an investment strategy, it's important to consider your risk tolerance, investment goals, and time horizon. It's also important to do your own research and due diligence before making any investment decisions.

- How to evaluate a crypto project and its potential

When evaluating a cryptocurrency project, there are several factors to consider. Here are some key areas to focus on:

1. Technology: One of the most important factors to consider is the technology behind the cryptocurrency. Is the technology innovative and capable of solving real-world problems? Is it secure and decentralised? Does it have a strong development team and community?

2. Adoption: Another important factor to consider is the level of adoption and use cases for the cryptocurrency. Are real-world businesses and individuals using it? Is there a strong ecosystem of developers and users supporting the project?

3. Competition: It's also important to consider the level of competition in the market. Are there other cryptocurrencies with similar features and use cases? How does the project differentiate itself from its competitors?

4. Partnerships: Partnerships can be a good indication of the potential for a cryptocurrency project. Are there any notable partnerships or collaborations with other companies or organisations?

5. Market demand: Finally, it's important to consider the market demand for the cryptocurrency. Is there a strong demand from investors and users? Is the project addressing a real need in the market?

When evaluating a cryptocurrency project, it's important to do your own research and due diligence. Look for reliable sources of information and consult with experts in the field.

Remember that investing in cryptocurrency is inherently risky, and there is no guarantee of returns.

- Diversification and portfolio management

Diversification and portfolio management are important concepts in cryptocurrency investment, just as they are in traditional finance. Diversification involves spreading your investments across multiple assets to reduce risk and protect against volatility.

In cryptocurrency, this can mean investing in a mix of different cryptocurrencies, as well as other asset classes such as stocks, bonds, and real estate.

Portfolio management involves actively managing your investments to optimise your returns and minimise risk. This can involve setting investment goals and strategies, monitoring market trends and news, and regularly rebalancing your portfolio to adjust your asset allocation. Here are some tips for diversification and portfolio management in cryptocurrency investment:

1. Define your investment goals: Before investing in cryptocurrency, it's important to define your investment goals and risk tolerance. Are you investing for short-term gains or long-term growth? What level of risk are you comfortable with?

2. Diversify across different cryptocurrencies: Invest in a mix of different cryptocurrencies to spread your risk. Consider investing in both well-established cryptocurrencies, such as Bitcoin and Ethereum, as well as newer, promising projects with growth potential.

3. Consider investing in other asset classes: Diversify your portfolio further by investing in other asset classes such as stocks, bonds, and real estate.

4. Regularly rebalance your portfolio: Monitor your portfolio regularly and adjust your asset allocation as needed. Rebalancing can help you optimise your returns and minimise risk.

5. Stay informed: Keep current on market trends and news related to cryptocurrency and other asset classes. Consult with experts and follow reliable sources of information to make informed investment decisions.

Remember that investing in cryptocurrency carries risks, and there is no guarantee of returns. It's important to do your own research, seek out expert advice, and invest only what you can afford to lose.

"I think investment psychology is by far the more important element, followed by risk control, with the least important consideration being the question of where to buy and sell."

Tom Basso

Week 9: Technical Tools

- Introduction to technical tools
- Trading bots, APIs, and other trading tools
- How to use technical tools to automate your trading.
- Understanding API keys and security

Week 9: Technical Tools

- Introduction to technical tools

Technical tools, also known as trading tools, are software-based programs or applications that traders use to assist in their analysis of financial instruments, including cryptocurrencies. Technical tools make use of mathematical algorithms and data to create visual representations of market trends, which traders can use to make more informed trading decisions.

There are many different types of technical tools available, and they can be grouped into categories based on their function. Some of the most commonly used technical tools in cryptocurrency trading include:

1. Charting tools: These tools are used to create charts of cryptocurrency prices over time. They help traders to identify trends and patterns that may indicate potential buying or selling opportunities.

2. Indicators: Indicators are mathematical calculations based on price and/or volume data. They are used to provide insight into market trends and can be used to identify potential entry and exit points.

3. Oscillators: Oscillators are a type of indicator that measures the momentum of price movements. They can be used to identify potential reversals in market trends.

4. Back testing tools: Back testing tools allow traders to test their trading strategies against historical market data. This can help traders to evaluate the effectiveness of their strategies and identify potential areas for improvement.

5. Automated trading tools: Automated trading tools are programs that allow traders to set up trading strategies and execute trades automatically. These tools use algorithms and data analysis to make trading decisions, which can be helpful

for traders who want to take advantage of market opportunities without constantly monitoring the market themselves.

Technical tools are an important part of cryptocurrency trading, and traders who use them effectively can gain a competitive edge in the market. However, it is important to remember that technical tools are only one part of a successful trading strategy, and they should be used in conjunction with fundamental analysis and risk management techniques.

- Trading bots, APIs, and other trading tools

Trading bots, APIs, and other trading tools are becoming increasingly popular in the world of cryptocurrency trading. These tools can help automate trading processes, increase efficiency, and provide more accurate analysis of market trends.

Trading bots are software programs that use various technical analysis indicators to identify trading opportunities and execute trades automatically. They can be customised to fit specific trading strategies and can operate 24/7, providing traders with a significant advantage in a market that never sleeps. However, trading bots can also be prone to errors, and they can be expensive to purchase and maintain.

APIs (Application Programming Interfaces) allow traders to access data and execute trades through an exchange's programming interface. APIs enable traders to build custom trading applications and connect with other trading tools, such as charting software and trading bots. They can also allow traders to automate their trading processes and execute trades more efficiently.

Other trading tools include charting software, which provides in-depth analysis of market trends and price movements, and news aggregators, which track news and events that may affect the cryptocurrency market.

While trading tools can provide significant advantages for traders, it is important to remember that they are just that: tools. Traders should still have a solid understanding of the market and trading strategies to make informed decisions. It is also important to thoroughly research and test any trading tools before incorporating them into a trading strategy.

- How to use technical tools to automate your trading.

Automated trading can be a useful tool for traders who want to execute trades automatically based on predefined rules and conditions. Traders can use several technical tools to automate their trading strategies.

1. Trading Bots: Trading bots are software programs that are designed to automatically execute trades based on predefined rules and conditions. These bots can analyse market data and execute trades faster than human traders. They can be set up to execute trades based on technical indicators, news events, or other market signals.

2. APIs: APIs (Application Programming Interfaces) are software tools that allow traders to access market data and execute trades programmatically. APIs can be used to create custom trading bots and other trading tools that can be integrated with different trading platforms.

3. Algorithmic Trading: Algorithmic trading involves using computer programs to execute trades automatically based on predefined rules and conditions. These programs can analyse market data and execute trades faster than human traders. They can be set up to execute trades based on technical indicators, news events, or other market signals.

4. Trading Signals: Trading signals are alerts generated by technical indicators, market data, or other market signals. These signals can be used to execute trades automatically or manually. Traders can use trading signals to automate their trading strategies or to make more informed trading decisions.

Automated trading can benefit traders who want to save time and execute trades faster. However, it is important to remember that automated trading strategies are only as good as the rules and conditions that are programmed into them. It is important to test and optimise automated trading strategies before using them with real money.

- Understanding API keys and security

API (Application Programming Interface) keys are used to allow third-party applications, such as trading bots, to access and interact with your exchange account. It is a secure way to access your account without sharing your login credentials.

When setting up API keys, it is important to keep security in mind. Here are some tips to keep your API keys secure:

1. Only use trusted and reputable third-party applications with a proven track record of security.

2. Only grant the necessary permissions required by the application. For example, if the application only needs to execute trades, do not grant it the ability to withdraw funds from your account.

3. Create a separate API key for each application and only use it for that application.

4. Use strong passwords and enable two-factor authentication (2FA) on your exchange account.

5. Monitor your account activity regularly and revoke any API keys that are no longer needed or suspicious.

Following these best practices, you can use API keys and other trading tools to automate your trading while keeping your account secure.

"You have to be willing to accept a certain level of risk, or else you will never pull the trigger.

You can't be afraid to take a loss.

The people who are successful in this business are the people who are willing to lose money."

Steve Watson

Week 10: Final Review and Assessment

- Review of all the concepts covered in the course.
- Practical Exercises and case studies
- Final assessment and feedback.

Note: This course is intended as an introduction to crypto trading and is not meant to be comprehensive or exhaustive. It's important to continue learning and adapting to the ever-changing crypto market.

Week 10: Final Review and Assessment

- Review of all the concepts covered in the course.

Over the past 10 weeks, you have learned a lot about trading cryptocurrencies. Here's a review of the concepts covered in this beginner trading course for crypto:

Week 1: What is cryptocurrency, and how does it work?

- Definition of cryptocurrency
- How blockchain technology enables cryptocurrency
- Types of cryptocurrencies

Week 2: Understanding blockchain technology.

- Definition of blockchain technology
- How blockchain works
- Benefits of blockchain technology

Week 3: Different types of cryptocurrencies

- Overview of the most popular cryptocurrencies
- Differences between major cryptocurrencies
- Considerations when choosing a cryptocurrency to trade.

Week 4: Basic concepts of trading, such as buying, selling, and holding.

- How to buy and sell cryptocurrencies
- Understanding order types
- Difference between long and short positions

Week 5: Setting up a crypto exchange account.

- Choosing the right crypto exchange
- Creating an account on a crypto exchange
- How to navigate the exchange's interface

Week 6: Introduction to technical analysis

- Definition of technical analysis
- How technical analysis is used in trading.
- Basic technical analysis tools

Week 7: Understanding price charts and candlesticks.

- Types of price charts
- Definition of candlesticks
- How to read candlestick charts

Week 8: Basic technical indicators such as Moving Averages, RSI, MACD, etc.

- Definition of technical indicators
- How to use Moving Averages, RSI, MACD, and other indicators
- Indicators that work best for cryptocurrency trading

Week 9: How to use technical analysis to make trading decisions.

- Combining technical indicators
- Identifying trends
- Setting entry and exit points.

Week 10: Introduction to fundamental analysis

- Definition of fundamental analysis
- How fundamental analysis is used in trading.
- Key factors to consider in fundamental analysis.

Congratulations on completing the beginner trading course for crypto! Always practice risk management and continue learning to improve your trading skills.

Practical Exercises and Case Studies

Practical exercises and case studies are an essential part of any trading course, including a beginner trading course for crypto. These exercises and case studies allow students to apply the concepts and techniques they have learned in the course to real-world scenarios.

Here are some examples of practical exercises and case studies that can be included in a beginner trading course for crypto:

1. Paper Trading: Students can use paper trading, which is a simulation of trading with virtual funds, to practice and test their trading strategies in a risk-free environment.

2. Technical Analysis Exercise: Students can be given a cryptocurrency price chart and asked to identify the trend, support and resistance levels, and potential entry and exit points based on technical analysis.

3. Fundamental Analysis Exercise: Students can be given news and events related to a cryptocurrency project and asked to analyse their impact on the project's future potential.

4. Risk Management Exercise: Students can be given a hypothetical trading scenario and asked to identify and manage the associated risks.

5. Trading Plan Exercise: Students can be asked to create a trading plan for a hypothetical trading scenario, including entry and exit points, stop-loss orders, and profit targets.

6. Portfolio Management Case Study: Students can be given a portfolio of cryptocurrencies and asked to rebalance it based on market conditions and their investment goals.

7. Trading Psychology Exercise: Students can be asked to identify and manage their emotions and biases in a hypothetical trading scenario.

These exercises and case studies can be conducted individually or in groups and reviewed and discussed in class or online forums. By applying the concepts and techniques they have learned in a practical setting, students can gain a deeper understanding of the course material and develop their trading skills.

Final assessment and feedback

After completing the 10-week beginner trading course for crypto, it is important to assess the progress your knowledge gained.

It important to summarise your performance, areas of strength, and areas for improvement. It is important to help identify your strengths and weaknesses and work on improving them. At the same time, it is equally important to acknowledge your progress and efforts.

Overall, this comprehensive evaluation of progress and the effectiveness of the course can be used to gauge your level of expertise. There are 3 Multiple choice quizzes based on the course over the next pages.

MULTIPLE CHOICE QUIZ BASED ON THE BEGINNER COURSE

Here's a multiple-choice quiz based on the topics covered in this course:

QUIZ 1

What is cryptocurrency?

A) A type of paper currency
B) A digital or virtual currency that uses cryptography for security

What is blockchain technology?

A) A type of encryption technology
B) A decentralised, digital ledger that records transactions on multiple computers
C) A type of cloud computing technology.

What is technical analysis?

A) The study of economic and financial factors to evaluate investments
B) The use of charts and technical indicators to analyse market trends and make trading decisions
C) The analysis of news and events to predict market movements

What is fundamental analysis?

A) The analysis of news and events to predict market movements.
B) The use of charts and technical indicators to analyse market trends and make trading decisions
C) The study of economic and financial factors to evaluate investments

What is leverage?

A) The use of borrowed funds to increase potential profits or losses
B) The process of buying and selling assets simultaneously to profit from market inefficiencies
C) The amount of money an investor has available for trading

What is the difference between trading and investing?

A) Trading involves buying and selling assets in the short term while investing involves holding assets for the long term
B) Trading involves holding assets for the long term, while investing involves buying and selling assets in the short term
C) Trading and investing are the same things

What is a trading plan?

A) A document that outlines a trader's strategy and goals
B) A tool used to automate trading decisions
C) A type of technical indicator

What is risk management?

A) The process of identifying and managing risks associated with trading
B) The process of buying and selling assets simultaneously to profit from market inefficiencies
C) The use of technical indicators to analyse market trends and make trading decisions

What is market psychology?

A) The study of the emotions and behaviour of market participants
B) The study of economic and financial factors to evaluate investments
C) The analysis of news and events to predict market movements

What is cryptocurrency investment?

A) The process of buying and holding cryptocurrencies for the long term
B) The process of buying and selling cryptocurrencies in the short term
C) The process of mining cryptocurrencies for profit.

QUIZ 1 ANSWERS:

1. B
2. B
3. B
4. C
5. A
6. A
7. A
8. A
9. A
10. A

MULTIPLE CHOICE QUIZ BASED ON THE BEGINNER COURSE

Here's a multiple-choice quiz based on the topics covered in this course:

QUIZ 2

What is cryptocurrency?

A) A physical currency like paper money.

B) A digital currency that uses encryption techniques to secure and verify transactions.

C) A precious metal like gold or silver.

What is blockchain technology?

A) A type of encryption used to secure online transactions.

B) A decentralised ledger that records all transactions securely and transparently.

C) A type of computer hardware used to mine cryptocurrency.

What is technical analysis?

A) The study of economic and financial factors that affect the price of cryptocurrency.

B) Using charts and technical indicators to analyse past market data and predict future price movements.

C) The process of analysing the underlying technology and adoption of a cryptocurrency project.

What is fundamental analysis?

A) Using charts and technical indicators to analyse past market data and predict future price movements.

B) The process of analysing the underlying technology and adoption of a cryptocurrency project.

C) The study of economic and financial factors that affect the price of cryptocurrency.

What is leverage trading?

A) A type of trading where you borrow funds to increase your trading position.

B) A type of trading where you only use your own funds to make trades.

C) A type of trading where you only hold your position for a short period of time

What is a trading plan?

A) A document that outlines your trading goals, strategies, and risk management rules

B) A software tool used to automate your trades

C)A typc of cryptocurrency wallet used to store your digital assets.

What is market psychology?

A) The study of how people make decisions and act in markets.

B) The study of how technology affects markets.

C) The study of how laws and regulations affect markets.

What is a trading bot?

A) A software tool used to automate your trades.

B) A type of cryptocurrency wallet used to store your digital assets.

C) A type of technical indicator used in trading.

What is diversification?

A) Spreading your investments across different assets to reduce risk.

B) Investing in a single asset to maximise profit.

C) Investing in assets that have a high correlation with each other reduces the risk.

What is an API key?

A) A password used to access your cryptocurrency exchange account.

B) A type of computer hardware used to mine cryptocurrency.

C)A code that allows you to access an exchange's trading interface and execute trades automatically.

Answers:

1. b
2. b
3. b
4. c
5. a
6. a
7. a
8. a
9. a
10. c
11.

MULTIPLE CHOICE QUIZ BASED ON THE BEGINNER COURSE

Here's a multiple-choice quiz based on the topics covered in this course:

QUIZ 3

What is cryptocurrency?

a. A physical currency like the dollar or euro
b. A digital currency that uses cryptography to secure and verify transactions.
c. A commodity like gold or silver
d. A stock or share in a company.

What is blockchain technology?

a. A digital wallet to store cryptocurrencies.
b. A computer network that verifies and records transactions on a decentralised ledger
c. An online exchange to buy and sell cryptocurrencies.
d. An investment fund that trades cryptocurrencies on behalf of clients

What is technical analysis?

a. Analysis of a company's financial statements and economic indicators to determine its value.
b. Analysis of news and events to predict price movements in the market.
c. Analysis of charts and patterns to identify potential trading opportunities.
d. Analysis of a company's management and operations to evaluate its potential growth.

What is fundamental analysis?

a. Analysis of charts and patterns to identify potential trading opportunities.
b. Analysis of news and events to predict price movements in the market.
c. Analysis of a company's financial statements and economic indicators to determine its valued. Analysis of a company's management and operations to evaluate its potential growth.

What is leverage in trading?

a. The amount of money you invest in a trade.
b. The percentage of profit you make on a trade.
c. Using borrowed money to increase the potential return on an investment.
d. The practice of buying and selling the same asset multiple times in a short period.

What is a trading plan?

a. A document that outlines your trading goals, strategies, and risk management rules
b. A software program that automatically buys and sells cryptocurrencies.
c. An online platform to track your portfolio and monitor market trends.
d. A social network for traders to share tips and insights.

What is diversification?

a. Investing in various assets to reduce risk and maximise return.
b. Investing in a single asset to maximise return and reduce risk.
c. Selling all your assets during a market downturn to avoid losses.
d. Borrowing money to invest in the market to increase potential returns.

What is market psychology?

a. The study of how market trends and sentiment affect price movements.
b. The study of how traders' emotions and behaviours affect their trading decisions.
c. The study of how economic indicators and news events affect market performance.
d. The study of how technical analysis and chart patterns can predict future price movements.

What is a trading bot?

a. A software program that automatically buys and sells cryptocurrencies based on pre-set rules.
b. A social network for traders to share tips and insights.
c. An online platform to track your portfolio and monitor market trends.
d. A tool to analyse charts and patterns to identify potential trading opportunities.

What is a candlestick chart?

a. A chart that displays an asset's opening and closing prices over time
b. A chart that displays the volume of trading activity for an asset over a period of time
c. A chart that displays the high and low prices of an asset over a period of time
d. A chart that displays the percentage change in the price of an asset over a period of time

Answers to the multiple-choice quiz based on the beginner trading course for crypto:

1. b. A digital currency that uses cryptography to secure and verify transactions.
2. b. A computer network that verifies and records transactions on a decentralised ledger
3. c. Analysis of charts and patterns to identify potential trading opportunities.
4. c. Analysis of a company's financial statements and economic indicators to determine its value.
5. c. Using borrowed money to increase the potential return on an investment.
6. a. A document outlining your trading goals, strategies, and risk management rules.
7. a. Investing in various assets to reduce risk and maximise return.
8. b. The study of how traders' emotions and behaviours affect their trading decisions.
9. a. A software program that automatically buys and sells cryptocurrencies based on pre-set rules.
10. a. A chart that displays the opening and closing prices of an asset over a period of time

"If you want something you've never had, you must be willing to do something you've never done."

Unknown

CONNECT WITH LISA N EDWARDS AT

- https://lisanedwards.com/
- https://thousandtomillions.com/
- https://linktr.ee/LisaNEdwards

21